# Laughter and Despair

# Laughter & Despair:

READINGS IN TEN NOVELS
OF THE VICTORIAN ERA

• • • • • • • • • • • • •

U. C. KNOEPFLMACHER

UNIVERSITY OF CALIFORNIA PRESS
BERKELEY · LOS ANGELES · LONDON · 1971

UNIVERSITY OF CALIFORNIA PRESS
BERKELEY AND LOS ANGELES, CALIFORNIA
UNIVERSITY OF CALIFORNIA PRESS, LTD.
LONDON, ENGLAND
COPYRIGHT © 1971, BY
THE REGENTS OF THE UNIVERSITY OF CALIFORNIA
ISBN: 0–520–01907–5
LIBRARY OF CONGRESS CATALOG CARD NUMBER: 73–145789
PRINTED IN THE UNITED STATES OF AMERICA

# Laughter and Despair: Readings in Ten Novels of the Victorian Era

# Preface

"An author," says Coleridge, "has three points to settle: to what sort his work belongs, for what description of readers it is intended, and the specific end or object, which it is to answer" (*Aids to Reflection*). Let me try to meet these standards.

This study contains critical readings of ten highly different Victorian novels (although the last work to be considered, Conrad's *The Secret Agent*, actually is "Victorian" only by virtue of its setting).

Victorian fiction relies on an exceptionally close interaction between reader, characters, and implied author. Uninitiated readers tend to overlook their active role in this exchange. Taught to regard novelists like Thackeray and Dickens as little more than faithful purveyors of sociohistorical facts, many intelligent twentieth-century readers underestimate the importance of their own involvement in the gratifying identifications and cathartic releases generated by these Showman–novelists. By undervaluing the extent of their participation, they fail to benefit from an illusionist act that depends on its audience's willing contribution for its full success. This study is designed to assist such readers. It is also addressed to those more sophisticated experts who, though already conversant with these novels and with the preoccupations of the nineteenth century, may nonetheless be interested in my method of analysis and in some of my results.

For the benefit of the first type of reader, there is a short Introduction which examines the opening of *Barchester Towers* in order to combat the tendency—still very much in evidence after forty years of New Criticism—of making a novel resemble an "objective" mirror of fact. The more seasoned reader who knows that the reality of a novel is largely shaped by its creator's accommodation of fears and yearnings can skip this introductory part without any great loss. Still, the Introduction may prove helpful as a specimen of the method and emphasis employed in the succeeding chapters. Most of these chapters follow the precedent of the Introduction by relying on a small, representative portion of each novel as a point of departure for a consideration of that novel's larger aspects (thus, for instance, Dobbin's fist-fight with Cuff and Lockwood's confusion at the Heights are treated in terms of the reader's own initiation into the fictional worlds devised by Thackeray and Emily Brontë). The Introduction's stress on the importance of setting and on the complications made possible by the manipulation of point of view is also retained throughout the book.

My immediate objectives, then, are twofold: by bringing together ten major novels by major Victorian novelists, I am eager to provide readers drawn to these and other novels of the era with some guidelines that might help them to appreciate more fully a genre unmatched perhaps in flexibility, variety, and riches; by devising a loose framework that enables me to draw analogies and differences among the ten "classics" expressly chosen for that purpose, I am equally eager to open some new areas of interest for the Victorian specialist.

The arrangement of this book is designed to establish connections I have never seen discussed before. By beginning with *Barchester Towers* and *Vanity Fair* I am able to use both of these works in my later chapters as a background against which the innovations of the other novelists can be measured. The contrasts developed as a result, like the deliberate pairings of *The Ordeal of Richard Feverel* with *The Mill on the Floss* in chapter four and of *Jude the Obscure* with *The Way of All Flesh* in chapter seven, yield vistas which, hopefully, can be extended by future students of the Victorian novel. Similarly, my slightly eccentric arrangement permits some new looks at works normally viewed from quite different angles: thus, readers who regard *Wuthering Heights* as a Gothic romance may be surprised by the significance I ascribe to the comic elements in that novel, while those formalists who stress the modernity of *The Secret Agent* may be startled to see that work discussed not in conjunction with *Ulysses* or *The Sound and the Fury* but rather as the culmination of a sequence which begins with that most placid of Victorian novels, *Barchester Towers*.

In my efforts to reproduce the effects on the reader of certain individual scenes, events, or descriptions, I am of course aware that no such universal reader exists. An American woman of 1970 who reads Thackeray's description of the fist-fight in Mr. Swishtail's establishment surely will not be moved by the same manly emotions that must have gripped a Victorian gentle-man—educated, like Dobbin, in a British public school and hence exposed to the codes of honor boys develop in the face of flogging and bullying—who read the same passage in 1847. The entity I have designated as "we" or as "the reader" can therefore at best remain a compromise. Still, the relativeness of that term should hardly invalidate my frequent efforts to act out the re-actions of a typical reader; nor, hopefully, will my persistent emphasis on the active role played by such a reader be dis-missed as a personal fad or critical hobbyhorse. If anything, my discussions of these ten novels should corroborate my convic-tion that one of the salient features of Victorian fiction was—and still is—its participatory quality.

The Victorian novelist entered into a tacit compact with his readers. His desire to resolve personal dilemmas and private doubts was congruent with a similar desire for affirmation held by his audience; he could share his fantasies and concessions to reality with his readers, yet to do so he had to create structures that would accommodate their needs as well as his own. The novel-reading public of the Victorian era was even vaster and more variegated than the multileveled audiences that had con-tributed to the success of Elizabethan and Jacobean drama more than two centuries before. To merge one's fears and hopes with those of such a vast public, to become that public's voice, seemed an unequaled literary achievement to the novelist—a unique op-portunity. The Victorian reading public welcomed the novelist's personal need to objectify inner tensions; it rewarded his fantasies with money and fame. On the other hand, it also exacted a psychological prize. For only a novelist's readers could lend full meaning to his imaginative rearrangements of reality; not only his financial success but also the success of his efforts to find sanity by wresting meaning out of chaos depended on the reactions, the participation, the catharsis of the novelist's readers.

The old Victorian writing formula of "Make 'em cry; make 'em laugh!" has often been adduced as evidence of the crass commercialism that motivated entertainers who ministered to their audience's need for escape and relief in a most calculated and programmatic way. A different construction, however, can be put on this same formula. The Victorian novelist desperately needed to be reassured that his audience shared his tears as well as his laughter, his fears as well as his defenses. Although he erected his fictions as bastions of sanity to protect himself against potential anarchy and meaninglessness, he needed constant proof of his prowess as fortress–builder. He was plagued by the possibility that he had merely built an insubstantial dream castle. Could he be sure that he had used building materials taken from the actual world? And, just as crucial, was the fastness he had constructed really strong enough to withstand the inconstancy of that external world?

Only the readers whom he had tried to persuade to share his shelter could furnish the novelist with the proof he required. The consuming desire shown by Charles Dickens in the later years of his career to possess the audiences of men and women that gathered to hear him read aloud from his written work illustrates most vividly, I think, the interdependence between author and reader that is so characteristic of the Victorian novel. Dickens wanted to be assured that his public had shared his despair as well as benefited from his laughter; he wanted to feel that he had implanted meaning in the dispiriting world of the Veneerings—to be convinced that he, Charles Dickens, remained confirmed as each reader's one, true, and only Mutual Friend. A public indifferent to his anxieties and unresponsive to his humor would deny the very sanity he had sought by writing. By holding live audiences under his mesmeric spell, Dickens the illusionist could personally test out the validity of his illusions. George Eliot, too, eagerly welcomed any hint or suggestion that her work had been meaningfully shared by others. Unlike Dickens, she remained screened from her public, unable to bear the disappointments that might come from such direct confrontations; nonetheless, like her great rival, she cherished all assurances that her work was not a lonely and subjective attempt to come to terms with reality. Full meaning and full identity could come only through the union of reader and author.

Reader and artist thus could fight the good fight with Giant Despair by jointly entering a fantasy world expressly erected for that combat—a fantasy world in which an actuality of change and disorder could be arrested, refined, and transmuted through wish fulfillment, balances, concessions, or, at least, through an ordered approximation of that disorder. Catharsis is at work in all the novels considered in this study—be it the catharsis that comes from laughter or from pathos or from terror. The Victorian reader could share Trollope's or Dickens' self-purgation by laughing away the threats represented by disruptive figures such as Mr. Slope or Silas Wegg; he could share the emotional release George Eliot felt when she wept over the martyrdom of that self called Maggie Tulliver; he could even derive a grim satisfaction from the knowledge that in Hardy's world our worst forebodings inevitably become true.

It is my contention that each of the novels examined in this study represents a variation of the struggle between the opposites I have called "laughter" and "despair"—a collision that not only underlies each author's transference of private quarrels into the realm of fiction but also becomes a dynamic part of our reading experience, our own intervention in this fictional realm. What, however, do these terms "laughter" and "despair" signify? Broadly, they represent the opposed impulses I have already been describing: each artist's apprehensions about a reality that seemed changeful, disjointed, loveless, gave rise to the endeavors—sanctioned and encouraged by the Victorian reading public—to devise alternate models of reality in which such anxieties could be scrutinized and, ideally, be allayed, arrested, or countered. I have used the terms of laughter and despair quite loosely to encompass such widely divergent novels. No inconsistency, however, exists in their application. Let me first dwell on the easier term of the two—despair.

Although in our post-Freudian world "despair" has become a fashionable equivalent of "angst" and "anxiety," the word's origin is theological. As a public moralist in a nominally Christian society, the Victorian novelist was the cultural heir of those earlier Protestant allegorists who had depicted despair as a deep-seated urge to escape the uncertainties of the human condition. (It is hardly a coincidence that *Paradise Lost* and *The Pilgrim's Progress* should be so frequently alluded to in these novels.) The death wish that temporarily possesses Spenser's Red Crosse Knight or Milton's Adam actually destroys Catherine Earnshaw, Sue Bridehead, Winnie Verloc—figures unable to find the purpose guaranteed to these earlier sojourners in a fallen world. Jude the Obscure never reaches the New Jerusalem he seeks as a pilgrim; Maggie and Tom Tulliver never recover Eden. Even those granted a makeshift substitute are subjected to states of mind that range from mild disorientation to deep and unmitigated pessimism: Mr. Harding's bewilderment, Dobbin's gradual disillusion, Heathcliff's Promethean rage, Sir Austin Feverel's blighted hope, Mortimer Lightwood's bitter self-derision, Lydgate's crushed idealism, Ernest Pontifex's mental collapse, all take place in an increasingly erratic world.

In a human reality no longer ordered by divine design, despair seemed harder to vanquish. Milton, buttressed by his personal belief in a just God, could compel his readers to share Adam and Eve's confidence in the penumbra that lay before them; the Victorian novelist who was forced to recover paradise in a world where social institutions could provide the only measure of stability found that his efforts to correct despondency were, by necessity, far more fragile. Dependent on society, the novelist also felt more deeply than his readers the alienation brought about by "loss of confidence in social man" (*The Excursion*, IV.261); like the Wordsworth who created the Solitary to rid himself of his inclination toward despair, the Victorian novelist struggled to exorcise a Hamletian self that was seductively logical yet crippled by loneliness and self-pity. By comparison with *Paradise Lost*, the gains attained in those two great Victorian epics *Vanity Fair* and *Middlemarch* seem deliberately muted. Though ejected from Eden, Milton's Adam and Eve carry within them the seeds for man's redemption; though granted a measure of fulfillment, Dobbin the idealist and Dorothea the reformer are forced to recognize that their effect, though diffusive, has been sorely limited by the temporal world. Paradise is far—very far—from being regained.

All efforts at affirmation, all the energy spent to overcome potential despair, all the devices to which the Victorian novelist resorted to satisfy his craving for a release of tension, I have called "laughter." José Ortega y Gasset maintained that "the nineteenth century was excessively inclined to see comedy on earth." George Meredith, on the contrary, complained in his "Essay on Comedy" (1877) that his Victorian contemporaries were losing the aid of a "powerful auxiliar" by "neglecting the cultivation of the comic idea." As my discussions of these ten novels should show, neither of these statements is wholly valid. Although Victorian novelists had inherited the comic conventions employed by their eighteenth-century predecessors, they found these conventions inadequate in their struggle to accommodate themselves to the disordered and potentially tragic world they saw around them. Of the nine novelists discussed here, only Trollope is able to appropriate for his own purposes the kind of comedy practiced by Smollett or Fielding.

Nonetheless, the relief provided by "laughter" was an objective deeply desired by all these writers. The shape and nature of that relief varies in accordance with the intensity of each author's preoccupation with the error, guilt, purposelessness, and obsession with death that give shape to his particular Vanity

Fair. Sometimes the laughter belongs to an adult and mature omniscience: the ironic comments made by the narrators of *Vanity Fair*, *Barchester Towers*, and *Middlemarch* have the effect of reconciling reader and author to the limitations which the characters are forced to accept. At other times, the laughter is deliberately regressive: in *Our Mutual Friend* the reader is forced to identify with the joyful antics of Boffin the child-man in order to dispel the anxieties Dickens has so superbly re-created. Laughter can act as a corrective for an excessive morbidity: Nelly Dean and Mrs. Berry act as a counter for the impulse towards self-destruction represented by Catherine Earnshaw and Richard Feverel. Even laughter of a vindictive and demonic kind can be channeled for purgative purposes: Becky Sharp punctures Amelia's illusions, Heathcliff revenges himself against civilization, Trollope's "female devil" ousts the "male devil" of his novel. An occasional laugh at the laughers, at cynical wits like Adrian Harley or Lockwood, can also provide a measure of relief. With Hardy and Conrad, laughter becomes ferocious; though still self-protective, it now blends with despair.

The ironies of plot are also a manifestation of laughter. The happy ending toward which so many Victorian novels aspire almost always results from two parallel plot developments: a removal of the disturbing element which the novelist has allowed to take shape in his fantasy world and, simultaneously, a corresponding reintegration or consolidation of harmonies that seemed threatened by discord. This fomula, which applies equally to novels as radically different as *Barchester Towers* and *Our Mutual Friend*, operates to some degree even in those novels in which the author refuses to smooth over the perturbations and sense of loss admitted in the course of the narrative. Thus, in a novel like *Wuthering Heights*, the tragedy of Heathcliff and of the first Catherine, though central and overpowering, is considerably softened by the concluding idyll of Cathy and Hareton and by Lockwood's exclusion from the world of these young lovers. Likewise in *Middlemarch*, a novel of infinite balances, the fulfillment of Fred and Mary offsets the joyless aftermath of Lydgate's marriage, and the enforced banishment of Bulstrode sweetens the bitterness of Dorothea's voluntary departure from Middlemarch.

Even in *The Secret Agent*, where Stevie and Winnie become the victims of an anarchic world, Conrad counters that anarchy by having the Assistant Commissioner track down and banish Vladimir, the man who has tried to unleash the terror of meaninglessness. Like so many of the quixotic figures in these novels —Dobbin, Austin Wentworth, Philip Wakem, John Harmon, Dorothea Brooke—Conrad's Assistant Commissioner is a benevolent outsider eager to restore harmony to the novelist's disrupted world. His instinct is to become a Wordsworthian Solitary, to flee absurdity and chaos by seeking refuge in the self—as do Richard Feverel, Maggie Tulliver, Eugene Wrayburn, Jude Fawley, and Sue Bridehead. Like the novelist of whom he is but a projection, he resists that urge and is spurred into resisting loneliness by immersing himself in the world around him. Like the novelist, he is therefore driven to re-create that world. He must rid it of meaninglessness for the sake of others and for his own peace of mind. His triumph, though partial and unobtrusive, is the triumph of the control that comes with laughter over the anarchy that stems from despair.

Conrad's recombination of "laughter" and "despair" in *The Secret Agent* thus rounds out the progression traced in this book. This progression starts with an examination of Trollope's successful creation of a comic form in *Barchester Towers* and then turns to Thackeray's and Emily Brontë's recourse to comic elements needed to check the disturbances set in motion through realism in *Vanity Fair* and through myth and romance in *Wuthering Heights*. The next chapter pairs two works which begin in a comic vein only to end in a tragic catastrophe: Meredith's *The Ordeal of Richard Feverel* and George Eliot's *The Mill on the Floss*. The succeeding chapters on Dickens' *Our Mutual Friend* and Eliot's *Middlemarch* show how a fantasist and a realist managed, in their greatest novels, to reconcile themselves and their readers to the darkened existence they found so threatening. The balances and compromises on which *Middle-march* is based are exploded by the unmitigated pessimism of *Jude the Obscure*; Dickens' unique ability to share an irrational comic world with his reading public is no longer possible for Samuel Butler in *The Way of All Flesh*. Hardy's tragedy and Butler's comedy illustrate the breakdown of the fusions attempted by the earlier novelists. It remained for Conrad in his "simple tale of the nineteenth century" to find a new mold for the old combat with Giant Despair.

Valuable work has been done in recent years by those critics of fiction who have established helpful categories of narrative modes through their scrupulous and precise distinctions. My own efforts, I fear, have been directed at blurring some of these distinctions. By showing how very different fictional structures can proceed from common intentions, the emphasis in these critical readings is, in Wordsworth's phrase, on "similitude in dissimilitude" rather than on "dissimilitude in similitude." The Victorian novel is a highly eclectic art form: comedy and tragedy are seldom found in a pure state; "realism" and "romance" invariably merge and interpenetrate. No matter how imperfectly executed, an approach such as I take here can bring together novels which unfortunately are all too often kept apart. The need for a book of this nature has been gradually impressed upon me by my interaction with demanding students—undergraduates, graduates, as well as some of the postgraduates enrolled in University of California correspondence courses. Since all these have been my unwitting and possibly unwilling contributors, it is only fitting that I should dedicate this volume to the students of English literature at Berkeley, past, present, and future.

U. C. K.

# Laughter and Despair

*And, I pray, with whom should I*
*fight this good fight, if not*
*with Giant Despair?*
Bunyan: *The Pilgrim's Progress*

# Introduction: Entering a Victorian Novel—
## *Barchester Towers*

The word "fiction" means a lie, a deception. Yet in reading a novel we too often tend to be deceived into mistaking its invented world for fact. From its very beginning in the eighteenth century the English novel has pretended to be either history or biography. Defoe, a journalist, skillfully disguised his fiction as an account of factual occurrences; Richardson likewise obscured his own imaginative control of his epistolary novels by pretending that they merely recorded the experiences of actual people. Even Fielding, who reacted against this simulation of actuality, nonetheless helped to perpetuate the notion of the novelist-historian. Writers like Smollett, Jane Austen, and Scott added to the same confusion. For a long time, their "realism" was held to be more veracious, because presumably truer to the conditions of actual life, than the illusory fabrications of "romance."

No novelist is ever able to reproduce a precise mirror image of actual life. Although the novelist may pretend to be nothing more than a faithful chronicler or biographer, although he may claim to be absolutely scientific and accurate, we ought to remember that "no mental method of daguerrotype or photography has yet been discovered, by which the characters of men can be reduced to writing and put into grammatical language with an unerring precision of truthful description."[1] The passage just quoted is taken from Anthony Trollope's *Barchester Towers*. It was written more than a century ago. Yet the confusion between the invented world of the novel and the actual world in which the novelist lived persists to this day. It has

1. Anthony Trollope, *Barchester Towers*, The Oxford Trollope, 2 vols. (Oxford, 1953), ch. 20. Future references in the text are to this edition.

become a particularly troublesome obstacle in the correct appreciation of Victorian fiction, for the Victorian novel—which by and large follows the tradition of Fielding and Smollett and of Scott's historical novels—can all too easily be misread as a kind of photographic replica of nineteenth-century life. More than half of the sophomores I once asked to comment on the relevance of the "love affair" between Pip and Estella in Dickens' *Great Expectations* wrote variations of what amounted to the same contemptuous answer: Dickens, a Victorian, and hence by definition a prude in sexual matters, had shied away from presenting a "mature heterosexual relationship"; presumably, his failure to depict a "frank" affair was attributable to the timidity and repression of his age. Perhaps so. But none of the students who wrote this answer ever asked themselves what the presentation of a candid love affair, portrayed in detail, might have done to the purpose, emphasis, and very mode of *Great Expectations*, a symbolic parable and fairy tale. In arriving at their conclusion, the students had mistaken art for sociology; they had leaned on secondhand historical generalizations, instead of availing themselves directly of the standards generated by the "reality" of the novel before them.

This mistake is not only attributable to innocent undergraduates. Nor can it be ascribed exclusively to those who might confuse a fantasy tale for a "realistic" novel. It is commonly made by all of us who are seduced by the novel's feigned reality into confusing fiction with fact. And it is made particularly by those who, deluded by the verisimilitude of Victorian art, tend to misconstrue the nature of its "realism." Notwithstanding the warning of the narrator of *Barchester Towers*, three highly reputable scholars who have written on Trollope's work have occasionally lapsed into the mistake of viewing his fiction as a "daguerrotype": Michael Sadleir regarded Trollope as being above all the "voice of an epoch," a chronicler, observer, and interpreter of his age who was "concerned, consciously and literally, to portray an actuality he knew";[2] Bonamy Dobrée

2. *Trollope: A Commentary* (Oxford, 1961), p. 15.

4

likewise felt that Trollope presented primarily "a fairly comprehensive and wholly comprehensible picture of the society in which he moved";[3] and Ralph H. Singleton, in his introduction to a recent edition of *Barchester Towers*, echoes these judgments and then goes on to assert that from that particular novel "we do get the clearest picture of mid-Victorian England, because Trollope was insistently preoccupied with producing just that."[4] Inherent in all three estimates is the same confusion between fact and the artist's deliberate transmutation of fact. Although there is certainly nothing wrong in reading a novel like *Barchester Towers* as a kind of document or historical record which may tell the student of the nineteenth century something about the squabbles which took place within the Church of England at the time, this information is not what gives the novel its comprehensibility, nor, I should add, its universality. (*The Warden*, of which *Barchester Towers* is the sequel, is actually more of a historical document. Though not for that reason alone, it also happens to be a lesser work of art than *Barchester Towers*.)

The world imagined by the novelist—whether drawn according to the norms of "realism" or cast in the mold of an improbable "romance"—always contains its own ground rules. To extract these rules we must participate in its invented reality. The novelist who shapes this reality refracts, metamorphoses, and transmutes. He filters the actual world impinging on him into the fictitious world he constructs. His novel is an artifact. It is distorted by a lens which never produces an accurate "picture" of the author's own times, but rather a refraction shaped by his own idiosyncrasies, by the ideals he yearns for as well as by the fears he wants to subdue. It is a "fiction," not a chronicle, and as such offers a dimension of experience different from an objective recording of fact. We must enter this experience not as students of external history but as readers willing to share

3. *The Victorians and After: 1830–1914*, rev. ed. (London, 1950), p. 83.
4. Introduction, Washington Square Press edition (New York, 1963), p. xi.

the novel's internal logic. Although separated by more than a century of changes in historical experience, the reader of today and the Trollope of 1857 can commune through their joint experience of the novel's unaltered reality.

In the remainder of this introduction, I should like to examine three devices essential to our understanding of a novel like *Barchester Towers*: setting, plot, and the elements that arise through the combination of the point of view of the characters with the novelist's use of a narrative voice. I begin with Trollope's fiction for two distinct reasons: first, since *Barchester Towers* is, as we have seen, so commonly extolled for the precise historical "picture" it reflects (a view at variance with Trollope's stated intentions), it provides me with an ideal example for my contention that the "reality" of any Victorian novel must, first of all, be viewed as an entity in itself, independent of any external historical considerations; secondly, the mode of *Barchester Towers*, with its indebtedness to the social comedy of the eighteenth century, furnishes me with a perfect starting point for the progression which I want to trace in the course of this study. The traditional comic form still employed by Trollope in 1857 will allow us to measure the innovations in form introduced by those nineteenth-century writers who used the novel to accommodate a vision far more precarious and pessimistic than his own.

## I

In *Barchester Towers*—as in most Victorian fiction—the novelist's device of setting discloses the primary characteristics of his created world. Trollope later called Barsetshire a "new shire which I added to the English counties," a "little bit of England which I myself have created." The county and its capital, the "cathedral town of Barchester," cannot be found on any map, despite their loose correspondence to Wiltshire or Hampshire, Salisbury or Winchester.[5] Rather than a reproduction of actual-

5. In *An Autobiography* (The Oxford Trollope, ed. Frederick Page [Oxford, 1950]), Trollope mentions that he conceived the story of *The Warden* while visiting Salisbury, but insists on the fictitiousness of the

ity, this placid rural society contains the novelist's reaction to that actuality. Neither a Utopia nor a realm as outlandish as Swift's Lilliput or Houyhnhnmland, Trollope's Barsetshire does nonetheless reflect its creator's peculiar idiosyncrasies and concerns. Its inhabitants belong to a probable world, as probable as Hardy's Wessex or George Eliot's Loamshire, or, in our times, as Faulkner's Yoknapatawpha County. Although the Barchesterians represent a mode of life which could have existed or might exist, they embody above all that quasi-mythical, quasi-pastoral existence that Englishmen still call "Merrie England."

The opening chapters of *Barchester Towers* repeatedly call our attention to the gap which separates the imagined reality of Trollope's novel from the world to which he and his readers belong. In his first two chapters Trollope establishes a contrast he will maintain throughout the entire book: he juxtaposes quiet, sleepy Barchester to a busy outer world, an urban society similar in its composition to that formed by a good portion of his Victorian reading public. Change is the rule in this outer world: cabinets and ministries rise and fall with mechanical regularity, partisan newspapers trump up a new cause every week. Whereas provincial Barchester is self-contained, self-sufficient, and self-engrossed, London, or what the narrator calls "the world at large" (ch. 3), constantly engages in causes it does not even understand. Its Prime Ministers and Parliaments and Church Officials and Newspapers of all affiliations are always meddling and interfering. Opinions abound. If a new bishop is to be appointed

---

county he created in that novel: "I never lived in any cathedral city,—except London" (p. 93). On writing *Framley Parsonage* (1861), the novelist was led to make a "map of the dear county" of Barsetshire (p. 154); many diligent Trollopians have since then followed his lead in trying to reconstruct its topography. In the concluding paragraphs of *The Last Chronicle of Barset* (1867), the author takes farewell of the province and again stresses its imaginary reality and personal relevance: "I may not boast that any beside myself have so realised the place. . . . But to me Barset has been a real county, and its city a real city, and the voices of the people are known to my ears, and the pavement of the city ways are familiar to my footsteps."

for remote Barchester, why, *The British Grandmother*, *The Anglican Devotee*, and *The Eastern Hemisphere* must all have their say on the matter.

Trollope's novel thrives on this initial contrast between a capricious "world at large" and a sluggish provincial enclave suddenly challenged by outward changes. His "London" is semifictional. Rather than a mimetic copy of the world in which he and his contemporaries move, it is above all a caricature that capitalizes on his readers' own associations of London. Trollope's public would immediately understand, for instance, that the powerful *Jupiter*, that all-knowing organ which molds the opinions of an entire British nation, is the author's satirical version of the London *Times*. But if Trollope's London is only slightly distorted by the lens of his satire, Barsetshire, where time seems to run so much more slowly, is far more removed from actuality. The lingering ways of its inhabitants are endorsed by the novelist himself, though even the most Quixotic among them come to realize their dependence on "the powers" ruling the nation's changeful capital. Trollope, however, creates still another setting, even more remote than the cathedral town. At Ullathorne Court and the parish of St. Ewold, situated at the novel's innermost center, time almost stands still. It is there, in the heart of the novel, where appropriately enough the affairs of the heart are eventually settled.

Though belonging to the same uniform "reality" which prevails in the novel, these various settings are arranged according to a kind of gradation which could be represented by a series of concentric circles. On the periphery of the first circle lies the actuality to which novelist and reader belong; within the confines of that first circle lies Trollope's version of the "world at large"; the middle circle contains Barsetshire and Barchester; the innermost sphere holds Ullathorne court. Each of these areas is related. The vanities of London soon find their counterpart in Barchester, whose clergymen and merchants are after all directly connected to the capital both by the railroad and by the new "Electric Telegraph." London is a battleground for busybody parties who do as they like while pretending to pursue the general good; but this same factionalism spreads to Barchester as soon as the London interlopers disturb the town's complacency. The new bishop and his secretary bring with them the unruliness of the outer world. With their arrival, Barchester becomes a battlefield for the duration of the novel.

Ullathorne, on the other hand, seems far more impregnable. The "Court" is properly named, "for the house itself formed two sides of a quadrangle, which was completed on the other sides by a wall about twenty feet high" (ch. 22). This archaic construction, which seems to block out the world beyond it, also safeguards the slower ways of its inhabitants. The Londoners descend on Barchester by the speedy railroad; the Barchesterians in turn pride themselves on the horse-drawn carriages they ride in even for the shortest distances. But no vehicle drawn by horses can ever pass Ullathorne's "iron gate": "If you enter Ullathorne at all, you must do so, fair reader, on foot, or at least in a bathchair" (ch. 22). And yet, though farthest from the outer world, this quaint medieval bastion can never be completely cut off from the motions of change which affect all life. Its residents may lack the convenience of an electric telegraph, but "the world at large might, if it so wished, walk or drive by their iron gates. That part of the world which availed itself of the privilege was however very small." As we shall see later, those few privileged to be drawn past Ullathorne's iron gates profit from their experience.

Trollope does not introduce Ullathorne until his novel is well under way. The clash which sets the story in motion is that between London and Barchester. London's ostensible representative in the novel will be Mr. Proudie; its actual representative, Mr. Slope. While chapters one and two juxtapose Barchester to London by setting Archdeacon Grantly and Mr. Harding against those undefined forces which affect their fates, chapters three and four introduce the figures of the two intruders. Mr. Proudie represents London's self-importance; Mr. Slope, its more oblique designs. Though appointed as a rural bishop, Mr. Proudie is above all a city man. He cannot part with London, for the capital is his domain, his sphere of action: "How otherwise could he keep himself before the world? how else give to the government, in matters theological, the full benefit of his weight and talents?" (ch. 3). At the end of the novel Mr. Proudie will be able to give the government the full benefit of his weighty opinions; appointed to the House of Lords, he manages to register an occasional vote "in favour of Government views on ecclesiastical matters" (ch. 51). But while the bishop represents the empty pomp of the capital, his secretary knows how to tap its true sources of power. This power lies in his ability to exploit the changefulness of "the world at large." Like the witty servants of Roman and Elizabethan comedy who are his prototypes, the bishop's chaplain can adapt himself to change, no matter how abrupt or unforeseen. His very name, Slope, we are told by our helpful narrator, has been changed from that of the good Dr. Slop, the Catholic physician who bungled the birth of Tristram Shandy. Just as Mr. Slope has changed that eminent physician's name, so has his family changed its religion. The future lies with the Low Church party and its innovations. It is to that faction, correspondingly, that Mr. Slope theologically inclines.

The Londoners who now move towards Barchester are for Trollope the representatives of social values that deserve to be mocked. London is a fair of vanities, the breeding ground for false values, but it remains a frame of reference only. It typifies an existence as mechanical and divisive as the imaginary world of Barchester is organic and cohesive. Still, its disorder and change can easily be transplanted. Although the "world at large" represents that confusion between means and ends which Matthew Arnold was to call "machinery," Barsetshire is by no means an ideal realm made up of sweetness and light. Connected by the electric telegraph, linked by the steam locomotive, Barchester is, as Archdeacon Grantly bitterly discovers, very much affected by the decisions so casually made in the capital. It, too, cannot escape change. London oscillates between conservative and liberal governments; the cathedral town hovers uneasily between the old and the new. In London, a conservative government can fall in a matter of minutes; in the slack atmosphere of the provinces, the dying bishop holds on to life for almost a month. To the chagrin of his son, the old man is rather poor at synchronizing his timetable with that of the "world at large."

The old Bishop on his deathbed is the first figure we meet in the novel. He is as much a symbol of the inevitability of change as of Barchester's resistance to change. While the nation asks itself what party will make up the new government, Barchester simply wants to know about its own immediate future. "Who Will Be the New Bishop," is the question it asks itself, rather selfishly, though with honest concern. Even in Barchester change is unavoidable, yet the town's permutations are more deliberate than the capricious shifts of fortune that occur in London life. The old bishop, neither dead nor alive, lingers on and on. When he dies, he does so "as he had lived, peaceably, slowly, without pain and without excitement" (ch. 1). His ways are those of Barsetshire.

## 2

The novel's contrasted settings, then, reflect degrees of antagonism between two distinct modes of life: the peaceful ways of Barchester and the offensive ways of London. Although in actual life most novelists undoubtedly prefer peace to war, a comic novel, like all comedy, relies on conflict and agitation. Trollope's aggressive Londoners are the movers of the plot. Their world at large impinges on the microcosm of Barchester and sets all characters in motion. The outsiders from that world —the Proudies, Mr. Slope, Signora Neroni, and the Stanhopes— stir up the dormant cathedral town almost as violently as the intrusion of the gigantic Gulliver stirred Lilliput. The reader, himself an outsider, is drawn into this miniscule society by venturing into Barchester, within the bishop's palace, and, eventually, past the iron gates of Ullathorne. Amused by the gyrations of the anthill that has been stirred up for him, the reader soon becomes entranced by its motions. He becomes a participant in

Barchester life, sharing its petty preoccupations and insignificant squabbles.

Strife is the essence of Trollope's comedy. Chapter six of the novel is called, quite simply, "WAR!" In it Archdeacon Grantly, who had until that point never bothered to examine his doctrinal views too closely, decides that he must fight Mr. Slope in a battle to the finish. "Proudieism" and "Grantlyism" are born in a flash. The battle lines are drawn. Mock-heroic similes and metaphors begin to build up: "contest," "fight," "adversary," "champion," "combat," are the words now adopted by Barchester, the same community that, at the opening of the book, merely wanted to be left alone. In *Gulliver's Travels*, peace existed among the Lilliputian parties as well as between Lilliput and Blefuscu. The strife and contention, which start immediately upon Gulliver's arrival, end only after the Man Mountain has returned to the outer world. Pretty much the same thing occurs in *Barchester Towers*, partly because the novel's mode harks back to eighteenth-century comedy and satire, and partly also because Anthony Trollope, like Swift, has the conservative outlook of the Tory (there is, however, a vast difference between his Victorian Toryism and that of the Augustans).[6]

At the end of the novel the town's slow ways reassert themselves. Peace returns to Barchester and with it the comedy is ended. The disruptive Mr. Slope is ejected, spewed out by the community: he leaves as "quickly" as he had come, and the town can return to its former immobility. Signora Neroni, that other alien, also leaves; less mobile than the nimble Mr. Slope, she departs in a far more dignified fashion and Barchester womanhood can breathe easier again. The Proudies, to be sure, do remain—some changes are inevitable. But the Bishop and his wife live mostly in London, where he can ceremoniously deliver his vote for the government in power. The only other outsider, Mr. Arabin, will become absorbed by Barchester. Its ways are his ways as well. He is an exile from London and not its deputy.

6. Cf. *An Autobiography*, p. 291: "I consider myself to be an advanced, but still a conservative Liberal."

Thus, the hostilities end as abruptly as they had begun. Mr. Grantly, Barchester's self-appointed champion, finds himself vindicated. "Grantlyism" can dissolve as a political party because with Mr. Slope's departure, "Proudieism," too, is dead. Though the archdeacon remains disappointed in his hopes of succeeding his father, he has never really hated the new bishop or Mrs. Proudie. It is Slope, the parvenu with clammy hands, who is his archenemy. Dr. Proudie, the archdeacon decides early in the novel, has after all "been in the church *these ten years*; and they used to be a little careful ten years ago." But Slope! "How on earth such a creature got ordained!—they'll ordain anybody *now*, I know" (ch. 6, italics added). To this champion of conservatism, the old, even if only dating ten years back, must by definition be better than the new.

To Mr. Grantly the bishop's chaplain is satanic, and clearly our narrator is not overfond of the devious Mr. Slope, who speaks with "the wiles of the serpent." Yet it would be all too easy to convert Mr. Grantly into the author's spokesman, to assume that his conservatism is also that of his creator. If Trollope's point of view were truly identical with that of Grantly, then the novelist's message—rendered in the style of the "electric telegraph"—might simply read:

> "MEN FROM BAD, BAD CITY COME TO GOOD, SIMPLE COUNTRY. DISRUPT ITS ANCIENT VIRTUES WITH THEIR EVIL CITY WAYS: OFFEND GOOD COUNTRYFOLK. AROUSED BARCHESTERIANS GET RID OF BAD CITY SLICKERS, RETURN TO THEIR HABITUAL WAYS. THUS GOOD TRIUMPHS OVER EVIL. REGARDS. ANTHONY TROLLOPE."

Obviously such a message would be far too reductive, for it completely ignores Trollope's subtle injection of his values, his presentation of his own point of view. We have so far discussed setting or place and also sketched out broadly the novel's general movement or plot. Although important for our understanding of *Barchester Towers*, neither setting nor plot are sufficient in themselves.

In his candid remarks about his practice as a novelist, Trollope wrote in his *Autobiography* that he regarded plot as being "the most insignificant part of a tale." The plotting of *Barchester Towers* is hardly as complex as that of Dickens' or George Eliot's novels. Trollope's characters interact, but their interaction is produced by a series of dramatic episodes, a string of separate meetings, incidents, conversations—each vivid and memorable in itself—rather than through a tightly knit sequence of events. The situations that give rise to each of these scenes are simple in themselves: the available bishopric, almost immediately filled by Mr. Proudie; the available wardenship, alternately promised to Mr. Harding and Mr. Quiverful; the available hand (and fortune) of Eleanor Bold, desired by three separate suitors; and, halfway through the novel, the available deanery of Barchester Cathedral, aspired to by Mr. Slope, turned down by Mr. Harding, and finally awarded to Mr. Arabin.

Will Mr. Harding or Mr. Quiverful get the wardenship? Will Mr. Slope or Bertie Stanhope or Mr. Arabin get Eleanor's hand? Will a Proudieite or a Grantlyite get the Deanship? The reader knows the answers to these questions. And he knows them because he is supposed to know them. For Trollope's narrator refuses to spring unforeseen surprises on the reader (as will Dickens in *Our Mutual Friend*). Quite to the contrary, this narrator is eager to let us into his confidence: "But let the gentle-hearted reader be under no apprehension whatsoever. It is not destined that Eleanor shall marry Slope or Bertie Stanhope" (ch. 15). The remark sets us at ease—having eliminated two of Eleanor's suitors at a single stroke, we can safely guess the identity of the happy man.

The narrator gives us his doctrine that author and reader ought to move along together in perfect confidence: "Let the personages of the drama undergo ever so complete a comedy of errors among themselves, but let the spectator never mistake the Syracusan for the Ephesian; otherwise he is one of the dupes, and the part of a dupe is never dignified" (ch. 15). Why should the narrator surprise us or keep us in suspense? A peek at the novel's conclusion or the casual remark of a previous reader might easily destroy all our precious illusions. And so the narrator prefers to let us in on the follies and misconceptions of his characters and allows us to believe that only they, and not we, are the dupes. To Henry James and to Jamesian critics of the novel, these narrative intrusions seemed a crime, a "betrayal of a sacred office." In his essay on the "The Art of Fiction" James wrote:

> I was lately struck, in reading over many pages of Anthony Trollope, with his want of discretion . . . In a digression, a parenthesis or an aside, he concedes to the reader that he and this trusting friend are only "making believe." He admits that the events he narrates have not really happened, and that he can give his narrative any turn the reader may like best.[7]

Possibly, James was thinking of passages such as that in chapter forty-three of *Barchester Towers*, where the narrator bemoans the fact that he has to dispose of "our friends" in the small remainder of "this one volume," and then goes on to wish that his publisher, Mr. Longman, would allow him a fourth volume to expatiate on further adventures (*Barchester Towers* was a so-called "three-decker," one of the three-volume novels in fashion until the end of the nineteenth century). This deliberate puncturing of our credulity occurs also in the remarks that introduce the last chapter of the book: "The end of a novel, like the end of a children's dinner-party, must be made up of sweetmeats and sugarplums." It is easy to see how such statements would have offended those who were dead serious about the art of fiction. To the outraged Henry James the mere notion that an artistic construct could be compared to the beneficent distribution of sweetmeats and sugarplums seemed a "terrible crime" indeed: "It implies that the novelist is less occupied in looking for the truth (the truth, of course I mean, that he assumes, the premises

7. "The Art of Fiction," *The Future of the Novel*, ed. Leon Edel (New York, 1950), p. 6.

that we grant him, whatever they may be) than the historian, and in doing so it deprives him at a stroke of all his standing room."[8] Later critics concurred. Assuming the Flaubertian notion (endorsed by Joyce) of a godlike artist who stands behind his handiwork, refined out of existence, they were as disturbed as James was by Trollope's unabashedly chatty narrator.

James' diagnosis is essentially correct. Trollope constantly calls our attention to the duping process of his art. But James' indignation is misplaced, for he failed to grant Trollope the very "premises" by which we come to place our trust in the delightful persona of the loquacious narrator. Although this narrator is indeed a spokesman for the novelist himself, he is also a character. His imperfections therefore link him both to the "dupes" in the novel and to those who, like the reader, live in an actual world of imperfection. Although he may pretend to take us into his full confidence, he can also be evasive, forcing us to make our own judgments: "My readers will guess from what I have written that I myself do not like Mr. Slope; but I am constrained to admit that he is a man of parts." The narrator's mock protestations (as in the famous incident of the slap), his calculated uncertainties, suggest that, far from destroying the "truth" of Trollope's novel, he complicates this truth for us. Like Mr. Slope, this narrator (who, as we shall later see, owes much to Thackeray's evasive Showman) can at times speak in a most "ambiguous manner."

The narrator's digressions about the course of the story do not in the least diminish our enjoyment of the novel. In fact it is precisely because his remarks allow us to anticipate the outcome of events, precisely because they establish the plot's predictability, that we cherish the individual episodes and vignettes all the more. Because we know that all will end well, that order will return to Barchester, we enjoy the disorder as long as it lasts. We take an interest in each situation and cling to the variations and complications that that situation affords. The disruptions pro-

8. *Ibid.*

duced by the discursive narrator only heighten our appreciation of the disruptions provided by the novel's plot.

If Trollope's narrator acts as a link between the characters and the reader, he also prevents us from becoming totally seduced by the enticing, lifelike quality of his fictive world. Although he describes and interprets the settings of the novel, although he does his very best to involve us in the events he unfolds for us, he never lets us forget that these settings and these events are feigned. The narrator thus invites us to participate in a fiction. He is a gamester who toys, for instance, with the notion that his novel is a "history." He tells us in great detail about the debates that led to the bill which regulates the administration of Hiram's Hospital, and his account sounds most authentic. But then he continues: "The bill, however, did pass, and at the time at which this history is *supposed* to commence, it had been ordained. . . ." Again and again, he maintains this pretended uncertitude. He tells us that our "present business at Barchester will not occupy us above a year *or two* at the furthest" (ch. 2, italics added). Or, in sketching Dr. Proudie's background, he informs us that the gentleman had "seven *or* eight children" (ch. 3, italics added).

The narrator also mocks our faith in the accuracy of his "history" by his repeated introduction of literary references. Squire Thorne, we are informed, is a "specimen" of the race "which a century ago was, as we are told, fairly represented by Squire Western" (ch. 22). The pretended unsureness produced by "as we are told" calls attention to the make-believe involved in a characterization that depends on literary cross-references. As mentioned above, Mr. Slope is a lineal descendant of another fictional character, Dr. Slop in *Tristram Shandy*. At least, the narrator tells us, so he has "heard it asserted." The fiction of the reporter is maintained with tongue-in-cheek: "All my researches on the subject have, however, failed in enabling me to fix the date on which the family changed its religion" (ch. 4). The effect of such statements is carefully calculated. Like the Fielding who buttonholes his readers in *Tom Jones* and *Joseph*

*Andrews*, Trollope wants us to realize that he is in complete control of his story—that we are reading not history but fiction, devised and directed by him.

The voice of Trollope's narrator, then, complicates our initial responses to setting and plot; what is more, it also complicates our reaction to the characters themselves. Victorian fiction depends above all on the profound appeal of its characters. The Victorian novelists relied on their representation of men and women to engage their readers and establish shared sympathies and aversions. By using their characters to bring out each reader's elementary need for identification and dissociation, the novelists were able to share gratifying wishes and defenses with their public. Trollope, too, relied essentially on characterization to mold our point of view and bring it in contact with his implied beliefs. He lets his figures think, act, and speak for themselves, yet also tells us (or, more often, pretends to tell us) through the voice of his narrator what our attitudes ought to be. In the following section we will examine Trollope's handling of Archdeacon Grantly and Mr. Harding in the opening chapter and try to determine how this initial contrast helps to set up attitudes that Trollope wants us to retain for the remainder of his novel.

### 3

The opening scene of *Barchester Towers* offers an excellent illustration of Trollope's ability to manipulate our responses toward his characters. The first pages introduce us to Archdeacon Grantly, who later becomes the nominal paladin of the Barchester forces, and who should, ostensibly, become the reader's paladin as well. A competent and dedicated clergyman, he has, in effect, ruled as unofficial bishop during his father's protracted illness and therefore deserves to be appointed by the government as the old man's successor. Grantly becomes understandably offended when the newly arrived Proudies foist their opinions on him: "The archdeacon," the narrator tells us dryly, "knew his subject, and really understood the business of bishop-ing, which the others did not." Still, despite the legality of Grantly's claims, Trollope deliberately undercuts his characterization. Although the narrator professes that we tolerate the archdeacon's weaknesses, he denies us all possible means for such an identification.

"Proud, wishful, worldly," are the three adjectives that the narrator attaches to Grantly in the opening pages of the book. The description is repeated at the end of the first chapter:

> Our archdeacon was worldly—who among us is not so? He was ambitious—who among us is ashamed to own that "last infirmity of noble minds!" He was avaricious, my readers will say. No—it was for no love of lucre that he wished to be bishop of Barchester. He was his father's only child, and his father had left him great wealth. His preferment brought him in nearly three thousand a year. The bishopric, as cut down by the Ecclesiastical Commission, was only five. He would be a richer man as archdeacon than he could be as bishop. But he certainly did desire to play first fiddle; he did desire to sit in full lawn sleeves among the peers of the realm; and he did desire, if the truth must out, to be called "My Lord" by his reverend brethren.

The description sticks in our minds. While the narrator exculpates Mr. Grantly from being avaricious, his defense only helps to indict the archdeacon and to link him with his London adversaries. Though cast as antagonists, Slope and Grantly are more alike than not (in fact, as we shall see in the next chapter, the two are the only masculine figures in a society where women fight the battles of their men). To be sure, the archdeacon is not avaricious. Slope is a fortune hunter because he wants power; Proudie is money-minded because he is vain, eager to parade his carriage before the eyes of fashionable Mayfair. But if Mr. Grantly is not avaricious, it is only because, unlike the Proudies or Slope, he happens to be rich. His ambitions, therefore, merely take a different outlet. Like Mr. Proudie, he is vain; like Mrs. Proudie or Slope, he wants to play first fiddle. He is as power-hungry as the man he shall try to unthrone.

What convinces us most strongly that we do not want Dr. Grantly as our future paladin is the situation Trollope dramatizes in the opening chapter. More than the mere words "proud," "wishful," "worldly," "ambitious," the dominant impression is that of a son wishing to hasten his father's death. Trollope handles the situation with tact and skill. The Bishop has for all intents and purposes been dead for a month; he is in a coma, and life and death seem so much alike to this good, old, virtuous man who is so sure to find his reward in heaven. And his son's predicament is, after all, so urgent. The conservative government may fall any minute; the archdeacon is in his fifties—clearly this is his last chance. The scene is delicately rendered. It is potentially tragic (one thinks of Edmund wishing Gloucester's death). Even to non-Freudians, the situation evokes deep-rooted emotions. Trollope avoids stirring our passions too violently, and yet, at the same time, forces the archdeacon to ask himself "whether he had really longed for his father's death." The question is now out in the open. And, then, with calculated ambivalence, the novelist suppresses the direct answer we have come to expect: "The proud, wishful, worldly man, sank on his knees by the bedside, and taking the bishop's hands within his own, prayed eagerly that his *sins* might be forgiven him" (italics added). It is Dr. Grantly who has used the word "sins," not the narrator—its usage is the only admission we are allowed to glimpse. For the kneeling archdeacon's humility is short-lived. When, moments later, his father does die, his thoughts turn worldly again. He thinks of the electric telegraph at the very same time that he remembers that he must maintain a doleful appearance: "how without appearing unfeeling was he to forget his father in the bishop—to overlook what he had lost and think of what he might possibly gain?" Obviously, the possibility of gain outweighs the reality of his loss.

When at the end of the chapter the narrator steps into the story in his own voice he contributes to our uneasiness about Mr. Grantly. The question asked (but not answered) by the archdeacon before his father's death is now raised again by the narrator: "Many will think that he was wicked to grieve for the loss of episcopal power, wicked to have coveted it, nay wicked even to have thought about it, in the way and at the moments he had done so." The triple repetition of the word "wicked" is disturbing, even though the narrator now tells us that he cannot "*completely* agree" with the "censures" he attributes to his readers. What is more, the nature of his defense is deliberately inconclusive: we are asked not to expect our clergymen to be "more than men," to recognize that a lawyer does not "*sin*" in seeking to be a judge, that a young diplomat trying to rise in an embassy "entertains a fair ambition." The chapter concludes with what purports to be a simple statement of fact: "His hopes, however, were they innocent or sinful, were not fated to be realised; and Dr. Proudie was consecrated Bishop of Barchester." The wedged-in clause, "were they innocent or sinful," is unsettling. The interjected words remind us that we as readers must make the judgment that the slippery narrator refuses to provide. "Innocent"? A man who is proud, wishful, and worldly, whose desire to play first fiddle has just been emphasized, cannot be considered innocent. "Sinful"? Dr. Grantly has himself used that word. As Trollope has suggested, and as he will stress again and again, the archdeacon is as fallible as most men. Even more than the too innocuous Mr. Proudie or than the too conniving Mr. Slope, this character can act as an apt representative of the vanities which the novelist wants us to recognize in ourselves. At the same time, however, Mr. Grantly can never be the spokesman of an author who addresses us through the voice of a narrator who inevitably refuses to pass judgment. Dr. Grantly is too sure, too self-righteous for that. Although we may think him to be on the right side of the battles of Barchester, we are led to discover that all "sides," all partisanship, merely cover up the same basic human vanities: pride, ambition, the desire for influence and power.

It is significant that this first chapter should also introduce Mr. Harding, the different, timid, evasive ex-warden. It is equally noteworthy that Trollope has the old bishop die in the presence of his old friend, as well as in that of his ambitious son. Indeed, the description of the bishop who ruled with such "meek authority" resembles rather strongly that of the warden who resigned his stewardship out of meekness. Ostensibly, it is the archdeacon who is in the foreground in chapter one. It is his drama that we are interested in. But Mr. Harding, passive, undramatic, forever a bystander, is just as important to the first chapter's architecture as the manly Barchester champion. The dying old man addresses both his friend and his son; he blesses them jointly before expiring.

Mr. Harding is the archdeacon's father-in-law, yet the relationship between the two men proves to be curiously qualified, as qualified as Dr. Grantly's grief for his father. In the same sentence in which we find the two mourners yoked to each other by the death of the bishop, we learn that they have not been at all close to each other in the past: "There was more fellowship between them at that moment than there had ever been before." Moreover, this momentary "fellowship" turns out to be quite one-sided. It is Mr. Harding who, contrary to his usual ways, takes the initiative when he grasps Grantly's hands and presses them warmly. His warmness, however, is not matched by any corresponding feelings in his son-in-law. The older man's innocence is jolted when he is asked to send the telegraph message that Grantly has been composing in his mind: "Mr. Harding who had really been somewhat surprised to find Dr. Grantly, as he thought, so much affected, was rather taken aback; but he made no objection. He knew that the archdeacon had some hope of succeeding to his father's place, though he by no means knew how highly raised that hope had been."

Mr. Harding cannot fathom the extent of his son-in-law's ambitions, because Grantly's mode of thinking is too removed from his own. If the one man is ruled by the power of feeling, the other is ruled by his awareness of the power of London. The devious archdeacon tells his father-in-law that Mr. Harding must sign the message he wants to send to the prime minister; he tells him how to deliver it to the telegraph office; he even gives him a half-crown: "Mr. Harding felt very much like an errand-boy and also felt that he was called on to perform his duties as such at rather an unseemly time." The older man is puzzled on seeing his name on the message, but is reassured by the archdeacon: "What name so proper as that of so old a friend as yourself? The Earl won't look at the name, you may be sure of that; but my dear Mr. Harding, pray don't lose any time."

The decisiveness of the younger man's tone admits no remonstration. Grantly is conscious of his dependence on "time," of the shifts of London, but it is Mr. Harding, and not the bishop's son, who is truly aware of the "unseemly time" and the unseemly gesture. We like the father-in-law, not the resolute son-in-law he only dares to address as "archdeacon," and Trollope makes us like him precisely because he is so meek and put-upon. We are therefore delighted at the sudden poetic justice that Trollope springs on us. As the old man obediently trots off to deliver the electric telegram for his scheming son-in-law—a telegram he neither composed nor wants to deliver, even though it has been signed in his own name—this aged and good-natured errand boy unwittingly gives the archdeacon the come-uppance Mr. Grantly so richly deserves. Almost by coincidence, Mr. Harding now remembers the news he had come to deliver but had forgotten in his excitement and grief over the death of his old friend: "He had found the moment so inopportune for any mundane tidings that he had repressed the words which were on his tongue." But now he recollects. " 'But archdeacon,' said he, turning back, 'I forgot to tell you—The ministry are out.' " The death of his father had raised the archdeacon's hopes; the death of the ministry kills them forever. And we rejoice.

The incident dramatized in this first chapter is a miniature of the entire novel. Mr. Harding's role in this episode is typical of his position throughout the book. Unworldly, naive, forgetful of "mundane tidings," the former warden is the exact opposite of his proud, wishful, worldly son-in-law. If Mr. Grantly wants to play first fiddle, the author of *Harding's Church Music* prefers to play his imaginary violincello. The old man is soon dragged into the clerical warfare of Barchester by the town's self-styled champion. His extraordinary timidity is laughable, his tendency to misconstrue the feelings and motives of others, almost exasperating. Still, Trollope's novel concludes with a description of him and not of his ambitious son-in-law. What is more, in the course of the story, Mr. Harding acquires a second son-in-law, a man almost as self-effacing as himself. Mr. Arabin compensates him for the intimidating Dr. Grantly. For Mr. Harding and Mr. Arabin (whom the warden might even dare to call by his first name) are unlike the leader of their camp, who, though a High Churchman, above all resembles Mr. Slope the Low Church evangelical. Like Slope, the archdeacon forgets the precept quoted in chapter four: "Blessed are the meek, for they shall inherit the earth." And in the invented, delightfully artificial world of Barchester, where Anthony Trollope pulls the strings, the meek actually can inherit the earth.

I have used *Barchester Towers* to illustrate the truism that a fiction is, above all, a fiction. Like all the Victorian novelists considered in this study, Trollope thrives on illusion. The world created by a novelist derives its fullest identity from each reader's wishfulness, from our need to resist the encroachments of a too restrictive view of actuality. The pleasure-evoking constructs each novelist devises become continuous with the private worlds that each of us creates to ward off the threat posed by uncertainty, doubt, and change.

We should not enter a Victorian novel like *Barchester Towers* by expecting to find a faithful replica of a fixed, external reality; instead, we should regard it as a fluid fantasy that enables author and audience to react jointly against an alienating world of change and disorder. As sharers and participants in an illusion of order, novelist and reader become tentative allies against chaos. Thus it is that the fight between Barchester and "London," examined in the chapter which follows, will prove to be emblematic of the fight of "laughter" against "despair" traced in the remainder of this book.

# I  *Barchester Towers*: The Comedy of Change

Like all the Victorian novels discussed in this book, *Barchester Towers* draws the reader into a fictive reality that simultaneously imitates and counters the disjunctions of the actual world. As representative of that disjunctive external world, Slope the Intruder acts as the novelist's agent as well as his antagonist. Though rendered laughable and, at the end, made to seem quite innocuous, Mr. Slope thus is cast in essentially the same role as those more serious perturbers, Thackeray's Becky Sharp and Conrad's Vladimir. In *Barchester Towers*, however, the placid pastoral world Trollope has invented ceases to be convulsed as soon as this outside agitator is removed; in *Vanity Fair* and in *The Secret Agent*, on the other hand, Becky Sharp and Vladimir merely mirror the dominant ways of an unstable and unsettling Vanity Fair. To use Trollope's quietistic comedy as the starting point for a progression that will immediately take us to Thackeray's grim panorama of flux and vanity and lead us, eventually, to Conrad's terrifying approximation of chaos may therefore seem an odd choice.

There is, furthermore, an odd breach in chronology: *Barchester Towers* was published in 1857, ten years after both *Vanity Fair* and *Wuthering Heights*. Compared with either of these works, Trollope's novel seems curiously antiquated in outlook as well as in its artistic form. Whereas Thackeray's satiric vignettes of urban mobility and Emily Brontë's romance about the decay of two country houses yield a vision of irreconcilables, Trollope's mildly disarrayed world seems all too easily restored. Barchester life proves to be only slightly affected by the rapid shifts of London, Trollope's inconstant "world at large." While Thackeray and Brontë seriously question the values on which modern civilization is predicated, Trollope relies on his notions of eighteenth-century decorum to placate his desire for order. To protect themselves against some of the same insecurities which Trollope fears, Thackeray and Emily Brontë were led to experiment with new fictional forms. Although, in a way, Trollope too is an improviser, his adaptation of Fielding and Smollett for his purposes hardly seemed innovative by 1857. As early as 1836–1837, in *The Pickwick Papers*, Dickens had tried to evoke the quaintness of the eighteenth-century in order to lend stability to that deranged and dehumanized world he was to portray with increasing intensity in his later work.

Why, then, should we begin with Trollope? It is precisely because he is so successful in his game, because he manages to delude us into thinking that he has provided us with nothing more than a throwback to an earlier, uncomplicated age, that his accomplishment is unique. His world of purgative laughter and complete poetic justice serves as an impregnable bastion against the same confusion that his contemporaries could not manage to screen as easily or as completely. Trollope does not, however, fence out that confusion; quite to the contrary, he invites it into his archaic bastion just as Miss Thorne admits "the world at large" into the walled interior of Ullathorne Court. Within the confines of *Barchester Towers* the same forces which other novelists magnified into gigantic proportions are starved into a Lilliputian shape. Trollope welcomes chaos because, through the mock-heroic and burlesque, he can reduce it and laugh it away.

The same tension underlying the novels we shall consider in later chapters thus exists in *Barchester Towers* in a simpler and more pristine shape. There is an alternation between threat and relief, between the fear of disintegration and the pleasure brought through the return of harmony. Compelled by Trollope to identify with Mr. Harding, we soon share his sense of dislocation, the anxiety that comes with the insider's displacement by the outsider. In *Barchester Towers*, however, Mr. Harding's alienation is at best potential; it is handled lightly by the jovial narrator whose presence assure us that relief is in sight. In other novels, where the fluctuations between laughter and

despair take on far more somber hues, the discordances that vex
Mr. Harding cannot as readily be reconstituted into harmony.
In these novels patterns similar to those employed by Trollope
will recur, yet with a quite altered emphasis. Thus, the fear of
dislocation we share with Mr. Harding becomes intensified
when his place is taken by a Maggie Tulliver or a Jude; the pleasure we derive from the expulsion of a Silas Wegg or Vladimir
must reconcile us to changes that are far more irreparable than
the slight alterations left in the wake of Mr. Slope's departure.
The homogeneity that reigns at the end of *Barchester Towers*,
though sought by the other novelists, can seldom be duplicated.
In Mr. Arabin, Mr. Harding finds a son in his own image. Such
continuity is impossible in all those novels which stress the gap
between fathers and children as a metaphor for the disruption so
strongly felt by the Victorians. Even in those novels where there
are similar attempts at continuity, the differences are palpable:
Fred Vincy fashions himself after his father-in-law and Hareton
becomes a humanized Heathcliff, but both are secondary figures, shaded by more pathetic counterparts.

Trollope himself was to write the far more gloomy, Thackerayan, *The Way We Live Now* in 1875. In 1857, however, he
fortified himself and his readers by writing a novel he might well
have entitled "The Way We Still May Live." In *Barchester
Towers* he calmly defused the despair that led other Victorian
novelists to defend themselves through constructs that were far
bolder, but also far more uneven in form.

## I

Thematically as well artistically, *Barchester Towers* relies on
the juxtaposition of the ostensible and the implied. Throughout
the novel, the narrator distinguishes between facade and motive,
between what he calls the "outer" and the "inner" man. He extends this distinction not only to dissemblers like Mr. Slope but
even to characters like Eleanor Bold or Mr. Arabin, who, though
far less fallible, are only imperfectly aware of their own inner
motives. It is significant, in this connection, that Trollope should

employ the mythical domain of Ullathorne to disengage the "inner" from the "outer" self. At Ullathorne, which rigorously filters the influx of the world at large, an honesty is possible which exists neither in London nor in Barchester. The small sphere of the Thornes seems hopelessly limited; it refines even further the stylized world of Trollope's comedy. Still, it is precisely because, in it, the characters "see so very very little"[1] that they also learn to recognize what may be most genuine and enduring.

It is at Ullathorne that Bertie Stanhope reveals truths he would not have dared to utter in Barchester; at Ullathorne, where Eleanor tells her father what she would not openly admit in Dr. Grantly's house; at Ullathorne, where the stiff Mr. Arabin finally manages to say "Eleanor" instead of "Mrs. Bold." At Ullathorne even Mr. Slope is led to abandon his indirections. He drops his ambiguous verbal allusions and puts his arm around Eleanor's waist. And she retaliates in kind: "quick as thought, she raised her little hand and dealt him a box on the ear with such right good will, that it sounded among the trees like a miniature thunder-clap" (ch. 40). The action, like many other actions in Trollope's world, is mock-heroic, but unlike the fulminations of the *Jupiter* or Mr. Grantly's oaths and imprecations, this miniature thunderclap, delivered by a dainty hand, is genuine. Ullathorne may be ludicrous, as outlandish as the Thornes themselves. Its very quaintness, however, allows Trollope to convert it into the center of feeling of his novel.

What seems salient and prominent in *Barchester Towers* is invariably not so. As we saw in the Introduction, the book's opening chapter ostensibly dramatizes the aspirations and plight of Archdeacon Grantly, whereas its primary effect is to introduce us to the undramatic, but truly central, figure of Grantly's father-in-law. Ostensibly again, the novel's main plot line seems to be built around the wardenship of Hiram's Hospital. Yet the competition for this office is secondary; it is created by Trollope

1. Anthony Trollope, *Barchester Towers*, The Oxford Trollope, 2 vols. (Oxford, 1953), ch. 48. Future references in the text are to this edition.

solely for the purpose of introducing complications that become so absorbing that the wardenship itself is made utterly insignificant. Even these complications, which presumably depict the battle between two clerical factions, soon turn out to conceal something else: the battle of the sexes.

The question of "Who Will Be the New Warden?" replaces, after the first chapter, the quickly answered question of "Who Will Be the New Bishop?" Trollope's handling of the plot soon makes this second question seem less and less compelling. The reader immediately sympathizes with Mr. Harding, whose claims to the position he had lost in *The Warden* seem rightful. When Mr. Harding, cleverly outmaneuvered by Slope, feels displaced and thrown out on the "rubbish cart" as outmoded dross, we are all the more drawn to his side. Yet the reader's sympathies are dampened as soon as we discover that, by supporting Harding, we are also supporting his vociferous son-in-law who vows that "we" must battle for the wardenship. We waver in our allegiances. The reader knows that Grantly's schemes to import Mr. Arabin and Dr. Gwynne to fight under his banner are meaningless: in the interim, the fickle Mr. Slope has altered his plans, having discovered that Mr. Harding is the father of a daughter as rich as she is beautiful. When new participants jump into the fray—with the enraged Mrs. Quiverful pleading for the intervention of Mrs. Proudie in the name of her fourteen little arrows—the contest for a position no longer desired by Mr. Harding himself becomes ludicrous. The three characters who ought to be most directly involved in the action —the bishop empowered to award the position and the two candidates for it—passively stand at the sidelines, displaced by a trio to whom the position itself is relevant only as a test for their strength. Thus, Dr. Proudie hovers insecurely between his secretary and his wife; Mr. Quiverful between Mr. Slope and his own wife; Mr. Harding between Slope and Grantly. Ultimately, Mr. Harding does not at all mind having the appointment go to his rival; diverted by other thoughts, he has become far more apprehensive about his daughter's status than his own. Quiverful, who really needs the job, thus gets it by default. The reader too has been diverted. The alliances, attacks, counterattacks, and capitulations have turned out to be far more absorbing than their prime mover—the wardenship itself. We care about Trollope's endless improvisations; separate episodes, separate conversations, separate character sketches and vignettes have engrossed us completely. The disputed wardenship has been but a ploy to engage us in the battle of the clergy.

Yet this battle, too, turns out to be a sham. Though Grantly declares war against Slope after their first and only meeting, the promised combat between the two men never takes place. For all his heroic speeches and posturings, Grantly is as wary a combatant as the enemy whose indirections he despises. He refuses to meet Slope head-on. Instead, he addresses his cohort, marshals it through meaningless exercises, and imports Arabin as a sure-fire ally, an "ecclesiastical knight before whose lance Mr. Slope was to fall and bite the dust" (ch. 47). The new paladin's fame rests solely on his rhetorical powers as a polemicist; Arabin has faced Slope only in the pages of a newspaper. When he and the bishop's chaplain meet at last, it is not as public jousters, but rather as two men privately competing for Eleanor Bold. Mr. Harding's public cause has been all but forgotten (indeed, Grantly and his allies do not even know that Slope, too, now wants Harding to become the warden). When Grantly brings in still another champion, Dr. Gwynne, the master of Lazarus College, neither he nor that gentleman suspects that the enemy they want (but do not dare) to fight openly has already fallen out of favor with the bishop.

Hence, at the end of the novel Mr. Grantly's inflated sense of victory is ridiculous. He has never met Slope directly, yet he assures himself that somehow he has led his forces to a triumph of epic proportions. The narrator slyly undermines the belligerent clergyman's self-aggrandizement. He first renders Grantly's thoughts in all their pomposity: "The archdeacon had trampled upon Mr. Slope, and had lifted to high honours the young clergyman whom he had induced to quit the retirement and comfort of the university." The narrator then adds, in his own voice: "So at least the archdeacon thought; though, to speak sooth, not he, but circumstances, had trampled on Mr. Slope" (ch. 52). The implications are clear. The archdeacon takes credit for a battle he has waged only in his own mind. For Slope, and Slope alone, has been the novel's actor. It is he who first disrupts the harmony of Barchester and he again who, by overreaching himself, brings about the restoration of peace and order.

In a tongue-in-cheek improvisation on *Paradise Lost*, Trollope's narrator tells us that every novel should have its male and female angels, as well as its male and female devils (ch. 26). Dr. Grantly unequivocally regards Slope as "a messenger from Satan." The narrator's more jocular use of demonic allusions throughout the story invites us to regard the chaplain as a ludicrous cousin of the conniver who, in *Paradise Lost*, forced God's angels into a similar position of reaction. Still, the archdeacon who prides himself on having trampled on his adversary is by no means one of the novel's "male angels." In *Paradise Lost* war was the fault of a single party; in Trollope's mock-epic world, Slope's "pride" is very much shared by Grantly. In Milton's heaven, the good angels became infected by Satan's unfair tactics; mountains began to fly all over the place. In Barchester, neither a heaven nor a paradise, the Grantlyites become even more confused. In Trollope's travesty an oily, carrot-headed minister with sweaty hands replaces Milton's heroic Satan, molehills replace flying mountains, and a well-applied slap is substituted for Michael's fiery sword. This unheroic world contains no peerless angels.

Like a good tactician, Mr. Slope knows how to exploit the element of surprise. He deliberately provokes the clergymen who have gathered in the cathedral to listen to his first sermon. Like Milton's fiend, who spoke in "ambiguous words,"[2] the crafty secretary speaks in an "ambiguous manner" (ch. 6); yet

2. *Paradise Lost*, VI.568.

his words are sufficiently unambiguous to reveal his objectives to his captive audience. Mr. Slope takes his sermon from St. Paul's text: "Study to show thyself approved unto God, a workman that needeth not to be ashamed, rightly dividing the word of truth."[3] Hiding behind both the authority of the Scriptures and the authority of the bishop who sits behind him, he uses this authority for divisive purposes. The new doctrines he advances merely mask his personal ambitions. (Mr. Arabin's text at St. Ewold, in Ullathorne, is the exact reverse of Slope's: "Whosoever transgresseth and abideth not in the doctrine of God, hath no God.")

Like his heroic cousin, "the damp, sandy-haired, saucer-eyed, red-fisted Mr. Slope" at first seems to exert a distinct power over "the female breast." The party now forming in Barchester on his "side of the question" consists "chiefly of ladies" (ch. 7). Satan, in the guise of the serpent, raised Eve's expectations by promising her unforeseen changes; this minister, who knows and uses "the wiles of the serpent" (ch. 8), promises to alter the "old humdrum way" of Barchester. The ladies of his party are willing to lend him their ears: "People in advance of their age now had new ideas, and it was high time that Barchester should go in advance" (ch. 7). Still, Mr. Slope's acquired power is precarious. The narrator risks a prediction: "Could Mr. Slope have adapted his manners to men as well as to women, could he ever have learnt the ways of a gentleman, he might have risen to great things" (ch. 8). The words are rather ironic, for it is by women and not by men that Mr. Slope will be defeated. Wounded by Eleanor's smart slap, deflated by Signora Neroni, and stripped of his powers by Mrs. Proudie, the novel's "male devil" becomes incongruous in his role. He is a Satan defeated by Eve.

The pride that caused both Satan's and Adam's fall is neatly distributed among all men in Trollope's comic universe. To remind us that Grantlyism and its quarrelsome flag-bearer are subject to Mr. Slope's own flaws, Trollope engages in a superb

3. 2 Timothy, 2:15.

parody of Milton's epic in chapter seven, "The Dean and Chapter Take Counsel." In *Paradise Lost* the fallen angels called a counsel to determine whether to fight God openly or with guile; but in the face of an all-seeing and omnipotent God, their heroism was futile. Trollope plays with a similar situation but deliberately reverses the parties: it is the "good" party, stung by Slope's sermon, who meet to hold a "high debate together as to how Mr. Slope should be put down." Milton's scene is anti-heroic; the warriors whose appeal to arms is so sonorous are secretly aware of their impotence. Trollope's scene exaggerates this same absurdity: the congregation of clergymen do not dare to engage an enemy shielded by the authority of their bishop. The best they can do is to hold on to their own self-respect. Just as Milton's angels vainly exulted in their former titles, Powers, Thrones, Dominions, so do dean, prebendary, vicar, and canon cling to their hierarchical positions. In Pandemonium, Satan rose to announce a safe course of action against God's divine authority; in the deanery, where there are neither archangels nor archfiends, it is the archdeacon who manfully tries to rally his dispirited forces. His introduction carries a Miltonic ring:

> Then up rose Dr. Grantly; and, having
> Thus collected the scattered wisdom
> Of his association, spoke forth with words
> Of deep authority.

But this epic note is quickly undermined by the narrator: "When I say up rose the archdeacon, I speak of the inner man, which then sprang up to more immediate action, for the doctor, had, bodily, been standing all along with his back to the dean's empty fire-grate, and the tails of his frock supported over his two arms. His hands were in his breeches pocket."

Milton's Satan asserted his power over his fallen band by promising to fight single-handed the warfare they eschew; eagerly, the fallen angels give up their authority to him. The scene in the deanery ends with a similar submission to Mr. Grantly:

"There was much more discussion among the learned conclave, all of which, of course, ended in obedience to the archdeacon's commands. They had too long been accustomed to his rule to shake it off so soon." Trollope's parody thus reinforces Milton's insight: in the face of change, men, like angels, gladly abdicate their freedom to those who promise them a restoration of their former prerogatives. Both scenes end with an illusion: the members of the fallen party, aware of their own inability to reverse change, rejoice in the notion that their leader will defy the authority they fear. In *Paradise Lost* this illusion is nurtured by Satan's majestic speech—a speech that will be followed by immediate action: the flight through Chaos and the Portals of Hell. In *Barchester Towers*, however, Mr. Grantly will never match words with actions. Instead, he merely indulges in vituperation. When he declares Slope's behavior to have been abominable, his pliant audience readily agrees: " 'Abominable,' groaned the dean. 'Abominable,' muttered the meagre doctor. 'Abominable,' re-echoed the chancellor." Even the pacific Mr. Harding is swept along: " 'I really think it was,' said Mr. Harding." The group's defiance, however, remains secret; Grantlyism is but a posture. Instead of an active hero, fighting an impossible cause, we are presented with a frocked clergyman whose hands are in his breeches pocket for the remainder of the novel.

Absolute perfection does not exist in Trollope's world. "Human ends," we are told at one point, "must be attained by human means." And these means are, as we are so often reminded, highly limited. Dr. Grantly may pride himself on his martial skills and import a retinue of champions, but his grandiose designs, like his verbiage, are inevitably deflated by the narrator: "Dr. Gwynne was the *Deus ex machina* who was to come upon the Barchester stage, and bring about deliverance from these terrible evils. But how can melodramatic *dénouements* be properly brought about, how can vice and Mr. Slope be punished, and virtue and the archdeacon be rewarded, while the avenging god is laid up with the gout?" (ch. 34). In the epic world of *Paradise Lost*, God is omniscient and omnipotent, even if He sits out the battle for a while. In a world where gods are laid up by the gout, the outcome of the contest between virtue and vice depends on the circumstances contrived by the novelist. And the circumstances which trample Mr. Slope into the ground take the shape of Eleanor, the signora, and Mrs. Proudie rather than that of the fierce archdeacon.

## 2

The real battle fought in Barchester is not the short-lived struggle between "Proudieism" and "Grantlyism" but rather the more elementary contest waged between men and women. While Mr. Grantly's fanfare is ostentatious, the skirmishes between the sexes are mostly conducted away from the public eye. In Trollope's handling, however, this competition is far more genuine than the empty scuffles of the two clerical factions. The battle of the clergy depends on a parity of power; in the battle of the sexes, however, the combatants are most unevenly matched. In Trollope's delightfully topsy-turvy world, women are by far the stronger sex.

It is Miss Thorne who comments at one point that "now-a-days the gentlemen were all women, and the ladies all men" (ch. 35). The narrator remarks that Charlotte Stanhope, had she been a man, "would have been a very fine young man" (ch. 9). And indeed the reader who comes to *Barchester Towers* expecting to find those delicate, self-effacing creatures we associate with Victorian womanhood will find that none of the Barchester ladies conforms to the stereotype of the frail female in a masculine world. This stereotype has come to be accepted as a historical fact—even though the Victorian era happens to owe its name to the resolute matron who ruled with absolute power for sixty-four years.[4] But whether Trollope relies on fact or fiction, he

4. As G. M. Young points out, it was in the nineteenth century that women rose to prominence in unprecedented numbers; see his *Victorian England: Portrait of An Age*, 2d ed. (London, 1960), pp. 2–3. And Trollope, the son of the indomitable Mrs. Frances Trollope, was surely aware of this fact.

gains some of his finest comic effects by inverting the traditional roles of the sexes.

From top to bottom, women dominate in Barchester. Everyone in the town knows that Mrs. Proudie rather than her husband is the real bishop. It is to the bishopess therefore that Mrs. Quiverful applies, indignant at her own quivering husband's abject passivity (to get the bishop's palace, Mrs. Quiverful appears to a farmer's wife, who in turn forces her mate to provide the transportation). At Ullathorne, Miss Thorne, the rural Britomart, arranges the manly sports her brother neglects. She distributes bows and arrows to the toxophilites and personally supervises the construction of the quintain: "She almost wished . . . to get on a saddle and have a tilt at it herself." In the Stanhope family, Charlotte takes over the duties evaded by her indolent father; she rules her weak brother Bertie and almost persuades him to overcome his aversion to the "tyranny" and "deceit" of marriage (ch. 15). Even Susan Grantly is far more influential than her husband realizes. She pretends to be a "pattern of obedience," but values power as much as the archdeacon himself. In battling the Proudieites, she is "as well prepared as her lord to carry on the battle without giving or taking quarter." In fact, she is better prepared: "Mrs. Grantly had lived the life of a wise, discreet, peace-making woman; and the people of Barchester were surprised at the amount of military vigour she displayed as a general of the feminine Grantlyite forces" (ch. 13).

The Barchester males are afraid of the opposite sex. Mr. Harding is terror-stricken at the thought that twelve old women and a matron will be added to the twelve old men at Hiram's Hospital. Mr. Lookaloft is so intimidated by his overbearing wife and daughters that he does not dare to come to the Ullathorne feast. Even Mr. Grantly, that fearless champion, admits that "when a woman is impertinent, one must . . . put up with it." Neither he nor Dr. Gwynne ever dares to challenge the authority of Mrs. Proudie. And Mr. Arabin, forty years old, whose "virgin lips" have never yet "tasted the luxury of a woman's cheek," is far more coy and maidenlike than Eleanor Bold who, for all her refreshing innocence, is the mother of a two-year-old child. When this gentleman finally clasps Eleanor to his bosom, Trollope's narrator wryly comments: "How this was done, whether the doing was with him or her . . . neither of them knew; nor can I declare" (ch. 48).

Unlike his Barchester brethren, Mr. Slope has too little respect for the supremacy of women.[5] Disdainful of those males who, like Proudie or Quiverful or Harding, passively hover between alternatives, he nonetheless finds himself alternating between Eleanor Bold and the enticing Signora Neroni. His indecision proves disastrous. The calculating fortune hunter (who had rejected one of Dr. Proudie's daughters because she lacked a dowry) discovers that his interests are also erotic. His sexuality —betokened by those clammy hands—first manifests itself when he surprises the lovely widow in a semi-innocent sport with her baby son. Smothering her child with kisses, admiring his "lovely legs," Eleanor provokes the child to twist her long glossy hair "hither and thither" (ch. 16). She is confused by Slope's sudden entrance; the chaplain is frankly aroused. His tasteless allusion to her silken tresses shows him to be no Victorian gentleman, but his words do show his desires. He too would like to assault those beautiful long tresses.

It is Signora Neroni, however, who begins to emasculate the chaplain who insisted on being a man in a female world. The smiling signora warns him that "Troilus loved and ceased to be a man." The preacher who had been so able to move the female heart becomes an awkward Ovidian monster seduced by a "couchant goddess": "Mr. Slope, taking the soft fair delicate hand in his, and very soft and fair and delicate it was, bowed over it his huge red head and kissed it. It was a sight to see . . . her hand in his looked like a rose lying among carrots, and when he kissed it he looked as a cow might do on finding such a flower among her food" (ch. 27). The Circe of Barchester is

5. Mr. Slope's disrespect extends to his sovereign: "He cares nothing, one way or the other, for the Queen's supremacy; these to his ears are empty words, meaning nothing" (ch. 4).

cruel, unsparingly satirical. She exposes the duplicity Slope has so successfully maintained and confronts him with the contradictions between his unworldly religion and his worldly aims: "Why do you want lands and income?" When Slope protests that he has the "natural ambitions of a man," she replies: "Of course you have, and the natural passions; and therefore I say that you don't believe the doctrine you preach." The horrified chaplain is speechless. Checked in his ardor, he returns to try his luck with Eleanor. The widow's slap only increases his frustration: "To him the blow from her little hand was as much an insult as a blow from a man would have been to another. It went direct to his pride. . . . He could almost have struck at her again in his rage. Even the pain was a great annoyance to him" (ch. 40). Like Satan smitten by Michael's sword, Mr. Slope has had his first experience of pain.

Able to divide others to further his ambitions, Slope discovers that his sexual passion has made him a divided man. Recoiling from Eleanor's slap, he turns to Madeline Neroni again, only to be slapped down far more cruelly. For the lady now publicly exposes the gap between his inner desires and outward professions. She reminds this apostle of newness that for once he has lingered too long on the old:

> It's gude to be off with the old love—Mr. Slope,
> Before you are on with the new.—

Escaping her room, Slope finds himself finished off by a third female, Mrs. Proudie, whom he has antagonized beyond repair by his attentions to the signora in Mrs. Proudie's drawing room. Slope comes to rue his passion for the two women to whom he has simultaneously attached himself, but "the pre-eminent place in his soul's hatred was usually allotted to the signora" (ch. 46). By divesting Slope of his mobility, the immobile signora becomes the most powerful figure in the novel. Her physical paralysis, emblematic of the Stanhope lassitude, also has come to represent the triumph of the stationary ways of Barchester. Once regarded as "very like an angel" (ch. 11), the signora whose eyes are "as bright as Lucifer's" (ch. 9) has assumed new characteristics in Mr. Slope's mind: "Whenever he again thought of her in his dreams, it was not as an angel with azure wings. He connected her rather with fire and brimstone" (ch. 46). Although the narrator assures us that Mrs. Proudie was not "all devil" (ch. 26), he does not challenge Slope's imputation. But even if Trollope means the signora to act as the novel's undisputed "female devil," he also makes her the agent of his own godlike dispensation of justice.

Eleanor Bold, the novel's female angel, impresses her superior strength on Mr. Harding and Mr. Arabin by forcing both men to live with her in the deanery; the signora, on the other hand, contributes to the happy ending by forcing the novel's would-be devil to live in perennial exile. In Barchester, Mr. Slope is ignominiously defeated. But outside its confines, in the external world of London, he is allowed to thrive. His marriage to the rich widow of a sugar refiner should sweeten the bitterness of the cinders that the signora and Trollope have made him swallow.

## 3

The peace between the sexes also marks the peace of the clergy—Mr. Proudie submits to his wife; Mr. Quiverful settles in Hiram's Hospital; Mr. Arabin's "virgin lips" meet those of Eleanor; the triumphant Madeline Neroni sets off for new conquests. In comedy, the return to normalcy is signified by marriage. Just as the union of Tom Jones to Sophia Western or Elizabeth Bennett's nuptials to Mr. Darcy repairs the temporary insanity of their world, so here too does marriage become emblematic of the restitution of order. The installment of Mr. Arabin and Eleanor in the deanery of the cathedral assures the reader of a continuity in the ways of Barchester; Mr. Slope's marriage to the sugar refiner's widow signifies that London, "the world at large," will also continue its own way. Each realm returns to its particular mode of life: Barchester will remain conservative, organic; London, innovative and mechanical. Mr.

Slope chooses as a seat for his future activities a "church in the vicinity of the *New* Road." His reputation as "one of the most eloquent preachers and pious clergymen in that part of the metropolis" is obviously false (ch. 51, italics added). Although, in Barchester, we have seen the hypocrisy masked by this piety, Slope's future deceptions are unimportant. The bishop's chaplain has served his purpose. Significantly enough, Trollope ends the stories of Slope and of the Proudies well before that of the Barchesterians. He devotes the last two chapters exclusively to their affairs.

For all his importance as a character, Mr. Slope is above all a tool for Trollope's comedy. Like the traditional "Vice" figure of the stage, he challenges an established order. In doing so he stirs up Barchester and induces its inhabitants to become his marionettes. Comedy thrives on making men seem stiff, mechanical, and therefore laughable. Trollope's brand of comedy nonetheless allows us to be kind to his puppets—we like Mr. Harding when he becomes Dr. Grantly's errand boy and sympathize with the former warden precisely when those who espouse his cause talk of him "as though he were a puppet" (ch. 39). Therefore, we rejoice when Mr. Harding, by withdrawing from public life, refuses to be a puppet any longer (the independent Eleanor has throughout rejected the role of marionette); and we rejoice all the more when Mr. Slope, Trollope's deputy puppeteer, becomes himself the puppet of Signora Neroni.

Although the signora's alien manners and mode of thinking clash with those of Barchester, it is she who enables the town to return to its former order. She resembles lethargic Barchester in the sense that both need an outside push—she to be lifted from one place to another, Barchester to be induced to make some progress. Yet this progress is minimal. Without Mr. Slope's urgings, Bishop Proudie will introduce no radical changes to disturb the town's habitual ways. Although the town accepts its new bishop, it is comforted by the thought that he, too, will one day be forced to become a traditionalist when "the new-fangled manners of the age have discovered him to be superannuated" (ch. 51). The changes that have occurred are hardly deplorable. There is a new warden at Hiram's Hospital, and there will be twelve old women and a matron in addition to the twelve male inmates. But this equality of numbers almost seems a male victory in a world in which women do not usually settle for such parity. There is also a new dean to replace Mr. Trefoil, but Francis Arabin, who comes from the Oxford of Newman and Arnold, is hardly a radical.[6]

At Ullathorne, shortly before declaring their love for each other, Eleanor and Mr. Arabin comment on their surroundings; their exchange bears quoting in its entirety:

> "Do you like Ullathorne?" said Mr. Arabin, speaking from the safely distant position which he had assumed on the hearth-rug.
>
> "Yes, indeed, very much!"
>
> "I don't mean Mr. and Miss Thorne. I know you like them; but the style of the house. There is something about old-fashioned mansions, built as this is, and old-fashioned gardens, that to me is especially delightful."
>
> "I like everything old-fashioned," said Eleanor; "old fashioned things are so much the honestest."
>
> "I don't know about that," said Mr. Arabin, gently laughing. "That is an opinion on which very much may be said on either side. It is strange how widely the world is divided on a subject which so nearly concerns us all, and which is so close beneath our eyes. Some think we are quickly progressing towards perfection, while others imagine that virtue is disappearing from the earth."
>
> "And you, Mr. Arabin, what do you think?" said Eleanor.

The pressed clergyman becomes even more evasive and circuitous than Trollope's own narrator:

> "What do I think, Mrs. Bold?" and then he rumbled his money with his hands in his trowsers pockets, and looked and spoke very little like a thriving lover. "It is the bane of

6. Oxford was still as much a "venerable seat of Learning, Orthodoxy, and Toryism" in the Victorian era as it had been when Boswell and Johnson visited in 1784.

my life that on important subjects I acquire no fixed opinion. I think, and think, and go on thinking; and yet my thoughts are running ever in different directions. I hardly know whether or no we do lean more confidently than our fathers did on those high hopes to which we profess to aspire." (ch. 48)

In this oblique and characteristically inconclusive fashion, Trollope introduces his own stand on a question that absorbed his age—a question that we shall see treated by all the other novelists discussed in this study. Like all major Victorian novels, *Barchester Towers* contains a reaction to a quickly shifting world in which traditional values and beliefs are in the process of being challenged, eroded, redefined. Though Trollope is as equivocal as Mr. Arabin, he clearly sides with Eleanor in preferring "old-fashioned things." The order to which Barchester returns does contain the novelist's own values and assumptions. Human nature is pretty much the same. Though Mr. Grantly may speak of having "girded himself and gone to war," he remains as proud, wishful, and worldly as before. Women will still retain their mastery over men; the merchants of Barchester will still be ruled by self-interest. No man is perfect and no man can be perfected by mere legislation—whether this legislation comes from the Ministry, Parliament, or the *Jupiter*. Change and progress are inevitable, but they must evolve through natural growth rather than through the imposition of arbitrary and mechanical rules. Like Dr. Johnson, Trollope is skeptical about excesses of all kinds, and he believes in social customs and social and religious institutions as the preservers of common sense and order. He is a conservative, not because he necessarily believes in the deterioration of the human race, or because he holds all old things to be better than the new, but rather because he assumes that whatever has been around for a long time has withstood the test of experience. The church music that Mr. Harding loves and Slope attacks has evolved for centuries; to prohibit it seems wanton and arbitrary. Even the "magnificent" violincello which Mr. Grantly, in the flush of victory, bestows on his father-in-law at the end of the novel proves to be useless to the old gentleman. Its "new-fashioned arrangements and expensive additions" baffle him so that he can never use the instrument "with satisfaction to his audience or pleasure to himself" (ch. 53).

Trollope's novel thus depicts a compromise. The superannuated inmates at Hiram's Hospital, confronted with a new warden and a dozen females, exclaim: "We be very old for any change . . . but we do suppose it be all for the best" (ch. 52). The statement can almost be taken as representing the novel's chief theme. In a world of change, the old must yield to the new, yet the new must recognize that experience and tradition contain the guidelines for all future growth. The norms of the past should not be cast on a rubbish cart in the name of "progress."

Despite this common-sense resolution, Trollope nonetheless does indulge in a nostalgic glance at an impossible past. It is no coincidence that the conversation between Eleanor and Arabin should be set in and stimulated by the chimerical world of Ullathorne. In Barchester, Grantlyism is favored by the town's rank and file not out of high principles but simply because the town's merchants do not care for a bishop who spends his money in London. Even those "high-souled ecstatic young ladies of thirty-five" who rally around Mr. Slope come to realize that their opposition to church music is wrong because "their welfare, and the welfare of the place, was connected in some mysterious manner with daily chants and bi-weekly anthems" (ch. 52). In Ullathorne, however, no such self-interest exists.

The Thorne's property is disconnected from merchants and trade and the feudal relationship between squire and tenant is still respected; Miss Thorne personally looks after the children and poor of the parish and fondly regards Harry Greenacre as a "pattern," an "excellent sample of an English yeoman" (ch. 35). The young man, in turn, is willing to act as her knight by tilting at the quintain, unafraid of being "powdered with flour in the service of his mistress" (ch. 36). Only upon being almost brained, does his gallantry abate a trifle. At her *Fête Champêtre* Miss Thorne entreats her steward, Mr. Plomacy, to be sure to admit all children if "they live near," as well as all the tenants and laborers of the estate. The command proves useless, for soon the park is overrun by apprentices from the city. On capturing one such intruder, Mr. Plomacy decides to eject him from Eden and send him "howling back to a Barchester pandemonium." The steward raises his stick, ready to see "the edict of banishment" carried out by conducting the culprit to the gate. But the justice of this Michael is tempered by mercy: the young man is allowed to stay at the entreaty of Farmer Greenacre. The overjoyed apprentice inwardly swears "that if ever Farmer Greenacre wanted a day's work done for nothing, he was the lad to do it for him" (ch. 39).

A world where people are willing to work for nothing is almost as chimerical as Miss Thorne's stout belief in the existence of men who have long been dead. To live in such a world is unthinkable: though Mr. Arabin and Eleanor are fond of Ullathorne's quaintness, they do not stay at St. Ewold's, but move to Barchester itself. Still, their union has been made possible by the matchmaking Miss Thorne; only upon being transported into the maiden lady's arrested world have the pair recognized their joint affection for old-fashioned mansions and gardens.

## 4

In *Barchester Towers* stability is achieved, to a large extent, by Trollope's adoption of the outlook and expression of a much earlier age. Miss Thorne's antiquated literary tastes can almost act as an index for the novel's own heritage: "She spoke of Addison, Swift, and Steele, as though they were still living, regarded De Foe as the best known novelist of his country, and thought of Fielding as a young but meritorious novice in the fields of romance. In poetry, she was familiar with names as late as Dryden, and had once been seduced into reading the 'Rape of the Lock'" (ch. 22).

Trollope's values, too, correspond to those held by earlier writers like Goldsmith or Fielding. A man should cultivate his own garden. He should be modest, have common sense, and perform his duties to the best of his abilities. He should recognize his own flaws and tolerate the imperfections of others. Mr. Harding, we are told in the novel's concluding paragraph, is not a man "who should be toasted at public dinners and spoken of with conventional absurdity as a perfect divine." Instead, he is—what is more important—"a good man without guile," cognizant of his shortcomings and therefore guided by "the precepts which he has striven to learn" (ch. 53).

This portrait of an unworldly clergyman is in the tradition of Fielding's Parson Adams or Goldsmith's Vicar of Wakefield. Not only the values implied in *Barchester Towers* but also the form of Trollope's novel reflect the literary conventions of an earlier age. Its mock-heroic depiction of the battles of the clergy and of the sexes owes much to such works as Swift's *Battle of the Books* or Pope's *Rape of the Lock*. Trollope's narrator is a direct descendant of the digressive commentator and theorist of *Tom Jones*; his episodic plotting is in the manner of Smollett's picaresque fiction. Eleanor's slap, Mrs. Proudie's torn gown, the tilting at the quintain are incidents which could easily have occurred in a novel like *Humphry Clinker*, where the structure lends itself to the portrayal of separate incidents, all vivid and memorable in themselves. The account of the checkered career of Bertie Stanhope (Protestant, Catholic, Jew, and Protestant again), like the thumbnail sketch of Miss Thorne's tastes and opinions, could have come straight out of the periodical essays of Addison and Steele. They render a type: the modern Dandy, the Tory Lady of the old school. Each detail contributes to this type until it is stamped and finished.

Trollope's handling of Bertie differs considerably from the presentation of Dickens' Richard Carstone, Emily Brontë's Lockwood, and George Eliot's Will Ladislaw, all versions of the aimless young man who suffers from *ennui*. Dickens fits Richard into a complex symbolic construct which displays the vanity of man's trust in chance; Brontë uses Lockwood to show the insufficiency of reason in an irrational world of romance; George Eliot penetrates Ladislaw's psychological make-up at the same time that she tries to determine his relation to the society from which he is alienated. Trollope's concerns are less grandiose. Bertie remains a type, laughable in his own right. His idiosyncrasies or "ruling passions" are fascinating in themselves. Each of Trollope's characters is reducible to certain basic humors or vanities. If Bertie stands for a kind of good-humored indolence and purposelessness, the archdeacon is proud, wishful, and worldly, the signora displays a desire for masterhood, Slope wants money, sex, and power. Only combined, can these individual types produce what Trollope at one point calls "the world's deceit" (ch. 44). Laughter can expose that deceit by piercing the social veneers of the outer man.

Trollope's deliberate use of flat characters carries certain limitations. George Eliot would have probed far more deeply into Dr. Grantly's guilt or Mr. Harding's self-doubts; Jane Austen would have exploited the misconceptions of Eleanor Bold and forced the young woman into a gradual recognition of her hasty impressions. Trollope does not altogether avoid the hidden recesses of the "inner man"; but he prefers to rely on inference and suggestion. Passion—so important to the Brontës or to Meredith—is used only mockingly in the figure of Slope, the grotesque, red-haired lover. For Trollope's mode is antiromantic. He eschews the complications of plot that Dickens delighted in and mocks the Gothic romances of Mrs. Radcliffe. In this sense, he is again the exact opposite of those writers who wanted to create a world of mystery and abnormality.

Trollope's limitations are of course his strengths. As a believer in moderation, he mocks excess of any kind. He resorts to parody, for instance, when in sketching Bertie's background he mentions the young man's encounter in Palestine with "one of the family of Sidonia, a most remarkable man" (ch. 9). In Disraeli's *Coningsby* (1844) and *Tancred* (1847), novels which mix their author's political ideals with the extravagances of romance, Sidonia is an exotic, Bedouinlike Jew who instructs two young English aristocrats in the ideals they will implant in their own country. In Trollope's handling, this noble character becomes utterly ridiculous. The signora wants to see the mysterious stranger who has so affected Bertie; she wants to have him at her feet. When Sidonia appears, however, he is hardly an exemplary idealist; he turns out to be a "dirty little old man" who demands payment for the bills which Bertie has contracted.

Trollope punctures all sentimental exaggerations. He gently mocks Victorian baby-worship when he renders Eleanor and Mary Bold's ecstatic chorus (" 'Diddle, diddle, diddle, diddle, dum, dum, dum: hasn't he got lovely legs?' said the rapturous mother. . . . 'H'm 'm 'm 'm 'm,' simmered the mama, burying her lips also in his fat round short legs."). He is less kind in exposing those distortions that stem from posturing and puffery. Throughout the novel, the signora invites her acquaintances to meet and comfort her fatherless child, the lonely descendant of the Neros and decadent remnant of a heroic race. Near the end of the novel, Mr. Thorne does see the little girl. She is dressed up extravagantly with a starched flouncy dress that spreads out horizontally from her hips: "It did not nearly cover her knees; but this was atoned by a loose pair of drawers which seemed made throughout of lace; then she had on pink little stockings." The squire is eager to make a favorable impression on the child's mother. Julia is thrust into his arms: "The lace and starch crumpled against his waistcoat and trowsers, the greasy, black curls hung upon his cheek, and one of the bracelet clasps scratched his ear." The bachelor gentleman, fifty years old, is somewhat at a loss; having, on other occasions, been compelled to fondle little nieces and nephews, he now sets about the task "in the mode he always had used":

> "Diddle, diddle, diddle, diddle," said he, putting the child on one knee, and working away with it as though he were turning a knife-grinder's wheel with his foot.
> "Mamma, mamma," said Julia crossly, "I don't want to be diddle diddled. Let me go, you naughty old man, you." (ch. 46)

Like Mr. Slope, this admirer must pay for his courtship of the exotic signora. The gallant squire finds himself in the uncomfortable position of a Humbert Humbert, denounced as a dirty old man by the Lolita he has bounced on his knees.

This kind of unmasking of the pretentious, the exaggerated, the oversentimental is one of Trollope's strengths. Though too gentle to be regarded as a satirist,[7] he can effectively expose the human animal that lies behind the social mask. His aim is to strip men of their affectations, to divest them of all the gaudy untruths with which they try to conceal their share of universal imperfections. By openly exhibiting his own imperfections, Trollope's narrator constantly reminds the reader that most men and women are reducible to the same flaws. Their follies and foibles persist in any age. Although change and innovation provide Trollope with the stimulus for his comedy, this emphasis on persistence leads him to portray life as an uninterrupted and unvarying process. He prefers similarity to difference, permanence to fluctuation. His art thrives on what is durable and constant.[8]

The history of the novel is one of change, of constant adaptation (the very name of the form connotes its capacities for perennial renovation). *Barchester Towers* appeared at a time when new social theories were burgeoning in England and when a new world picture began to threaten the cosmology accepted by Trollope's clergymen. Around this time, George Meredith and George Eliot were beginning their careers. Even earlier, other novelists had carried the novel beyond its eighteenth-

7. In his *An Autobiography* (Oxford, 1950), Trollope contends that the novelist ought not to create vice "in order that it may be lashed" (p. 95). He therefore censures Thackeray for "that dash of satire which he felt to be demanded by the weaknesses he saw around him" (p. 185) and seems to disapprove of his own satirical harshness in *The Way We Live Now*.

8. This steadfast rejection of all that is precarious and unstable may well be why Trollope's work held such an enormous appeal for Englishmen during the grim and unpredictable years of World War II. As Elizabeth Bowen suggests in her fine playlet, *Anthony Trollope: A New Judgment* (London, 1946), it is paradoxical that the bastion which Trollope constructed for himself and his mildly harassed Victorian readers should offer shelter to those besieged by changes far more drastic and violent than those witnessed by his age.

century roots. Though starting in the tradition of Smollett and Fielding, Dickens had soon wandered into the hallucinatory realm of romance; the Brontës had published their own Gothic romances a decade before the appearance of *Barchester Towers*. What is more, *Vanity Fair* had been published in 1847. Trollope regarded himself as a kind of disciple of Thackeray's; in later life, he wrote an excellent study of the master. Like *Barchester Towers*, Thackeray's masterpiece relies on parody, burlesque, and satire; it too harks back to the mode of the eighteenth-century humorists. But Thackeray's novel displays the darker, more pessimistic vision that underlies so much of Victorian art: "it has to be confessed," wrote Trollope, "that Thackeray did allow his intellect to be too thoroughly saturated with the aspect of the ill side of things."[9] In *Barchester Towers* Thackeray's disciple stoutly refused to yield to a capricious and changeful world; by allowing his intellect to defend itself through laughter he successfully resisted that "ill side of things."

9. *Thackeray* (London, 1879), p. 207.

# II  *Vanity Fair*: The Bitterness of Retrospection

"Vanity Fair may make me," wrote Thackeray shortly before the first installment of his novel appeared in January 1847.[1] In the same year Trollope ventured into fiction with *The Macdermots of Ballycloran*; it was an abysmal failure. While Thackeray reaped the fruits of a ten-year period of apprenticeship as a free-lance writer, editor, and cartoonist, Trollope casually dismissed his own stillborn novel as an unsuccessful experiment which, in his words, "did not in the least interfere with my life or with my determination to make the best I could of the Post Office."[2] Years later, upon Trollope's own success as a novelist, Thackeray asked the younger writer to contribute to his *Cornhill Magazine*; the two men became friends, and, after Thackeray's death, Trollope wrote a biographical and critical study of his predecessor for the English Men of Letters series.

Trollope and Thackeray had much in common: as novelists, both were at home in the eighteenth century. The differences between the contented civil servant who regarded his fiction as an avocation and the professional writer who depended on his pen and pencil do, however, outweigh the similarities between them. Thackeray is a far more divided figure than Trollope, and it is no coincidence that so many studies of his work have been biographical in their emphasis. In some of his later novels, such as *Pendennis* and *Philip*, Thackeray tried to depict the precarious life of the man of letters who, though a gentleman by birth, becomes an outcast because of his indigence, bluntness, and unconventionality. In 1848 Thackeray was briefly con-

1. Quoted by Geoffrey and Kathleen Tillotson in their introduction to the Riverside Edition of *Vanity Fair* (Boston, 1963), p. xviii. All future references in the text are to this edition.
2. *An Autobiography* (Oxford, 1950), p. 75.

sidered for a position in the Post Office; in 1854 he was turned down for a job in the British Embassy at Washington. These reversals seem justified: the author of *Vanity Fair* would never have succeeded as a civil servant. The writer who thrived on disorder could not have led a life of discipline and routine. As Trollope points out in his study of Thackeray: "There was never a man less fit for the Queen's coat."[3]

This disparity in temperament is reflected in the differences that characterize each man's literary productions. Though both mock the vanities of their puppets, Thackeray uses his fiction in a far more exploratory way. *Vanity Fair* is hardly a conventional comic novel. Like Trollope, Thackeray studied the work of the eighteenth-century satirists.[4] But his great novel reflects above all the doubts of his own era. Whereas Trollope regards himself in the traditional role of the moralist, Thackeray is less sure about his function as an artist. He wants to attack English Philistinism, yet at the same time he is aware of his dependence on a public composed of middle-class readers. In this sense, his is the more typical dilemma of the Victorian intellectual. His position in *Vanity Fair* resembles that adopted two decades later by Matthew Arnold, who attacks middle-class values with irony and sarcasm, while calling himself a "Philistine and the son of a Philistine."[5] Just as the witty ironist of *Culture and Anarchy* hides the despairing Romantic of "Dover Beach," so does the detached humorist of *Vanity Fair* conceal an anguished man, unsure of his identity as an artist.

In *Vanity Fair* Thackeray is straining to define his relation to a reality that offers only illusions, a world of memories containing, in Arnold's words, "neither joy, nor love, nor light,/

3. *Thackeray* (London, 1879), p. 36.
4. Thackeray's only longer novel before *Vanity Fair*, *Barry Lyndon* (1844), is modeled after Fielding's *Jonathan Wild*. *Henry Esmond* (1852) and *The Virginians* (1858–1859) are set in the eighteenth century. Like the writers he discussed in *The English Humorists of the Eighteenth Century* (1853), Thackeray was involved in periodical writing; like them, he wrote sketches, parodies, satires, and burlesques.
5. *Culture and Anarchy* (Cambridge, 1961), p. 106.

Nor certitude, nor peace, nor help for pain." Although, as we shall see, this grim picture is diffused and complicated by the novelist, the very title of his work, drawn from *The Pilgrim's Progress*, is indicative of its negative emphasis.[6] In Bunyan's allegorical scheme Vanity Fair represents a stage in the soul's journey to purification. Christian and his companion Faithful are detained in this city of "merchandisers," where they are tortured and defamed. For Bunyan, this mortification is necessary: Christian and a new travel companion, Hopeful, can now proceed to the Celestial City. In Thackeray's handling, however, Vanity Fair becomes the only realm of existence. There is no promised transcendence; no earthly perfection. Amelia professes: "George is my husband, here and in heaven" (ch. 59), but the heaven where she supposes George to be seems very distant indeed. Nor is her belated marriage to Dobbin made to seem a sufficient, this-worldly reward for his hopefulness and faith.

Thackeray takes for his province the bustling "world at large" which Trollope sidestepped in *Barchester Towers*. There is no such separable microcosm as Ullathorne in *Vanity Fair*: despite our movement from Miss Pinkerton's school at Chiswick Mall to the fashionable homes of the Sedleys and Osbornes, to Vauxhall, to the country estate, Queen's Crawley, to Brussels and Paris, to Germany and even India, we are always within the compass of the same fairground. Vice and folly are universal in this novel. The mover of its plot is not a ludicrous intruder defeated by passion, but rather one who calmly exploits the sentimentality and greed that exist everywhere. At the end of *Barchester Towers*, Trollope removes the exploiting Mr. Slope from the sphere of Eleanor and Arabin; at the end of *Vanity Fair*, Thackeray has Becky Sharp remain at the very center of the "reality" he has created. While Dobbin and Amelia, Janey and George, stand outside, she is safely ensconced within her stall. To be sure, Thackeray also pretends that his version of the world-as-is is only the world-as-was. King George, and not

6. Thackeray changed the novel's original subtitle, "Pen and Pencil Sketches of English Society," to "A Novel without a Hero."

*Virtue rewarded: A booth in Vanity Fair.*

Queen Victoria, is the monarch introduced to Becky. Thackeray simulates a kind of historical verisimilitude by sprinkling allusions to actual men and women of the Regency era—artists, prizefighters, politicians, freaks, quacks, diplomats, historians— and by referring to the novels, songs, plays, and operas of that time. But the vanities of this earlier age, when morals were presumably much looser, are visibly similar to the values of his own time. The characters of the first generation, old Sedley, old Osborne, the elder Sir Pitt, and Miss Crawley, do not live to see the present to which author and reader belong. But those belonging to the second and third generations do. The vanities of one era are passed on to the next; they are perpetuated by time, which, as we shall eventually come to see, is the true protagonist of this time-conscious and time-consuming novel.

Like *Barchester Towers*, *Vanity Fair* is a novel without a hero; like that comedy, Thackeray's satire relies on the use of a fallible narrator. In Trollope's benevolent scheme, however, Mr. Harding almost becomes an ideal figure; his weaknesses, shared by narrator and reader, are meant to evoke our approval. Though every bit as good-natured as Trollope's warden, Thackeray's Dobbin is not at all endorsed by the narrator. In a world where all ideals may be illusory, Trollope's distinctions between "angels" and "devils" become even more suspect. Though Thackeray's equivocal Showman is the model for Trollope's own narrator, there is a vast difference between this uncertain jester and the jolly narrator who invites the reader to move with perfect confidence in the author. Unlike *Barchester Towers*, *Vanity Fair* relies on the unexpected. It tricks us into ambivalent responses; it asks us to toss out the ordinary dictionary definitions by which most men order their lives. The very structure of the novel contributes to this calculated confusion.

## I

Unlike Trollope's three-volume novel, *Vanity Fair* was published in nineteen monthly parts.[7] The reading experience of its

7. For a more elaborate discussion of the practice of part-publication,

contemporary audience thus differed considerably from that undergone by Trollope's readers who, as he tells us, could easily have turned to the book's last pages to determine its outcome. (This reading experience, of course, differs also from that of the modern reader of *Vanity Fair*. It is sometimes assumed that the bulky novels of the Victorian period were intended for a public who had the leisure to read several hundred pages in one sitting. But the Victorians were at least as harried as twentieth-century readers. The reader of 1847 who enjoyed his monthly installment of thirty-two pages had nineteen months to absorb what the modern college student—or teacher—is forced to devour in a week and a half!)

Thackeray gains some of his finest effects through this method of part-publication. Like Trollope, he tries to encompass an entire society and comment on its values. But where Trollope's picture is compact, predictable, adhering to a uniform setting in which the chief characters are constantly before us, Thackeray's panoramic novel exploits the pauses, shifts, and alternation of settings made possible by the narrative's division into separate units. His novel relies on counterpoint: we move from the battlefield of Waterloo at the end of the ninth number to Miss Crawley reading a newspaper account of her nephew's promotion in number ten. The transition is skillfully handled; through it the event we have witnessed loses the significance it held for the combatants at this time. The point of view shifts from that of the "dauntless English infantry" tossed about in the commotion of the battle (ch. 32) to the opinion of a rich and hypochondriacal spinster who is "very moderately moved by the great events that were going on" (ch. 33). The tone of this chapter clashes with the ringing battle description which ended the ninth number. Neither Miss Briggs' romantic exaggerations nor Miss Crawley's unforgiving attitude toward her brave nephew can do justice to the scene we had briefly

---

see Kathleen Tillotson, *Novels of the Eighteen-Forties* (Oxford, 1961), pp. 20–53, and the introduction to the Riverside edition of *Vanity Fair*.

glimpsed. The "vanities" of Brighton life obscure all heroism; the battle of Waterloo itself has in retrospect become an exercise in futility. The narrator's earlier description of war as the "alternations of successful and unsuccessful murder" (ch. 32) seemed unduly cynical; it was forgotten in the sweep of his brilliant account of the battle. Now, with Miss Crawley's values at the fore again, the cynicism becomes justified. It is for her and her ilk that Englishmen and Frenchmen have successfully slaughtered each other. The irony is bitter.

The endless alternations and juxtapositions of *Vanity Fair* give the illusion of change, of the passage of time. The diffusiveness of the novel, accentuated by its publication in monthly parts, constantly forces the reader to reassemble and reassess what he has previously experienced; he must move along with the characters themselves, in spurts, without a clear foresight of their future—their vanities, hopes, illusions must therefore temporarily become his as well. Whereas the narrator of *Barchester Towers* lets us into his confidence by allowing us to anticipate the ending towards which his comedy is moving, the Showman of Vanity Fair does his best to hide this destination.

At the end of the novel's first number, Joseph Sedley is on the verge of proposing to Becky Sharp, but his courage fails. The narrator comments that, had Jos been less timid and George and Amelia farther away, "bachelorhood would have been at an end, and this work would never have been written" (ch. 4). The remark recalls a very similar situation in *Barchester Towers*. When Mr. Arabin fails to blurt out his love for Eleanor, Trollope's narrator confides: "had she but heard the whole truth from Mr. Arabin. But then where would have been my novel?" (ch. 30). At first glance, the situations and each author's comments seem identical. In Trollope's novel, however, we are assured that Eleanor and Mr. Arabin will eventually marry; our interest is engaged by the obstacles strewn in their path. We are amused by the increasing complications and misunderstandings devised by the novelist and are relieved by their eventual dissolution. Nonetheless, the nature of our expectations is never

*Mr. Joseph entangled.*

fundamentally challenged; we are asked to maintain these expectations for the duration of Trollope's comedy.

In *Vanity Fair*, on the other hand, we do not know what to expect. Instead of facing two equally confused lovers, we are engaged by a resourceful female strategist about to snare a fat prize. Fresh from Miss Pinkerton's academy, Becky still is transparent. Even Amelia sees through her scheme; the sketch of Joseph being entangled by a smiling Becky's thread is eloquent in itself. Yet the reader is undecided about his reaction. Becky is so sly, so amusing; Jos, so stolid and unimaginative. We should like to see more of this little temptress; we do not want her to succeed in her very first encounter. So, when by the end of the first number we expect a climax of sorts, we are delighted to see that none has come. The relation is still indefinite; Jos postpones his proposal: "Gad, I'll pop the question at Vauxhall." We gladly accept this uncertainty. Unsure of the novelist's design, we are more than willing to place our trust in fortune, the unpredictable shape of future events.

Jos, of course, does not pop the question at Vauxhall. Instead of asking for Becky's hand, he requests a bowl of rack punch. The narrator makes this request seem momentous:

> That bowl of rack punch was the cause of all this history. And why not a bowl of rack punch as well as any other cause? . . . Was not a bowl of wine the cause of the demise of Alexander the Great, or at least, does not Dr. Lempriere say so?— so did this bowl of rack punch influence the fates of all the principal characters in this "Novel without a Hero," which we are now relating. It influenced their life, although most of them did not taste a drop of it. (ch. 6)

The protestation seems a delightful exaggeration, a piece of mockery akin to Trollope's heroic incantations about Mrs. Proudie's torn gown. We laugh at it and disregard it. Soon, Jos Sedley's own importance seems to have faded. He disappears from the story, the victim of his stupid prudery. Only much later do we come to recognize that Jos' inability to hold his

*An Elephant for Sale.*

liquor has indeed affected the lives of characters who did not taste a drop of rack punch; had Becky married Jos, most of the other characters would have been spared much misery and delusion.

At the time, Jos' disappearance leads us to believe that his importance in the novel has ended. Becky must now go to a different setting and find a different testing ground for her wits. But Thackeray's novel is not a picaresque account of a pilgrimage through independent episodes. Jos eventually does pop the question he could not utter at Vauxhall. He does so, to be exact, eighteen numbers later, but by that time, both Becky Sharp and our attitude toward her have altered. All sorts of changes have intervened. Becky has been married and unmarried; she has risen above the Sedley's social scale only to fall beneath Jos again. The Madame de Raudon who stays at an inn called "The Elephant" in chapter sixty-three turns out to be the same unnamed young woman who, as a joke, had bought the picture of an elephant and its rider in the auction of the Sedley belongings in chapter seventeen. At that time her purchase seemed irrelevant (though it merited Thackeray's humorous illustration of "An Elephant For Sale"); we were far more engrossed by Captain Dobbin's purchase of a miniature piano than by Becky's acquisition of a painting of the man who had jilted her after the Vauxhall incident. Now, however, Rawdon's wife gets a return for this long-forgotten investment: she leads her old friend, Mr. Sedley, to her room at the inn, and, to his delight, shows him a picture hanging on the wall: "It was the portrait of a gentleman in pencil, his face having the advantage of being painted up in pink. He was riding on an elephant" (ch. 67).

Becky's devotion does not go unrewarded. But she is no longer the little conniver we were so reluctant to yield to Jos Sedley in chapter four. He has become her last straw, not her first try. She has seen King George, been Lord Steyne's friend, lost Rawdon, left her son, gone to Paris, and lived in a Bohemian garret, accosted by two German students. The outcome of this delayed

No. III.]   MARCH.   [Price 1s.

# VANITY FAIR:

## PEN AND PENCIL SKETCHES OF ENGLISH SOCIETY.

—◆—

### BY W. M. THACKERAY;

Author of " The Irish Sketch Book :" " Journey from Cornhill to Grand Cairo :" of " Jeames's Diary
and the "Snob Papers" in " Punch :" &c. &c.

LONDON:
PUBLISHED AT THE PUNCH OFFICE, 85, FLEET STREET.
J. MENZIES, EDINBURGH ; J. M'LEOD, GLASGOW ; J. M'GLASHAN, DUBLIN.
1847.

[Bradbury & Evans, Printers, Whitefriars.]

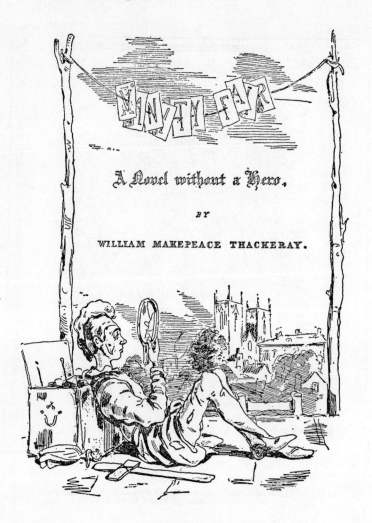

proposal can no longer be the same. Had Jos popped the question at Vauxhall he might not later die in mysterious circumstances. Vanity Fair has been Becky's teacher. By the end of the novel she may not have changed substantially from the girl who insinuated her way into the Sedley home, but we, who have followed her ups and downs, have changed our attitudes toward her and toward her laughing creator. A bowl of rack punch has had all the significance attributed to it by the Showman. Our inability to understand that significance at the time has turned out to be a mark of our innocence and not a mark of the novelist's lack of design.

## 2

*Vanity Fair* is a novel that forces the reader into a constant process of questioning. The Showman delights in puncturing the complacency of his audience. He refuses to instruct us in what to think or how to react to the bustling fair before us; he tells us that he can at best point out its "shops" and "shows"—to make us laugh and yet to force us also to "be perfectly miserable in private" (ch. 18). In the original title page of his novel, Thackeray drew a jester expounding on the follies of an audience which lives in a topsy-turvy world (in the background of the drawing is the Duke of York standing upside down on his column in Waterloo Place) and which possesses the same donkey ears that adorn the jester's cap. The title page for the completed novel in 1848 shows a rather different design. The jester now leans on a box of puppets and looks at his own image in a cracked mirror. In chapter nine, at the end of a passage in which the narrator has mocked the value that all men, including himself, place on money, Thackeray introduces a third picture of his Showman. The jester's stick is still in evidence, but the clown's comic mask is removed. Exposed is a sketch of the face of William Makepeace Thackery himself. The mask is smiling; the face is doleful and melancholic—beneath laughter lies a quiet despair.

The Showman who addresses us as his "brother wearers of motley" no more permits the conventional relationship between author and reader than he allows the conventional relation between the reader and the novel's characters. He refuses to judge the characters for us and, what is more, denies us the means by which we can ourselves arrive at a complete and unequivocal judgment. Are we to despise Becky or like her a little? Are we to like Amelia or despise her a lot? What is our attitude towards Dobbin meant to be? Is he the hero of a novel without a hero, or is he, as his name indicates, a gawky, benevolent, but dull workhorse? These are the crucial questions that have divided most readers of this novel. They have led some of these readers to denounce, alternately, Thackeray's cynicism as well as his sentimentality; they have led others to complain that the novelist is eternally equivocating.

There are more specific questions to which we are given no answers. Is Becky an adulteress? Is she or is she not a murderess? The narrator professes to have no point of view on these matters. Thackeray's illustrations of Becky—in which her features deteriorate almost as much as Satan's appearance degenerates in the course of *Paradise Lost*—only add to the general ambivalence. In the novel's last full-page drawing she seems young again, demurely proclaiming her innocence to the world. In *Barchester Towers* we know what our responses are meant to be; we are not confused when the narrator protests that he is shocked by Eleanor's uncouth behavior in slapping Mr. Slope or when he professes to be impressed by the chaplain's rhetorical powers.

But in *Vanity Fair* the Showman constantly tricks us into reactions which may turn out to be incorrect or incomplete. We have seen one such instance in the Vauxhall incident. I should like to examine another by looking at Thackeray's treatment of Dobbin in the opening pages of the novel's second number.

Dobbin's first appearance in chapter five parallels our introduction to Becky in chapter one.[8] In each case our attitude becomes modified through the contrasts which ensue: just as our initial response to Becky is soon qualified by her interaction with Amelia Sedley, so is our reaction to Dobbin affected by his subsequent relation to George Osborne. We see these characters at their simplest and most innocent: Amelia and Becky are leaving Miss Pinkerton's academy with the world still lying before them; Dobbin and George still are schoolboys at Mr. Swishtail's establishment. The inexperience of the characters is matched by the reader's own innocence. We are novices, as yet uninitiated in the ways of Vanity Fair. Our first encounter with these characters is therefore far less guarded than it would be later in the novel when our familiarity with Thackeray's narrative method and the cumulative effect of further episodes have greatly complicated our attitudes. Still, these opening chapters set the pattern for those later attitudes. The novel's first two chapters convince us of the insufficiency of our impressions. We waver between two heroines and find neither to our liking. Becky, whom we instinctively admire for her defiance of Miss Pinkerton, soon shows a disturbing disregard for sentiment when she bruises the feelings of the gentle Miss Jemima; by way of contrast, Amelia, whom we branded as being too insipid and conventional, seems less repulsive. We become wary. Amelia is all heart—she has no brains; Becky is all brain—she lacks a heart. The reader of Thackeray's first installment discovers that he must use both heart and brain to sort out the experiences he is asked to witness.

8. In their introduction to the Riverside Edition the editors point out that Thackeray may not even have contemplated Dobbin in the original scheme of his novel.

By the time we come to chapter five and the novel's second installment we may already have lost some of that earlier caution. The chapter is entitled "Dobbin of Ours"; its intimacy seems promising. Here at last we shall find a protagonist with whom we can identify: the childhood setting augurs a return to innocence. Disappointed in our previous attempts to sympathize with Becky the Orphan, we are now elated to find another outcast in the figure of the poor grocer's son. Dobbin seems more deserving of the reader's unqualified regard. If Becky seemed capable of defending herself against all comers, this child is awkward and unresisting. Becky possesses a rapierlike wit; Dobbin lisps and stammers. Becky pretends to be a Montmorency in order to counter the sneers of Miss Pinkerton and her pupils; Dobbin meekly accepts the name of "Figs" bestowed upon him by his snobbish schoolmates. He lets himself be teased by their unfunny allusions to his horselike name, "Heigh-ho Dobbin" and "Gee-ho Dobbin." If Becky sets out to conquer the world which rejects her, the scion of Dobbin & Rudge, Grocers and Oilmen, Thames Street, London, chooses to isolate himself from that world. Sitting apart from the other boys, be becomes engrossed in the make-believe world of the Arabian Nights. More than in Becky's case, we want to espouse the cause of this underdog, to have young Dobbin become the carrier for our own romantic sensibilities. We are delighted, therefore, when he is roused to challenge the school bully.

Had Dickens depicted the fight between Cuff and Dobbin, he would have shamelessly exploited our sympathy for the ungainly underdog. But Thackeray undercuts our sentimental identification with Dobbin of Ours precisely at those points where the reader most wants to convert the boy into the novel's future hero. Dobbin's actions in this chapter are prophetic of his behavior as an adult. He is already what he will be throughout the novel, the lonely outsider who takes refuge in impossible dreams. Just as he now sits apart from the other boys, so will he later separate himself from the members of his regiment, write poetry, and play the flute. And, just as the cries of a "little fellow weeping" now lead him to forget Sindbad the Sailor in the Valley of Diamonds, so is he later stirred into the "every day life" before him by his inability to bear the pain of others.

The situation unfolding before our eyes seems fit for *Tom Brown's Schooldays*. "Honest William" notices a large boy beating a little boy with a cricket stump. The older boy turns out to be Cuff, the school's much-feared "cock"; the smaller boy is George Osborne, one of Dobbin's most persistent hecklers. We are led to ask the obvious questions. Will this awkward, but honest youth defend an underdog? Will he dare to face George's oppressor when he realizes that his antagonist is the bully whose tyranny he has meekly borne in the past? And, finally, will he defend George when he realizes that Cuff's victim is none other than his old tormentor? The situation is ready-made. The reader builds his answers in advance. Dobbin must fight and triumph; by beating Cuff, he must teach George Osborne a lesson and humble his former tormentor into becoming his indebted and grateful friend.

Thackeray employs the incident neither to build up Dobbin's character nor to educate George Osborne, but rather to shake our sentimental presuppositions about human nature. He pretends to milk the scene for its melodrama by focussing on George's "distorted" face, Dobbin's "quivering" anxiety, the crashing cricket stump, yet quickly shifts from the beating in order to confront his readers: "Don't be horrified, ladies, every boy at a public school has done it. Your children will so do and be done by, in all probability." Nor does he allow the reader to over-empathize with the grocer's son. The awaited challenge takes too long to come; it is delayed even further by the narrator's sudden urge to endorse Dobbin. In his endorsement the narrator only complicates what we had expected to be forthright and simple. Pretended uncertainty, sarcasm, and a final flurry of bombastic exaggerations undermine our desire for a swift and earnest approval of our champion:

I can't tell what his motive was. Torture in a public school is as much licensed as the knout in Russia. It would be un-gentlemanlike (in a manner) to resist it. Perhaps Dobbin's foolish soul revolted against that exercise of tyranny; or perhaps he had a hankering feeling of revenge in his mind, and longed to measure himself against that splendid bully and tyrant, who had all the glory, pride, pomp, circumstance, banners flying, drums beating, guards saluting, in the place.

When Dobbin finally challenges Cuff, it becomes evident that he has yet to earn the gratitude of the little boy he wants to pro-tect. Sure that his defender will lose, George merely anticipates a worse beating for himself. Nor has his snobbery abated. He grudgingly becomes Dobbin's bottle-holder: "for you see his papa kept a carriage, and he was rather ashamed of his champion."

Thus, what starts out as a stock situation in which we are ready to sympathize with Dobbin of Ours becomes a satire on vanity in which we are gradually forced to recognize that our sentimentality is as foolish as that of "honest William." When the fight takes place, no boy dares to cheer the clumsy fighter who cannot parry Cuff's "scientific" blows. As soon as Dobbin shakes off his passivity and knocks Cuff down, however, *almost* as many fellows shout, "Go it, Figs," as there are youths ex-claiming, "Go it, Cuff." In a boy's school, as much as in the adult Vanity Fair, people are sure to back a winner. The reader cheering Dobbin finds himself a trifle uneasy; he is now in the company of those who had looked down on the lowly "Figs." Our discomfort mounts when we discover that Thackeray's narrator does not even permit us to participate in the fight. Lapsing into a mock-heroic style, he tells us that he would like to describe this combat properly by likening it to the last charge of the Guard, only that he remembers that Waterloo had not yet taken place. Still, he persists and continues in this vein. His exag-gerated allusions to "ten thousand bayonets" and "twenty eagles" diminish our involvement with a childish fight; his ref-erence to the "shout of the beef-eating British" prevents us from patriotically cheering "Figs," our Dobbin, the true-blooded Englishman of yeoman stock.

Nor does the burlesque end with Dobbin's triumph. After Cuff's defeat, the school's principal threatens to flog the winner and not the instigator of this fight. Our beef-eating British hearts palpitate at this new injustice. But Cuff speaks out nobly: "It's my fault sir—not Figs—not Dobbin's. I was bullying a little boy; and he served me right." We are led to admire what we falsely regard as a noble speech; even the switch from "not Figs'" to "not Dobbin's" has not gone unperceived. Surely the distasteful nickname will now be dropped forever; surely Cuff has learned his lesson, and so, undoubtedly, has George Osborne, the little snob. But the next line completely undercuts our sense of relief, for we discover that there is policy in Cuff's honesty: "By which magnanimous speech he [Cuff] not only saved his conqueror a whipping, but got back all his ascendancy over the boys which his defeat had nearly cost him." We are shocked: Cuff, the blackguard, had played on the emotions of beef-eating British schoolboys. They have been duped. And so have we. And so, it turns out, has Dobbin.

Vanity and delusion persist undisturbed by a black eye. Cuff is still the school's cock; like the ever-adaptable Becky Sharp, he has merely altered his methods of persuasion. Nor has George Osborne at all profited from his experience. When he writes to his rich Mama in Richmond, he suggests that she buy her groceries from—not Dobbin & Rudge—but "Figs and Rudge, Thames St., City—I think as he fought for me you ought to buy your Tea & Sugar at his father's." George's sudden condescension toward his champion hardly matches his unshaken respect for his tormentor. For Cuff is a gentleman's son; his father's wealth is enviable: "He has a white Pony to come and fetch him, and a groom in livery on a bay mare." George ends his letter with a fervent request which shows the persistence of his former values: "I wish my Papa would let me have a Pony, and I am, Your dutiful Son, GEORGE SEDLEY OSBORNE." The insertion of the boy's middle name introduces an ironic touch which the reader comes to appreciate only after George's marriage to the "little Emmy" remembered in a postscript. When George marries his godfather's penniless daughter, he will be disowned by his father, even though Osborne owes his wealth to Mr. Sedley. On striking George's name from the family Bible, Osborne comes across his son's early letters, requesting cakes, shillings, and a pony. Like so much in this novel, the puerile message sent by the schoolboy at Swishtail's academy acquires its fullest significance only in retrospect.

Even in its immediate context, the letter reveals that the fight against vanity is never won. Helplessly, the reader is forced to admit Dobbin's foolishness. More than grateful to be patronized by Cuff and George, honest William gladly bears the nickname of "Figs" as a badge of his popularity and attributes his "good fortune to the sole agency and benevolence of little George Osborne." By flinging himself at the little boy's feet and loving him, Dobbin the victor has become Dobbin the victim. His love for George, like his later love for Amelia, is perverse. It is his single vanity. Dobbin is a virtuous character—the best in the novel. But though Thackeray establishes William's goodness in chapter five, he will never allow the reader to identify himself fully and unreservedly with the "male angel" of his novel. The foolish boy who projects his benevolence on others becomes the foolish man whose acts of goodness only help to perpetuate vanity. By trying to protect George from Cuff, Dobbin only succeeds in making George admire Cuff; by later trying to shield Amelia from grasping George's true character, he only succeeds in making her worship a false idol. The child proves to be the father of the man. To show his love for George, Dobbin the boy gives little Osborne money and buys gifts he can ill afford; to express his love for Amelia, Dobbin the man gives her a husband, retrieves her piano, and furtively maintains her and her child. Unlike most of the other characters in the novel, Dobbin is not a materialist, but the dreamer is forced to use money to express his love, for money is the only expression understood by Vanity

Fair. In a society ruled by greed, "Dobbin of Ours" can never be a victor.

## 3

The characters in *Vanity Fair* are moved by either of two impulses: greed (or what the Showman at one point calls "this race for money") or love (or those feelings which the characters mistake for love). Speaking of the auction at the Sedley home, the narrator argues that such public assemblies afford the novelist with an opportunity to "light on the strangest contrasts laughable and tearful" (ch. 17). To be sure, the auction provides the Showman with a perfect miniature spectacle which Satire and Sentiment can visit arm in arm together. The narrator can simultaneously expose two different kinds of appetite: the voraciousness of the bargain-hunters who rummage through the belongings of the Sedleys and the hunger of those sentimentalists who rummage through the associations held by these remnants of a lost past.

Money and material goods possess a kind of permanence in Vanity Fair. The acquisition or loss of wealth may alter the characters, but the cult of money is unvarying. As long as Dobbin's father runs a modest shop he is looked down upon by the sons of gentlemen, but when his profits rise he is made Alderman Dobbin and knighted. The distance separating the onetime grocer and Mr. Osborne is thus considerably reduced; their sons are no longer as far apart on the social scale as they seemed at Mr. Swishtail's establishment. On the other hand, the bonds that once existed between Osborne and his benefactor, John Sedley, vanish after Sedley's financial ruin.

On visiting Amelia's fallen father, Dobbin admits that his own father and sisters, who would in earlier years have been most grateful to be noticed by Mr. Sedley, now snub him. In turn, the old man scrapes and bows before Dobbin. In a pathetic mixture of abasement and vanity, he alludes to "the worthy alderman, and my lady, your excellent mother" (ch. 20) in order to be overheard by a waiter in the shabby coffeehouse. Mr. Sedley blames his collapse on Napoleon, the British government, and the Kings and Emperors of Austria, Russia, and Prussia. His accusation is an attempt to aggrandize himself by obscuring his own imprudence. But his statement also carries a meaning unintended by him: the kings and emperors of this world *are* on a par with him; they too are warring merchants eager to gain economic supremacy. From top to bottom, money determines alliances and attractions. Just as the rival powers who join to fight the returning Napoleon are willing to overcome their contempt of each other, so is old Osborne more than willing to overlook the social ineligibility of an heiress with 200,000 pounds. In the political world, unequal nations consolidate against a common competitor; in the world of society, unequal marriages are made for money, and undesirable relatives are wooed for their fortunes. Mr. Osborne commands his son to marry Miss Swartz before some aristocrat will snatch her away. Conversely, aristocrats like Rawdon feel that it is their duty to take as much "tin" as possible from gambling "city-men." The Bute Crawleys abjectly court Miss Crawley, although they secretly despise her. Miss Crawley, in turn, unfairly accuses Miss Briggs of waiting for her death to receive a legacy; she assumes that her devoted housekeeper is pleading for Rawdon and Becky because of a bribe. To the materially minded, there can be no disinterested attachments.

Nobody understands better the commodity that sentiment can be than Becky Sharp. Her financial gains are always achieved through her exploitation of the affections of others. She wheedles a gift out of Mr. Sedley by tearfully alluding to herself as a penniless orphan; on reaching the street, she wipes her tears and counts her guineas. The one time she weeps in earnest is on discovering that she could have married Sir Pitt, an ailing man with a title and sure income, instead of sharing the increasingly doubtful expectations of his younger son. Becky's obsession with money is contrasted to the naïvete of Amelia who regards two thousand pounds as "an immense deal of money" that will last for a lifetime. Unlike Becky, who thinks that she could be a good woman on five thousand pounds a year, Amelia never even wonders where the funds maintaining her and Georgy are coming from.

Becky's money-mindedness is also contrasted to Rawdon's disregard for his earnings as a gambler. When we first see the couple living on "nothing a year," Becky's indifference to money seems like Rawdon's. Gradually, however, their attitudes prove to be totally dissimilar. In chapter twenty-five Rawdon stops to think about the future. The impending war makes him pity the newly wed Amelia: "I say, what'll Mrs. O. do, when O. goes out with the regiment?" Becky, too, has thought of the possibility of George's departure. But her foresight takes a significantly different shape: "Rawdon, dear—don't you think—you'd better get that—money from Cupid, before he goes?" While cajoling her husband to claim his bill, she is "fixing on a killing bow" to impress the same man whose death she has so calmly considered.

This same contrast is elaborated in "The Girl I Left Behind" (ch. 30), in which Becky's relation to Rawdon is brilliantly juxtaposed to Mrs. O'Dowd's and Amelia's farewells to their respective husbands. The chapter begins with Mrs. O'Dowd's preparations. The woman who wakes up her husband "as soon as the hands of the 'repayther' pointed to half past one" is acutely aware of time. Like Becky, who is the next wife to be described, she also seems to be realistic and unsentimental, devoid of "the fits of tears and hysterics by which more sensitive females exhibited their love." But as soon as we shift to Becky's leave-taking from Rawdon we realize that Mrs. O'Dowd, for all her outward calm, may in fact be closer to the hysterical Amelia. Despite their matter-of-factness, Mrs. O'Dowd's preparations "betokened affection." Not so Becky's. Sentences which would have aptly described Mrs. O'Dowd's stoic refusal to yield to sentimentality become heavily ironic when applied to Becky: "Knowing how useless regrets are, and how the indulgence of sentiment only serves to make people more miserable, Mrs. Rebecca wisely determined to give way to no vain feelings of sorrow, and bore the parting from her husband with quite a Spartan equanimity. Indeed Captain Rawdon himself was much more affected at the leave-taking than the resolute little woman to whom he bade farewell."

Rebecca's good humor grates on the reader as much as it does on Rawdon. Sensing that her manner has "hurt the feelings" of her husband, she mollifies him by "hastily dashing something from her eyes"; but if Rawdon is convinced, the reader is not. There is something moving in Rawdon's sudden metamorphosis from spendthrift into provider: " 'Look here,' said he. 'If I drop, let us see what there is for you. I have had a pretty good run of luck here, and here's two hundred and thirty pounds. I have got ten Napoleons in my pocket. That is as much as I shall want; for the General pays everything like a prince; and if I'm hit, why you know I cost nothing. Don't cry, little woman; I may live to vex you yet.' " Becky remains quite unvexed. Rawdon trots off to battle, wearing his oldest and shabbiest uniform, "leaving the newest behind, under his wife's (or it might be his widow's) guardianship," while Becky, who, "as we have said, wisely determined not to give way to unavailing sentimentality," goes back to bed. After her beauty sleep, she resumes Rawdon's "calculations" beyond any plane imagined by him. Rawdon has given her all his earthly belongings down to his coat and duelling pistols. But we now discover that she, unbeknown to him, has stashed away a fortune in "valuables" given to her by other admirers. Satisfied, she concludes that she can easily "begin the world" again. Rummaging through Rawdon's notes, she finds a twenty pound draft on Osborne: " 'I will go and get the draft cashed,' she said, 'and pay a visit afterwards to poor little Emmy.' " Becky is a far more astute economist than her husband: whereas his "plan of economy" is an expression of love, her own calculations show only self-interest.

Rawdon does not die on the battlefield; he lives to vex his

wife. What is only implicit in "The Girl I Left Behind" finally becomes explicit when Rawdon surprises Becky with Lord Steyne. Earlier, on being imprisoned, he had asked her to pay his debts; her reply—written "in bed"—dwelt on her difficulties in liberating *"mon pauvre prisonnier"* (ch. 53). Now, after Rawdon is released by his sister-in-law, he not only discovers Becky with Lord Steyne but also discovers that the nobleman regards him as a pander who has profited from his wife's prostitution. Forcing Becky to open her desk, Rawdon lights on her hoard: "It contained papers, love-letters many years old—all sorts of small trinkets and woman's memoranda. And it contained a pocket-book with bank notes. Some of these were dated ten years back, too, and one was quite a fresh note—a note for a thousand pounds which Lord Steyne had given her" (ch. 53). The scene is one of the high points of the novel; its position—at the three-quarter point—shows the extent of Becky's progress. The wife who murders Rawdon's love is closer to the survivor who eargerly cashes Jos Sedley's insurance policy than to the girl who had flung the dictionary at the kind-hearted Miss Jemima in the first chapter of the novel. Her protestation, "I am innocent," seems less and less believable. Her innocence diminishes in proportion to the pain she inflicts. Although we are forced to make our own surmises, it is clear that the girl whose wit once seemed so delightful has become a woman capable of adultery and murder.

But in a sense, Becky *is* "innocent." She has merely carried the outlook of Vanity Fair to its logical extremes. The reader who belongs to a society as acquisitive as her own finds himself yoked to Becky's cruel logic. Even Rawdon's words upon discovering her treasure reinforce the inescapability of material considerations: "You might have spared me a hundred pounds, Becky, out of all of this—I have always shared with you." Morally, Rawdon is far more innocent than his calculating wife, yet even he must express his affection through the values of Vanity Fair. His words confirm Becky's cynicism. Love, gratitude, affection are to her meaningless abstractions by which most men disguise their true values. At the end of the novel, when the insurance company backs down and pays Becky her claim for Jos' policy, the Showman comment laconically: "The money was paid, and her character established" (ch. 67).

Becky thrives by disregarding sentiment. She knows that emotions are salable wares in the mart of Vanity Fair. She is logical and clear-eyed. But what of those who are illogical because they are moved by feeling? Rawdon, Amelia, Dobbin, Lady Jane, Miss Briggs go against the grain of Vanity Fair. They do not care for money. Nonetheless, these characters do not escape the ironic treatment accorded to the materialists of Thackeray's world. Unlike the Trollope who rewards the unworldliness of Dr. Harding, Arabin, and Eleanor, Thackeray refuses to dispense sweetmeats and sugar plums. His Amelia is not the model of perfection that her namesake was in Fielding's novel.[9] In his more realistic treatment, love, too, can prove to be a crippling vanity.

While Becky disregards all considerations beyond the self, Amelia's love presumably is directed at others. And yet her childlike and naïve obsession with love resembles Becky's adult and cynical obsession with money. Becky the opportunist thinks ahead, aware of change; Amelia the sentimentalist tries to arrest all growth, to deny change. She refuses to admit that her childhood sweetheart has developed into a man unworthy of her devotion; she loves this man all the more when his death allows her to be true to a fixed and unchanging image. Thackeray makes sure to have Amelia disillusioned in George before his death, for he wants us to see that she knows that her husband is not the ideal she had worshiped. Her distortion of George's character

9. For a discussion of the relation between Fielding's *Amelia* and Thackeray's novel, see R. W. Rader, "Thackeray's Injustice to Fielding," *Journal of English and Germanic Philology*, LVI (1957), 203-212, and E. D. H. Johnson, "*Vanity Fair* and *Amelia*: Thackeray in the Perspective of the Eighteenth Century," *Modern Philology*, LIX (1961), 100-113.

after his death is therefore all the more reprehensible. His death is a blessing to her because it allows her to avoid the reality she was about to face and to revert to her former cult.

Amelia's love, like Becky's, thus is self-love. Although, unlike Becky, she is a dutiful mother, she smothers her son and almost ruins Georgy by fashioning him in the image of his snobbish father. Becky's cynicism leads her to deny all bonds; Amelia's love of love results in similar denials. She is uninterested in the European cataclysm which ruins her father; she is too self-pitying to show commiseration for Mr. Sedley's misfortune; she refuses to acknowledge her debts to Dobbin. Like Becky, she takes without offering a return. And, since her self-love involves an act of self-blinding, we almost prefer Becky's frank egotism—almost, until we realize that such empathy can also lead us to empathize with adultery and murder. Still, just as Becky helps the author to satirize the greed that rules Vanity Fair, so does she allow him to puncture Amelia's false love. Becky is cruel in destroying George's memory, yet for once the reader rejoices in her lack of pity: "Why, the man was weary of you, and would have jilted you, but that Dobbin forced him to keep his word. . . . . He used to sneer about you to me, time after time; and made love to me the week after he married you." Becky produces the evidence of George's infidelity by forcing Amelia to look at the letter she has kept: "He wrote that to me—wanted me to run away with him—gave it me under your nose, the day before he was shot—and served him right!" (ch. 67).

Becky's savagery is necessary. Yet, though we want her to prick Amelia's illusions, we cannot rejoice in the union she makes possible. The sense of fulfillment we derive when, under similar circumstances, Signora Neroni brings about the marriage of Eleanor and Mr. Arabin, is absent here. The union of Dobbin and Amelia is not a triumph. It merely mitigates Dobbin's misery and chastens Amelia's self-love. The marriage is belated. Amelia is not a prize like Eleanor Bold. The matron who now becomes Dobbin's wife is but a shade of the vision to which he had clung over the years. When Dobbin finally admits that he, and not George, had retrieved Amelia's piano, he unwillingly calls attention to the disparity between past and present:

> "Amelia, Amelia," he said, "I did buy it for you. I loved you then as I do now. I must tell you. I think I loved you from the first minute that I saw you, when George brought me to your house, to show me the Amelia whom he was engaged to. You were but a girl in white, with large ringlets; you came down singing—do you remember?—and we went to Vauxhall. Since then I have thought of but one woman in the world, and that was you." (ch. 59)

Dobbin's recollection exposes the vanity of his own love. Though more intelligent than Amelia, though far more aware of the ways of Vanity Fair, he too is guilty of attributing his own emotions to others. In one of the novel's key ironies, this silent lover forces George into marrying Amelia by bringing him a letter from her thanking George for the gift of the piano: "I shall often play upon the piano—your piano. It was like you to send it." Amelia's sentimental words—words which apply to Dobbin and not to George—are exploited by Dobbin in order to move Amelia's reluctant groom. In delivering the message, Dobbin is overcome by emotion: " 'George, she is dying,' William Dobbin said,—and could speak no more" (ch. 18). Amelia is hardly dying. Unaware of Bonaparte's fall, unconcerned with Mr. Sedley's plight, the girl who mopes in her room is dimly conscious that her father's ruin somehow prevents her from marrying George. Dobbin is using hyperbole for a calculated effect—his exaggeration, like those of Becky Sharp, has the effect of touching his listener. George is infected by his friend's genuine emotion. He writes a note: "Dearest Emmy—dearest love—dearest wife—come to me." He is happy with himself. He will defy his father and marry the poor and virtuous Amelia. But his pose crumbles to pieces after he discovers that his father remains firm. Vindictively, George turns on Dobbin: "A beggar, by Jove, and all in consequence of my d – – d sentimentality" (ch. 25).

George's remark is as ugly as his sudden disenchantment with his wife. It is permeated by his love of money. His recrimination is just, nonetheless. He has been blinded by Dobbin's sentimentality. Dobbin has muddled things up. He is responsible for a father's disavowal of his son; he has forced Amelia into a marriage saved only by George's death. And why? "Because he loved her so much that he could not bear to see her unhappy: or because his own sufferings of suspense were so unendurable that he was glad to crush them at once—as we hasten a funeral after a death" (ch. 24). Love is selfish even in its unselfishness. Had Dobbin been more cruel and less kind (as Becky will be when she finally crushes Amelia's illusions), he could have spared Amelia this unfortunate marriage. What is more, he could have spared himself the years of misery that now await him. In due time, he admits his mistake. Unlike Amelia's recognition, which must be forced on her by Becky, his admission comes unaided: "It was myself I deluded, and persisted in cajoling; had she been worthy of the love I gave her, she would have returned it long ago. It was a fond mistake. Isn't the whole course of life made up of such?" (ch. 67).

Dobbin's recognition cannot be altered. Even after he gets his Amelia he can never love her as he had loved her before. She is no longer the girl in white he had sentimentalized as much as she had sentimentalized George Osborne. Resigned, he weds the querulous mother of a teen-age son. His hopefulness must be placed in his own child, who, significantly, is named after another woman, Lady Jane, in a novel where all other children bear the name of their parents. Dobbin is fonder of Janey "than of anything in the world—fonder even than of his 'History of the Punjaub'" (ch. 67). Amelia is envious: "Fonder that he is of me," she thinks rightly. Still, the narrator renders her point of view only to insist, in his own voice, that Dobbin remained a model husband: "he never said a word to Amelia, that was not kind and gentle; or thought of a want of hers that he did not try to gratify" (ch. 67).

The narrator avoids a final summing up. He refuses to enter

Dobbin's inner life. But, as in the concluding description of Becky's charitable activities, what remains unsaid is as important as what is being said. We are not allowed to forget the stoicism of Dobbin's earlier concession in the same chapter: "I have 'geliebt and gelebet' as the girl in Wallenstein says. I am done.— Pay the bills and get me a cigar" (ch. 67). The tone of his statement strongly resembles the narrator's parting words in the novel's last paragraph: "Ah! *Vanitas Vanitatum*! Which of us is happy in this world? Which of us has his desire? or, having it, is satisfied?—Come children, let us shut up the box and the puppets, for our play is played out."

Like the narrator and like the ideal reader demanded by the Showman, Dobbin, the man of feeling, must remain a spectator at the perpetual fair of vanities. The man with the horselike name is a Houyhnhnm among the Yahoos. He has lived as an exile during most of the novel; on tasting the fruits enjoyed by others he finds them insufficient. The goal he has maintained so long, Amelia, proves a mere illusion. Though resigned to his present, Dobbin finds comfort in his observation of the past and his trust in a better future. He writes his 'History of the Punjaub' and also hopes that he may benefit from his past mistakes by making Janey a wiser child than her parents. Like the reader of *Vanity Fair*, this observer of life finds meaning through the act of retrospection. Though the search for happiness proves to be futile, the search itself has not been in vain. As in that other treatise on the vanity of human wishes, Dr. Johnson's *Rasselas*, we are left with a conclusion that is no conclusion. The novel's movement is circular. Time, which both perpetuates and annihilates human vanity, is the protagonist of this novel without a hero.

### 4

No work before *Vanity Fair* illustrates so extensively and impressively the passage of time. The very bulk of the panoramic novel allows Thackeray to create the impression of the flow of years. The weight of time affects characters and reader alike,

modifying their initial assumptions and threatening their security. Becky destroys Amelia's denial of the past by producing
George's faded letter; her bills and letters rupture Rawdon's
long-held belief in her innocence. Throughout the novel, time-
past mocks the illusions of those who would deny change. Miss
Briggs still cherishes the "hectic" love letters of a writing master
she flirted with twenty-four years ago. The letters remind the
spinster not only of the dead man who could have been hers but
also of other dead hopes and expectations. Old Osborne looks at
the parcel of letters written by George; young Georgy, in his
grandfather's house, sees the initials "G.O." scratched upon a
windowpane. The initials are his father's; they establish a link
between the failings of Amelia's husband and the potential failings of her son. The recovery of the little piano, the reappearance of Jos' picture, the reemergence of Jos' flowery vests and
of the scar on Lord Steyne's forehead help to create a rhythm in
which the emphasis is less on the continuity that arises from
repetition than it is on the disconnectedness between hope and
regret, expectation and disappointment. The narrator wishes
that this gap were less apparent; sardonically, he implores men
to destroy the record of their onetime feelings:

> Perhaps in Vanity Fair there are no better satires than letters.
> Take a bundle of your dear friend's of ten years back—your
> dear friend whom you hate now. Look at a file of your
> sister's: how you clung to each other till you quarrelled about
> the twenty pound legacy! Get down the round-hand scrawls
> of your son who has half broken your heart with selfish un-
> dutifulness since; or a parcel of your own, breathing endless
> ardour and love eternal, which were sent back by your mis-
> tress when she married the Nabob—your mistress for whom
> you now care no more than for Queen Elizabeth. Vows, love,
> promises, confidences, gratitude, how queerly they read after
> a while! There ought to be a law in Vanity Fair ordering the
> destruction of every written document (except receipted
> tradesmen's bills) after a certain brief and proper interval.
> (ch. 19)

Change is all in Vanity Fair. The passage of time exposes all human vanity. Although time perpetuates the same aspirations from generation to generation, it also modifies them and ends them. The novel's many death scenes are not due to a mawkish Victorian fascination with such situations, but rather stem from Thackeray's desire to remind the reader that death, the end of life, is the only true vanquisher of vanity. Osborne, aloof and powerful, and Sedley, low and powerless, die on the same day. Miss Crawley's fortune and the elder Sir Pitt's title change hands after their deaths. Alive, they have used these ornaments as a bait; dead, they are soon forgotten.

Becky and Dobbin, antagonists in so many other ways, can be contrasted in relation to their attitude towards time. Becky always lives in the present; she never permits herself "much useless and unseemly sorrow for the irrevocable past" (ch. 15). Her reversals only spur her on—the world is forever before her. Immutable because of her very mutability, she posses a chameleonlike ability to adapt herself to new environs. Jos' fortune renovates her; even her features seem youthful again in Thackeray's last illustration. Dobbin, on the other hand, does age. Though he climbs from Lieutenant to Captain to Major and Colonel, his rise in rank and his father's changed social position are equally irrelevant to him. The civilian who faces Becky with such disgust in the last drawing looks more dignified than the awkward Major Sugarplums depicted earlier. But he also looks wearier, more pained. Becky's experiences have increased her flexibility; Dobbin's experiences have increased his rigidity. The spectator who stands outside Becky's booth is incapable of anchoring his ideals in the ever-shifting bustle of the Fair.

*Vanity Fair* is primarily a satire. In it, the author of a book on *The Four Georges* tries to laugh at the unheroic age of George IV in the same way that Pope had laughed at the age of George II: "Yes, we saw him. Fate cannot deprive us of *that*. Others have seen Napoleon. Some few still exist who have beheld Frederick the Great, Doctor Johnson, Marie Antoinette, &c.—be it our reasonable boast to our children, that we saw George the Good, the Magnificent, the Great" (ch. 48). Yet the irony that

Thackeray maintains throughout his masterpiece does not really lead to the purgative laughter of a Swift or Pope. Although, strictly speaking, *Vanity Fair* is neither a religious nor a philosophical work, it raises questions about human existence that are not posed in Trollope's comic world of clergymen. Under the guise of laughter, it laments the external and internal barriers which conspire against freedom and depicts a world of flux in which being is pitted against becoming. Unlike the Brontës, Meredith, George Eliot, or Dickens, Thackeray refuses to impose a moral order on the erratic universe he portrays. Instead, he puts his Amelia doll, Becky puppet, and Dobbin figure back into their box, content to have illustrated the contradictions inherent in human nature.

## III  *Wuthering Heights*: A Tragicomic Romance

The modern reader who has come to regard *Wuthering Heights* as one of the finest Victorian novels cannot but wonder why the public which responded to Dickens, Thackeray, and George Eliot failed to recognize the excellence of Emily Brontë's work. *Wuthering Heights* was published in 1847, the same year which marked the publication of Thackeray's successful *Vanity Fair* and Trollope's unsuccessful *The Macdermots of Ballycloran*, as well as of Charlotte Brontë's *Jane Eyre* and Anne Brontë's *Agnes Grey*. Like Trollope's, Emily Brontë's first novel was published by Thomas Newby; despite Newby's attempt to capitalize on the success of *Jane Eyre* (by pretending that "Currer Bell," its author, and "Ellis Bell," the pseudonymous author of *Wuthering Heights*, were one and the same), Emily Brontë's masterpiece was as ill received as Trollope's clumsy *Macdermots*. Yet while Trollope tried again and again until he succeeded later with *The Warden*, Emily Brontë was granted no second chance to conquer the Victorian reading public. She died of tuberculosis on December 19, 1848.

The notion that *Wuthering Heights* was too much removed from the ordinary "reality" that Victorian readers could find in the novels of Trollope and Thackeray is belied by the contemporary success of Charlotte's own work, *Jane Eyre*, which—with its supernatural omens and eerie voices, the madwoman in the attic, the split chestnut tree, the burning manor, and the maimed Rochester—depends far more unequivocally on mystery and melodrama than does *Wuthering Heights*. In her preface to a posthumous edition of *Wuthering Heights* (1850) in which she capitalized on her own prestige to draw attention to Emily's work, Charlotte deplored her sister's unfamiliarity with "what is called 'the world' " and guardedly defended the novel as a "rude and strange production."[1] According to Charlotte, Emily was possessed by a daemon she could not master, working "passively under dictates you neither delivered nor could question."[2] Her attempts to excuse the supposed excesses of Emily's imagination miss the mark as much as her efforts to moralize *Wuthering Heights*.[3] Charlotte had once shared the childhood dreamworld of Emily, yet either she never quite penetrated the qualities of her sister's imagination, or, if she did, she shrank from them in her eagerness to make Emily's novel palatable to the Victorian reader.

Charlotte's reprinting of her sister's novel did not help to persuade Victorian readers of its merits. *Wuthering Heights* continued to be neglected. In 1860, one of Emily's cousins wrote: "I wish my cousin had never written *Wuthering Heights*, although it is considered clever by some." Why did the novel fail to attract a contemporary audience? The reasons for its failure in the nineteenth century are probably the reasons for its success in the twentieth century.[4] The Victorians did not reject Emily's work because, as Charlotte assumed, they found it to be too fantastic and subjective a work. (Charlotte also made the mistake of declaring Thackeray to be a Jane-Eyre-like reformer, "the first social regenerator of the day.") They rejected it because under the guise of the comic amusement of the novel, which they had come to expect, they found a disturbing, unexplained vision of anarchy and decay.

1. "Editor's Preface to the New Edition of Wuthering Heights," reprinted in *Wuthering Heights: An Authoritative Text With Essays in Criticism,* Norton Critical Edition, ed. William M. Sale, Jr. (New York, 1963), pp. 10, 9. All future references in the text are to this edition.
2. *Ibid.,* p. 12.
3. "For a specimen of true benevolence and homely fidelity, look at the character of Nelly Dean; for an example of constancy and tenderness, remark that of Edgar Linton" (*Ibid.,* p. 11).
4. *Wuthering Heights* has stimulated a greater variety of distinguished critical essays than most other Victorian novels. The reader is referred to the essays reproduced in the Norton Critical Edition, as well as to the more comprehensive selection by Richard Lettis and William E. Morris in *A Wuthering Heights Handbook* (New York, 1961).

Both *Jane Eyre* and *Wuthering Heights* can be traced back to the mythical domain of "Angria" invented by the Brontë children after their readings in Shakespeare and Byron. When Angria was dissolved in 1831 with Charlotte's departure for school, Emily and Anne proceeded to form a second fantasy world, the island of Gondal.[5] The poems that Emily wrote about the inhabitants of this imaginary realm were discovered by the surprised Charlotte, who found them to be "condensed, vigorous and genuine" (the same adjectives apply to *Wuthering Heights*).[6] The Gondal cycle, recently reconstructed by Mrs. Fannie Ratchford,[7] demonstrates that Emily's imagination, far from being lyrical and subjective, was essentially dramatic, relying on complementary points of view.

In writing *Wuthering Heights* Emily relied on this same dramatic talent to objectify her vision. Unlike the earnest Charlotte, who projected her fantasies and aspirations through the single-minded figure of Jane Eyre, Emily relied on irony and self-division to complicate her own responses to reality. The indignant feminist who acts as Charlotte's narrator is treated without the protective irony enforced by Lockwood and Nelly Dean, the two narrators of Emily's novel. In *Wuthering Heights*, as in *Barchester Towers* and in *Vanity Fair*, the mode is dramatic; there is no direct spokesman for the implied author. Whereas the self-righteous Jane Eyre imposes, through the forcefulness of her personality, her own order on the world around her, and her own view on us, the pair of comic observers who act as our guides in *Wuthering Heights* are even more fallible than Thackeray's equivocal Showman or Trollope's evasive narrator. The civilized Lockwood and the commonsensible Mrs. Dean qualify, and are qualified by, the turbulent, irrational world of Cathy and Heathcliff.

5. For the full story of "Angria" and "Gondal," see Fannie E. Ratchford, *The Brontës' Web of Childhood* (New York, 1941).

6. "Biographical Notice of Ellis and Acton Bell," *Ibid.*, p. 4.

7. In *Gondal's Queen: A Novel in Verse by Emily Jane Brontë* (Austin, 1955).

Emily Brontë knew that her bent, like Charlotte's, was romance; yet she was also astute enough to recognize that the dominant mode of the English novel was comic. Byron, who had written "Childe Harold" and *Manfred*, had also composed the comic *Don Juan*; Shakespeare, whose *King Lear* Lockwood remembers so incongruously when he is beset by Heathcliff's dogs, had blended humor and melodrama, laughter and terror. Emily's dramatic powers allowed her to control the fantasy world she had once shared with her brother and sisters. Her inventiveness allowed her to devise a framework in which the outer veneer of social comedy encases the truths of fantasy and myth.

In *Vanity Fair*, as we have seen, Thackeray was able to express his pessimistic outlook within the traditional framework of the comic novel by throwing out the dictionary definitions of good and evil and thereby forcing the reader to reassess reality itself. Though sharing this aim, Emily Brontë is far more radical in her departures. Thackeray's Showman refuses to act as our moral guide; yet his equivocations help to establish definable attitudes in the reader. The guide provided to the reader in the opening pages of *Wuthering Heights* proves to be totally unreliable. We cross the threshold of Heathcliff's mansion together with Lockwood only to find that the assumptions we have shared with this city man become totally untenable. Lockwood is a refugee from civilized society. His witty tone and extreme self-consciousness make him a distinct cousin of the jesting misanthropist who acts as Thackeray's narrator. Yet this Thackerayan figure, whose manners are urbane and whose outlook is comic, cannot cope with the asocial world he finds beyond the "threshold" of Wuthering Heights. His education becomes the reader's own, although, eventually, our understanding will surpass his.

Once inside the mansion Lockwood commits one blunder after another. Each overture, each phrase that he utters, results in a new misconception. In desperation, Lockwood cries out to the girl he has twice misidentified: "I want you to *tell* me my way, not to *show* it" (ch. 2). He demands to be led back to the sanity of Thrushcross Grange. After Lockwood is imprisoned by the snowstorm, the guide he demands will appear to him in a nightmare. Although the disturbing dream which he defends himself against was intended for Heathcliff—whose sensibilities are totally unlike his own, despite Lockwood's earlier, jocular identification of his host—the dream, though not telling Lockwood the way out of the labyrinth he has entered, begins to show us a new way of creating order. Lockwood, however, bound by his ordinary perceptions, fails to see that the creature outside the window is, potentially, a guide whose call for pity can rescue him from the "sin no Christian need pardon." Next day he relies on Heathcliff to conduct him back to the Grange. The snow-covered landscape has become treacherous: a "billowy, white ocean" has erased all landmarks, covering "rises and depressions in the ground: many pits, at least, were filled to a level" (ch. 3). Heathcliff follows stones erected to "serve as guides in the dark"; he warns the stumbling Lockwood to "steer to the right or left, when I imagined I was following, correctly, the winding of the road." Just as the external topography has altered from what "yesterday's walk left pictured" in Lockwood's mind, so has his neatly ordered inner world been disrupted by contradictions he has yet to sort out. Heathcliff stops at the gate of the Grange. Within its confines the exhausted Lockwood yields to a new "guide," Nelly Dean. Yet even her more sedate attempts to impose order and sanity on the reality he has experienced prove to be insufficient.

The reader is lured with Lockwood into the irrational world of *Wuthering Heights*. Like Lockwood, we have had barely time to take note of the lavish engravings on the front door, the date "1500," and the name "Hareton Earnshaw" before we are faced with incongruities we must decipher. The Heights lacks any "introductory lobby or passage," just as Emily Brontë's novel lacks the introductory passages furnished by a Trollope or Thackeray. Lockwood's initial experience is our own. As we stand on the threshold with him we too ponder between "speedy entrance" or "complete departure." On crossing the threshold we are mystified. Unsure of the causes for our mystification, we, like Lockwood, make the mistake of being overconfident. Soon, however, we are on the defensive. Our instinctive reaction is to flee, to be told the way out. Emily Brontë's Victorian readers took this way out. Confused by the discrepancy between Lockwood's polite diction and the atmosphere into which he is thrust, they must have been as confused as he is to find that a lady's furry "favourites" turn out to be a heap of dead rabbits. Yet the modern reader, more attuned to incongruity, gradually accepts the challenge. Whereas Lockwood represses the meaning of the two dreams he has experienced, we are willing to analyze their content. While Lockwood is content to lie on his back for most of the novel, willing to be entertained by Nelly's account, we continue to wander through a maze of conflicting attitudes, shifts in point of view, and abrupt changes in tone.

For a long while the reader is thwarted. Expectations misfire. Doors that seem open are shut; gates that seem closed turn out to provide us with an unexpected means of passage. Hovering between comic realism and the exaggerations of melodrama, this novel constantly avoids either extreme. In Thackeray's scheme, too, satire and sentiment qualify each other. But in *Wuthering Heights* these two modes merge and interpenetrate. Unlike *Vanity Fair*, Emily Brontë's novel moves toward a resolution. The social-comical realism of Lockwood and Nelly clashes with the asocial tragic myth enacted by Cathy and Heathcliff, but a new comic mode—represented by the idyll of the second Cathy and Hareton—bridges the chasm and ultimately provides the passage that seemed so impossible to find. In the novel's closing scene, Lockwood flees through the back door of the Heights. The reader, however, is rewarded for his endurance. He welcomes the restoration of order, and he wonders, with the departing Lockwood, how anarchy could ever have disrupted the benign face of "that quiet earth" (ch. 34).

# I

Like *Vanity Fair*, *Wuthering Heights* traces the fortunes of three generations. Whereas time moves in a straightforward progression in Thackeray's novel, Emily Brontë's use of two narrators permits her to devise a more subtle time scheme. The novel begins in the winter of 1801; but after chapter three, when Lockwood yields to Nelly's narrative, the plot moves simultaneously in two directions. Nelly's long flashback accounts for the "some quarter of a century" (ch. 3) that separates Lockwood's present from the events recorded in the notebook he has read; at the same time, as the prostrate Lockwood listens to the housekeeper's story, the weeks keep gliding by. By the end of chapter thirty, after Nelly has finished her tale, Lockwood decides to spend the "next six months in London." He returns in September of 1802, and, in a new flashback, Nelly now fills him in on the events that have occurred in his absence. The novel finishes on a forward thrust. Heathcliff's agony has ended, and the union of a new set of lovers promises a future far more wholesome than the one projected in *Vanity Fair*.

Thus it is that although the novel carries the reader through almost three decades it gives us the impression that only a year has elapsed. In *Vanity Fair* (where the nineteen monthly parts contributed to the sense of wasted decades which Thackeray wants to produce) the reader is asked to share the weariness felt by Dobbin and the Showman. The reader of *Wuthering Heights*, however, can shake off Lockwood as soon as he recognizes that the destructive past fits into a cycle of regeneration. Refreshed by the abrupt turn of events which have taken place during Lockwood's absence and without Nelly's usual interference, we thus are finally freed from our dependence on the two narrators who have until then controlled our responses.

For the first thirty chapters, however, we depend on Lockwood's and Nelly's points of view. Both characters fail us precisely at those points where they could have taken an active part in the story. Although their own actions are significant, both are

essentially passive figures. Lockwood comes to the country because he has resisted involvement. Having toyed with the affections of a "most fascinating creature, a real goddess," he fled her
company as soon as this imaginary attachment threatened to be
confounded by actuality. His evasion has gained him "the reputation of deliberate heartlessness" (ch. 1). He makes two trips to
Wuthering Heights in the opening chapters and but two more
in the final portions of the book. The rest of the time, between
these visits, he is either laid up in bed or away in London. Only
his "fancy" (the term he uses in contradistinction to Heathcliff's
term, "imagination") remains active. After his unsettling experience at the Heights, Lockwood is diverted by Nelly's story of
the Earnshaw and Linton families. Although his tone is patroniz-
ing ("Excepting a few provincialisms of slight consequence, you
have no marks of the manners which I am habituated to consider
as peculiar to your class" [ch. 7]), Lockwood actually wants
Nelly to simplify experience for him. To him she is an uncomplicated rustic who lives "more in earnest . . . and less in surface
change, and frivolous external things" than the Londoners of his
acquaintance (ch. 7). Lockwood the city man needs Nelly the
provincial. Her story permits him to order his excited mind; it
allows him to fan his fancy in safe and unviolent ways.

Lockwood's reactions remain as stereotyped as before; his
involvements continue to be imaginary. After Nelly's account
of the two Catherines, he finds it possible to consider the young
woman he has met at the Heights in a completely new light. He
tells himself to "beware of the fascination that lurks in Catherine
Heathcliff's brilliant eyes" (ch. 14). From his earlier pose of "a
fixed unbeliever in any love of a year's standing," he lapses into
fancying "a love for life here almost possible" (ch. 7). But as his
bodily health returns, Lockwood's fancy abates. He goes to the
Heights and looks at the real Cathy, and he is relieved to find
that actuality does not match his romantic preconceptions:
"She's a beauty, it is true, but not an angel." The union of Cathy
and Hareton defeats his constructing more mental castles. In
the opening part of the book, on finding himself locked out by

Joseph, this wooden Lockean angrily protests: "I would not keep my doors barred in the day time" (ch. 2). Yet at the end of the novel, it is Lockwood himself who deliberately bars the door and hastily escapes romance in plain daylight.

Nelly, on the surface, seems a far more active character than Lockwood. She bustles around as a go-between and acts as an officious duenna; she is a witness to all the crucial scenes. Yet, for all her meddling, Nelly remains curiously inactive whenever she might have exerted a crucial influence on events through compassion and feeling. Her first reaction to the alien child brought by Mr. Earnshaw is as defensive as Lockwood's reaction to the child in his dream. She ignores the little intruder, hoping that it might leave the Heights. As the adult Heathcliff says sarcastically to her, later in the novel: "you'll force me to pinch the baby, and make it scream, before it moves your charity" (ch. 27). When the elder Catherine dies, Nelly reports the event casually, without any display of emotion.

The dire effect of Nelly's inaction is best illustrated in the crucial scene in which Catherine confides to her that she will marry Edgar Linton although she loves Heathcliff. The housekeeper knows that Heathcliff has overheard the first part of Catherine's speech, yet instead of recalling Heathcliff or telling Catherine to run after him, she remains silent, thus contributing to the misfortunes that will be visited on two generations of Earnshaws and Lintons. Not only does she refuse to acknowledge that her passivity has contributed to Heathcliff's misunderstanding and escape but she also self-righteously lays "the blame of his disappearance on [Catherine] (where indeed it belonged ...)" (ch. 9). After Heathcliff's return she refuses her sympathy to the morbid trio at the Grange: Isabella, in love with love, secludes herself, "always silent"; Edgar, in love with Catherine, locks himself in his study "among books that he never opened"; Catherine, in love with Heathcliff, shuts herself in her chambers and fasts for three full days. Yet Nelly, the talkative meddler, holds off all communication and merely congratulates herself for her own sanity amidst this disorder: "I went about my household duties, convinced that the Grange had but one sensible soul in its walls, and that lodged in my body" (ch. 12).

Although Nelly, like Lockwood, distrusts passion and emotion, she is by no means the villainess that at least one critic has made her out to be.[8] Of all characters, she best loves the second Cathy, "my own sweet little mistress," and is willing to serve the girl's interests. But, significantly enough, Nelly can do nothing to avoid this Cathy's subjection to Heathcliff. Whereas she could easily have prevented the first Catherine's union to Edgar Linton and thereby have helped to avert her mistress' irresolvable conflict of allegiances, Nelly cannot, despite her efforts to the contrary, prevent the second Catherine's unfortunate marriage to Heathcliff's son. Nelly falls sick precisely during the time that her ward steals away for her visits with Linton Heathcliff ("I was laid up, and during three weeks I remained incapacitated . . . a calamity never experienced prior to that period, and never, I am thankful to say, since" [ch. 23]). She is locked in by Heathcliff during Cathy's nuptials and kept a prisoner for five days (ch. 27). When she returns to the Grange, she is incapable of altering the dying Edgar Linton's testament. Her self-induced inaction contributed to the first Catherine's alienation from Heathcliff; her enforced inaction now contributes to the second Catherine's suffering—even though this suffering proves to be a necessary prelude for the younger Cathy's growth to a stage beyond the arrested development of her mother.

Lockwood's own paralysis is, as we have already seen, amply suggested in the opening chapters. Like the gregarious Nelly, he is, for all his antisocial pose, an eminently social creature with little understanding for the isolatoes dwelling at the Heights. Although he professes to be a misanthrope eager to be "removed from the stir or society," he cannot really identify himself with that "capital fellow," Heathcliff: "It is astonishing how sociable I feel myself compared with him" (ch. 1). Lockwood's second

---

8. James Hafley, "The Villain in *Wuthering Heights*," *Nineteenth-Century Fiction*, XIII (December 1958), 199–215; reprinted in Lettis and Morris, *A Wuthering Heights Handbook*, pp. 182–197.

visit to the Heights incapacitates him even further. His new impressions confirm his inability to penetrate the drama of its inhabitants. His frame of reference proves to be wholly inadequate. His diction is full of the formulas of polite conversation: "amiable lady," "proper person," "ministering angel." He is as shocked by the incivilities of Joseph, Hareton, Heathcliff, and Cathy as he is rattled by his discovery that by no stretch of his "fancy" can a heap of dead rabbits be construed to be a lady's pets.

Like Nelly, Lockwood finds that only "by assuming the cheerful" (ch. 2) can he manage to settle his mind. Threatened by the nightmare in Cathy's chamber, he tries on awaking to bring his imagination under control. Heathcliff, on hearing about the dream, strikes his "forehead with rage"; Lockwood, on the other hand, steadfastly refuses to yield to his host's "access of violent emotion" (ch. 3). He looks at his watch, that symbol of regularity, and self-consciously begins to soliloquize on the length of the night: "Not three o'clock yet! I could have taken oath it had been six. Time stagnates here—we must surely have retired to rest at eight!" (ch. 3). Lockwood's obdurate cheerfulness sets off Heathcliff's melodramatic outburst somewhat in the way that Becky Sharp's calculated good humor qualifies and yet is qualified by Amelia's tear-floods. Taken by itself, Heathcliff's action of beating his forehead may seem excessively histrionic; yet the turbulence of his emotions seems preferable to the complacency of Lockwood, who looks at his watch so methodically and refuses to betray the violence which had led him to rub the bloody wrists of the apparition in his nightmare. He merely "fancies" a tear in Heathcliff's eyes. By way of contrast, the unbridled, irrational behavior of his host seems preferable by far.

Lockwood's external calmness, however, is deceptive. He has been shaken by his encounter with visions more unusual than those his rational fancy is able to concoct. When he returns to the Grange he gratefully yields to Nelly Dean's ministrations, almost too feeble to enjoy "the cheerful fire" prepared for him (ch. 3). His ailments are not purely physical: "I was excited, almost to a pitch of foolishness, through my nerves and brain" (ch. 4). He relies on Nelly to purge this unwanted "foolishness"; her logic must counter the illogic he has experienced. The housekeeper who is so proud of her "sensible soul" is glad to oblige. Her reaction to dreams is, after all, not unlike Lockwood's own (to Catherine's query about "queer dreams," she rejoins, "Come, come, be merry, and like yourself!" [ch. 9]); when, "half dreaming," she yields to fantasies of her own, she welcomes the dawn that restores her to "common sense" (ch. 34). Bodily health and the mental sanity that come with such health are what she prizes most. Nelly delights in nursing the strong; she rejects the weak and abnormal. Heathcliff appeals to her only after the "dangerously sick" boy responds to her care (ch. 4); she likes the second Catherine because—like Hareton whom she has bottle-fed—this child is healthy, a far better investment for her sympathies than the shrieking Catherine or the stupid Frances, Hareton's tubercular mother, who is insensible of her approaching death. Like Dr. Kenneth the physician, Nelly can be cruelly blunt. She dismisses Linton Heathcliff as a "bit of a sickly slip" (ch. 23) and tries to intimidate the morose youngster: "do you imagine that beautiful young lady, that *healthy*, hearty girl, will tie herself to a little *perishing* monkey like you?" (ch. 27; italics added).

Although the woman who reserves her heart for those who are healthy, sensible, and sane shares Lockwood's shortcomings, her point of view cannot be dismissed as easily as that of her "heartless" listener. Lockwood flees; Nelly remains firmly anchored in the world of Cathy and Hareton. Her view of life ultimately blends with that of her favorites. She is most reliable, because most intimately involved, when she tells the younger Cathy's story; she is a far less able interpreter of the romance of Catherine and Heathcliff. Still, even if her indifference to the first set of lovers reveals her limitations, Nelly Dean also becomes the vehicle for Emily Brontë's own definite reservations about the romantic exaggerations of Heathcliff and Catherine.

Her comic stance, unlike Lockwood's, helps to preserve the novel's balance. When the enraged Hindley tries to force his carving knife down Nelly's throat, she tells him that she would much prefer to be shot, "if you please," since she dislikes the taste of his blade (ch. 9). Her answer has the effect of reducing bombast into slapstick. We are disarmed by Nelly's cheerfulness because, by converting this "blasphemer" against God and the universe into a harmless fool, she has helped us to disarm Hindley's nihilism. The reader who listens with Lockwood to Nelly's story gradually is led to acknowledge that her instinct of self-preservation saves us from the vortex of self-destruction that engulfs her romantic counterparts.

Wordsworth, a Romantic, claimed that in his sonnets, Shakespeare had "unlocked his heart"; Browning, a Victorian, ridiculed that claim. In *Wuthering Heights*, a work that is both Romantic and Victorian, Nelly Dean and Lockwood provide the ironic frame which encases the novel's heart. This outer frame is not detachable. If the passion of Heathcliff and Catherine lies at the emotional core of the novel, Nelly's comic vision is vindicated by her two nurslings, Cathy and Hareton. We are allowed to unlock the novel's inner core only through Nelly's guarded account. Paradoxically enough, it is this balanced housekeeper who provides us with the keys to a story about the imbalances of the heart.

## 2

*Wuthering Heights* ultimately relies on the comic convention of a happy ending through the harmony of marriage. Just as the marriage of Mr. Arabin and Eleanor Bold in *Barchester Towers* erases the conflicts that agitated poor Mr. Harding, so does the union of Hareton and the second Cathy help to restore the happiness denied to the previous inhabitants of Wuthering Heights and Thrushcross Grange. But the losses incurred in this novel are far more severe than those that disrupt Trollope's world of provincial clergymen. At the center of *Wuthering Heights* lies a tragic vision of waste and disjunction which even goes beyond

the grim picture of irreconcilables that Thackeray had presented in *Vanity Fair*. This tragedy relies on severance—the severance between old Earnshaw and his children, between the worlds
of the Heights and the Grange, and, most cruelly, between
Catherine and the two men in her life: Heathcliff and Edgar
Linton.

Catherine Earnshaw tries to explain to Nelly the nature of her
oneness with Heathcliff by resorting to an account of one of her
"queer dreams." Nelly, "superstitious about dreams," quickly rejects this irrational means of explanation. In desperation, Catherine is thus forced to express herself in metaphoric terms:

> I was only going to say that heaven did not seem to be my
> home; and I broke my heart with weeping to come back to
> earth; and the angels were so angry that they flung me out,
> into the middle of the heath on the top of Wuthering Heights;
> where I woke sobbing for joy. That will do to explain my
> secret, as well as the other. I've no more business to marry
> Edgar Linton than I have to be in heaven; and if the wicked
> man in there had not brought Heathcliff so low, I shouldn't
> have thought of it. It would degrade me to marry Heathcliff
> now; so he shall never know how I love him; and that, not
> because he's handsome, Nelly, but because he's more myself
> than I am. (ch. 9)

Catherine assumes that her marriage to Edgar Linton will not
destroy her essential oneness with Heathcliff: "Nelly, I *am*
Heathcliff—he's always, always in my mind—not as a pleasure,
any more than I am always a pleasure to myself—but as my own
being—so, don't talk of our separation again." Catherine's very
diction is expressive of her own internal division, her split between the two antithetical realities that William Blake had la-
beled "innocence" and "experience." The girl who tries to rely
on irrational dreams to explain her feelings, whose semiconscious
being responds to the asocial energies represented by Heathcliff,
nonetheless finds her conscious, social self yielding to the ordered existence represented by Edgar Linton, Nelly's favorite.
She hovers between stasis and change, between the intuitive af-

97

finities of a world of essences ("My love for Heathcliff resembles the eternal rocks") and the self-conscious acceptance of a temporal world of growth ("My love for Linton is like the foliage in the woods. Time will change it"). Unable to exist in both of these orders, she falls from innocence into experience and thus precipitates Heathcliff's own self-division and incompleteness. She argues that if he were annihilated, "the Universe would turn to a mighty stranger" for her. Her words apply to Heathcliff's own estrangement after her death: until his own demise, Heathcliff will live in that estranged universe. He searches for Cathy in the dreamworld she failed to maintain. Only in that realm, re-created by Heathcliff's superior imagination, can the two lovers eventually be reunited and attain the oneness of mythical beings, freed from time and change. Unlike the second generation of lovers, they cannot find fulfillment in a temporal world of change and disruption.

This disruption begins with Heathcliff's introduction to the Heights. The foundling enters a world no longer bound by the reasonable social and ethical values still operating in Trollope's Barsetshire. The Christian ethic, so often invoked by Nelly to counter Catherine's and Heathcliff's presumed heresies, has lost its hold; by the end of the novel, Nelly informs us laconically that Gimmerton Kirk no longer has a "minister now." Instead of Trollope's benevolent bishop, the figure who opens Nelly's narrative is that of the "severe" and forbidding Old-Testament "master," Mr. Earnshaw. The door latch is raised, the master appears, and his expectant family confront the alien creature hidden in his greatcoat.

A century earlier, old Earnshaw would have been represented by Fielding's Squire Allworthy as an emblem of natural benevolence. In Emily Brontë's darkened world, however, Earnshaw's kindness is suspect: "I was never so beaten with anything in my life; but you must e'en take it as a gift of God, though it's dark almost as if it came from the devil" (ch. 4). The provider who had earlier promised gifts to the children eating porridge at his table and promised a "pocketful of apples and pears" to Nelly herself soon starves the affection of his dependents. Oblivious of the crushed fiddle expected by Hindley, impervious to having lost the whip Cathy had demanded, he becomes strangely obsessed by the sullen boy who shows no signs of gratitude. His irrational attraction to Heathcliff puzzles Nelly as much as Heathcliff's attraction for Catherine. Earnshaw indulges his adopted son, but he is unduly harsh to the daughter who later claims that she is Heathcliff. Through Nelly's eyes, we witness the incongruity of the master's behavior. Yielding to the influences of the curate and of the canting Joseph, the old man frowns on Cathy's laughter, is jealous of her vigor, and wishes that she be tamed by sickness: "I cannot love thee; thou'rt worse than thy brother" (ch. 5). When he reproaches her for not always being a good lass, Cathy pertly asks, "Why cannot you always be a good man, father?" Conventional goodness—still desired by Heathcliff when he asks Nelly to make him "decent" so that he can be "good"—can no longer order existence at the Heights.

After old Earnshaw's death, the energies he had stifled burst out. Hindley and Catherine cannot take their place in the adult institutional world now represented by the Grange. Both revert to the freedom and unrestraint of childhood. Hindley chooses the vapid Frances, a figure of perennial mirth, as a partner in his attempts to regress into a world of childhood games, but this world proves too frail to resist the realities of death and change. Incapable of assuming the role of a mother, Frances dies on giving birth to a son; bereft of a playmate, Hindley eschews the responsibilities of master and father. Losing the "benefit of his early education," he sinks into the chaos of total irrationality: Hareton, his son, runs a chance of either "being squeezed and kissed to death" or of "being flung into the fire, or dashed against the wall" (ch. 9).

Unlike her older brother, Catherine retains the companionship and affection of her own mate, Heathcliff. Whereas Hindley's attachment to Frances is an infantile regression, Cathy and Heathcliff are children who live a life of healthy unconstraint; "rude as savages," they are stronger by far than the new master of the Heights. Yet Cathy's division is not totally unlike her brother's. Hindley shakes off his education and reverts to savagery; Catherine, though secure in the "absolute heathenism" she shares with Heathcliff, becomes attracted to the civilizing influences of the Grange. Whereas Hindley capriciously hovers between alternate moods, his sister's conflicting allegiances make her far more deeply and irreconcilably divided. Hindley's childhood games merely signified an evasion of his adult role; Cathy, on the other hand, refuses to be arrested in her development. In her speech to Nelly she implies that she feels she can somehow retain her identity with all that which is represented by Heathcliff while moving into the different order of reality to which she now aspires. Her wishes prove to be impossible. By expecting that she can possess both Edgar Linton and Heathcliff she becomes untrue to each man and to the antithetical modes of existence each stands for.

Heathcliff's return only confirms the discord Catherine has created. He, too, has tried to submerge his earlier self by adopting the ways of civilization. But his genteel exterior only disguises the energies he shared with Cathy. These energies are now bent on destruction. He exploits Isabella's affections and deprives Hindley's son of his patrimony. Even at his most satanic and brutal, however, Heathcliff still remains true to that self which is Catherine. Like Hindley, he lashes out against a universe that has become meaningless. His recriminations to the dying Catherine are made, ironically enough, against the background provided by the chiming bells of the Gimmerton church, where Edgar and Nelly have gone for their devotions. Heathcliff bitterly accuses Catherine for having betrayed her own instincts: "You have killed yourself" (ch. 15). Upon her death, he accuses Edgar of being her murderer. Yet it is he who, by returning, has induced the woman who is pregnant with Edgar's child to long for her old freedom. This freedom is, for her, now only possible through the release of death.

When Nelly informs Heathcliff that Catherine has died on giving birth to the second Cathy, he rejects the housekeeper's pious hope that she may wake "in another world." He asks that she may wake "in torment" and demands that her ghost haunt him "as long as I am living" (ch. 16). His fullest expression of his love thus comes in a curse. In life, their union was denied by all kinds of barriers and obstacles. Catherine's death creates a new barrier, but Heathcliff denies the physical barrier of the grave as well as the spiritual barrier implied in Nelly's allusion to "another world." Catherine's notion of retaining Heathcliff while married to Edgar Linton proved to be an impossible longing; Heathcliff's desire to have her ghost with him at all times seems even more fantastic. Throughout the novel, however, he incessantly seeks out her ghost: he pushes Lockwood aside after he finds that the apparition in Lockwood's dream had claimed to be walking the earth "these twenty years" (ch. 3); he almost kills Hindley when his former tormentor tries to lock him out of the Heights.

Heathcliff's devotion to a Cathy who has been liberated from the confinement of time and space is finally rewarded. Wishing to die, Catherine had fasted for three days upon Heathcliff's return; after her death, we discover from Isabella that Heathcliff failed to eat a meal for nearly a week (ch. 17). At the end of the novel, the Heathcliff who refuses Nelly's food ("seemingly, I must not eat") dies in his paneled bed with the window swung open besides his corpse (ch. 34). Has he been recalled by Cathy? Before expiring, he stated that he was near sight of his haven—"hardly three feet to sever me!" His reunion with Catherine's ghost may be imaginary, but his imagination belongs to a different order than Isabella's fancied love for him or Lockwood's fancied love for the second Cathy. It is capable of breaking barriers. He and Cathy may well have fused in a world of myth that defies ordinary understanding.

The story of Heathcliff and Catherine thus ends as mysteriously as it had begun. Nelly dismisses the account of the little shepherd boy who claims to have seen "Heathcliff and a woman, yonder." The rational housekeeper who is so afraid of dreams remarks that the child "probably raised the phantoms from thinking, as he traversed on the moors alone, on the nonsense he had heard his parents and companions repeat" (ch. 34). Relying on her own eyes, she sees "nothing." Nelly's skepticism seems too defensive, too assertive in her need to vindicate common sense at the expense of inexplicable powers of intuition. Although her report is confirmed by Lockwood, who wonders how any one could ever imagine "unquiet slumbers" for the sleepers buried next to the moor, we remember that, on closing his eyes, Lockwood had stared at the ghostly "child's face" in his dream. Phantoms, it would seem, are raised, not "from thinking," but from the suspension of thought. It is significant that the pair who, in life, found that their union was possible only as thoughtless children, "half savage, hardy, and free," should be seen, after death, by another small child.

## 3

Heathcliff's and Catherine's love has proved mutually destructive; it is resolved only through their survival as mythical creatures roaming the moors. As phantoms whose essence is denied by both Nelly Dean and Lockwood, they exist in a reality removed from ordinary experience. Their afterlife is not that affirmed by orthodox Christian belief—be it Nelly's unquestioning belief in a beneficent Providence or Joseph's fanatical belief in a God of damnation. Organized religion deteriorates in the course of the novel: old Earnshaw's loveless righteousness degenerates into Heathcliff's frank cult of hate. Gimmerton Kirk, whose curate had originally set Earnshaw against his children and later failed to soothe Edgar's bereavement over the loss of his wife, crumbles into ruins by the end of the novel. Only through the love of Hareton, a Heathcliff who does not degenerate, and of the second Cathy, a Catherine who survives an error in judgment, can Emily Brontë lend meaning to the temporal world the first pair of lovers have vacated.

The union of Hareton and Cathy provides a fulfillment that does not require a suspension of disbelief, but, quite to the contrary, can be achieved in the ordinary, probable world presided over by Nelly Dean. The restoration effected by Hareton and his bride completes a cycle. Hindley's son and Catherine's daughter correct the imbalance of the previous two Earnshaw generations and manage to counter the changes introduced by Heathcliff and his offspring. Heathcliff recognizes his own Catherine in both Hareton and the second Cathy. In both, the infusion of outside blood, that of Frances and of Edgar Linton, has humanized the Earnshaw strain. The second Cathy is blond like her father; like Edgar, she is capable of extending love to others. In marked contradiction to her mother, who married Edgar Linton in order to receive from him the solicitude she had been denied by her father and her elder brother, Cathy first marries the younger Linton Heathcliff out of an almost maternal need to give the sickly youth the same affection and care she has received from her own father: "I'm certain Linton would recover quickly if he had me to look after him" (ch. 23). Secure about her father's love for her, Cathy cannot be persuaded by Heathcliff that Edgar must have hated her for being the cause of her mother's death. Moreover, her intuition allows her to divine that Heathcliff's own professions of hate are but expressions of his own thwarted love. She says to him: "I don't hate you. Have you ever loved *anybody*, in all your life, uncle? *never?*" (ch. 27). Her words cause Heathcliff to flee. She triumphs over Heathcliff again when she reminds him that her strength comes from the reciprocation of love: "I know he loves me and for that reason I love him. Mr. Heathcliff, *you* have *nobody* to love you . . . *nobody* will cry for you, when you die! I wouldn't be you!" (ch. 29).

Cathy—the daughter of the woman who wanted to "be" Heathcliff—is wrong in assuming that he will die uncried for. She has not yet taken notice of Hareton's own capacity for love. On seeing Heathcliff's corpse, Nelly's reaction is one of fear—she is afraid of the face that has been contorted into a sneer and afraid that Dr. Kenneth may blame her for not having fed her master. Hareton, on the other hand, sits by Heathcliff's corpse "weeping in bitter earnest" (ch. 34). Heathcliff's attempt to revenge himself on the third generation of Earnshaws by converting them into haters thus proves to be unsuccessful. Though brutalized as a Caliban, Hareton loves the master who tried to supplant his father.

The laughter of Cathy and Hareton comes to signify the restoration of sanity in the disrupted world of *Wuthering Heights*. This laughter is that of comedy, closer in tone to that of Nelly Dean than to that so seldom indulged in by the previous tenants at the Heights. The first Catherine's merriment grates on her father, who preferred the serious Heathcliff to the little girl who was always "singing, laughing, and plaguing everybody who would not do the same" (ch. 5). Heathcliff's first alienation from his former playmate occurred when she returned from the Grange and declared him to be "funny and grim." Like Dickens' Pip, mocked by Estella, Heathcliff cannot bear her ridicule: "I shall not stand to be laughed at" (ch. 7). When he returns, it is he who wants to laugh at others, although his laughter is bitter and hollow. Heathcliff banishes the cheerful Nelly. He taunts Isabella and Hindley, mocks Lockwood, deprecates Edgar, and sneers at Linton, his own son. Significantly enough, his revenge misfires when the more healthy laughter of others again penetrates Wuthering Heights.

In chapter thirty-three the second Cathy is sticking primroses in Hareton's plate of porridge. A "smothered laugh" is heard. When Heathcliff turns fiercely on Cathy and says, "I thought I had cured you of laughing," Hareton sheepishly admits that it was he who had laughed. Despite the sternness of old Earnshaw and the sullenness of Joseph, who distrusts any form of amusement, laughter—imported from the social world of the Grange—intrudes in the asocial world of the Heights. Ironically enough, it is Hareton, whom Heathcliff has tried to degrade into a replica of the crude being that the first Catherine had laughed at after her contact with the Grange, who now defies his master's attempt to smother joy.

The fact that Hareton's laugh occurs over a plate of food is equally significant. We have seen how the death wishes of the first Catherine and of Heathcliff find expression through their deliberate starvation. Hareton and the second Catherine, on the other hand, feed each other. Sure that "she was starved," Hareton clumsily presses some food on the second Catherine when she comes to the Heights as Heathcliff's captive (ch. 30). Cathy admits that she has been "starved a month and more," but she fails to recognize Hareton's own starvation for love and his hunger for knowledge. When Hareton asks her to read to him, she mistakes his overture as a "pretence at kindness" (ch. 30). Soon, however, she discovers that his kindness is unfeigned. Like Heathcliff, Hareton is compacted of good and evil; but unlike Catherine, Cathy does not reject his coarseness, but proceeds to civilize him and to bring out the good. Together, they uproot the twisted bushes at the Heights and import "plants from the Grange." Presumably, in moving to the Grange, they will in turn implant Earnshaw vitality into the too-ordered gardens of the Lintons.

Although it is false to ignore the positive ending made possible by Cathy's ability to reclaim Hareton, it is equally easy to exaggerate the happiness of this happy ending. Emily Brontë's return to a comic mode allows her to illustrate the redemptive powers of a quasi-Christian love. Still, the story of Hareton and Cathy is clearly subordinated to that of the first set of lovers. Heathcliff's tragedy cannot be dispelled. As a denier, a Faustian figure who questions the meaning of existence in this world and in the next, Heathcliff, though checked and countered by Emily Brontë's art, remains a self-projection who acts out some of her own anguish and doubt. It is the withering of love, more than its eventual restoration, that remains at the emotional core of *Wuthering Heights*.

In his first dream in the third chapter, Lockwood, "with Joseph for a guide," had entered the Chapel of Gimmerton Sough to hear the preacher Jabes Branderham. The sermon is on "Seventy Times Seven," the unpardonable sin. The text is taken from Matthew, 18:21–22: "Then came Peter to him, and said, Lord, how often shall my brother sin against me, and I forgive him? till seven times? / Jesus saith unto him, I say not unto thee, Until seven times: but, Until seventy times seven." Lockwood is bored by the preacher's interminable sermon; the man who later uses Nelly to divert him from boredom accuses the preacher of the "sin no Christian need pardon." The preacher in turn accuses Lockwood of challenging his authority. But the unpardonable sin is committed by Lockwood in his next dream, when he rejects the child that pleads to be let in from the cold. Lockwood's failure to respond to the "child's face looking through the window" makes him guilty of the same lovelessness which was so ruinous to the descendants of the man who admitted the alien child into his house. In the same chapter of Matthew, Jesus tells His disciples that "whoso shall receive one such little child in my name receiveth me." To those who deny love to the innocent, damnation will occur: "But whoso shall offend one of these little ones which believe in me, it were better for him that a millstone were hanged about his neck, and that he were drowned in the depth of the sea" (18:5–6).

Cruelty toward the innocent is the chief sin in *Wuthering Heights*. This cruelty is shared by almost all the adult characters; moreover, it is often self-inflicted. There is no original sin, no absolute evil; no character is purely and wantonly malicious. In a novel in which the characters themselves are constantly blaming someone else for their misfortunes, the reader, prevented from pointing an accusing finger at any one of them, cannot declare, "Thou art the man!" Heathcliff blames Catherine for her willingness to marry Edgar; Catherine, in turn, blames Hindley for forcing her into a union with a man she cannot really love. Hindley has his own scapegoats. He blames God, his Heavenly Father, for killing the one object of his love, Frances, just as he blames old Earnshaw, his earthly father, for loving Heathcliff the Ishmaelite instead of his rightful son. Earnshaw, however, has merely rationalized his perverse attraction to the foundling by telling himself that he is following the dictates of a just God. It is in that Justicer's spirit that he reproaches Nelly for her cruelty to the boy. But the deity he believes in is devoid of feeling. Out of justice comes injustice. Although this process proves reversible, Emily Brontë's novel nonetheless relies on this cruel arch-paradox.

Despite the novelist's efforts to vindicate her belief in goodness and love, *Wuthering Heights* achieves its harmony not because of its final synthesis but rather because of its recognition of paradox and contradiction. Although the plot represents a triumph for the benign social forces of the Grange, it is in the garden at that Grange, and not at the Heights, that the cleavage which will separate Catherine from Heathcliff first becomes manifest. By having Edgar and Isabella fight over their dog so fiercely that they almost tear the animal apart, the author shows that the Lintons' civilized ways are only skin deep. Emily Brontë seems to share Heathcliff's disgust with the "petted things" who quarrel over a "heap of warm hair" (ch. 6). His mockery, to Nelly, of these "good children" only helps to expose the incongruity of the housekeeper's notions of what constitutes conventional "good."

The vitality of Heathcliff and the first Catherine is used as a foil to expose the precariousness of the Lintons' ordered way of life. As the second Cathy's "uncle," Heathcliff merely parodies the family structure on which life at the Grange is based. It is no coincidence that the elder Mrs. Linton, who nurses Catherine after the girl's unsuccessful search for Heathcliff in the rainstorm, should have "reason to repent of her kindness" (ch. 9). Both she and her husband die from the fever Catherine had contracted. Good can come out of evil, but the test of anarchy and disease seems necessary. Edgar Linton must confront such a test and suffer in its process before the author is willing to endorse his humaneness.

By her willingness to interpenetrate opposites, Emily Brontë achieves artistically what Catherine Earnshaw was unable to do. Catherine wanted to retain Edgar and Heathcliff, to live suspended between responsibility and freedom, civilization and eros, Victorian acquiescence and Romantic rebellion. Finding herself unable to span Edgar's social order and the life of instinct that she shared with Heathcliff, Cathy chooses to die, hoping to transcend a finite world of irreconcilables. The suspension she despairs of, however, is made possible by the novelist's construction of a form which encompasses these same alternatives. *Wuthering Heights* relies on the resemblances between opposites and the disjunction of alikes. Opposites blend: the Heathcliff who oppresses Hindley's son eventually matches the Hindley who oppressed Heathcliff; victim and tyrant become alike. Similarities are sundered: the Catherine who vows that she *is* Heathcliff survives, yet becomes altered, in the Linton daughter hated by Heathcliff. Only Joseph, oblivious to paradox and contradiction, always remains himself, unswerving in his self-righteousness, as eager to depreciate Heathcliff in the eyes of Hindley as he is to depreciate Hindley's son in the eyes of his new master. Joseph the fanatic, sure of his point of view, is an anomaly in Brontë's world.

By blending the illogic of Heathcliff's story with the logical realism of Nelly Dean and her nurslings, by fusing pessimism and hope, tragedy and comedy, Emily Brontë was able to resist the formulas by which her characters want to reduce reality. It is a tribute to the reality of *Wuthering Heights*, as well as to the novelist's integrity, that she was able to control the polarities on which her vision is built. The novelists we shall consider in the next chapter were unable to follow her example. In Meredith's *The Ordeal of Richard Feverel* and in George Eliot's *The Mill on the Floss*, the tension maintained in Emily Brontë's novel is no longer possible; in both works, the equipoise between romance and realism breaks down as comedy yields to pathos and the sins of the fathers irrevocably destroy their children.

# IV   The Intrusion of Tragedy: *The Ordeal of Richard Feverel* and *The Mill on the Floss*

*The Ordeal of Richard Feverel: A History of Father and Son* (1859) and *The Mill on the Floss* (1860) are shaped by a vision of change and disorder which, though inherent also in the comedy of Trollope and Thackeray and in Emily Brontë's romance, acquires far more despairing overtones in the form chosen by George Meredith and George Eliot. Both novels are relatively early works written by intellectuals who were newcomers to the field of Victorian fiction. Meredith, who started out in the romance tradition of the Brontës, had written the Arabian extravaganza *The Shaving of Shagpat* in 1855 and *Farina: A Legend of Cologne* in 1857. George Eliot, continuing the more "realistic" vein of Thackeray, conquered the Victorian reading public with her sketches of provincial life in *Scenes of Clerical Life* (1857–1858) and *Adam Bede* (1859). For their third work each novelist chose the form of the *Bildungsroman* or novel of education, a form popular with Victorian novelists ever since Thomas Carlyle had translated Goethe's *Wilhelm Meister* in his *Specimens of German Romance* (1827).

Goethe's *Bildungsroman* had served as a model for several major English novels written before *The Ordeal* and *The Mill*.[1] Dickens' *David Copperfield* (1849–1850), Charlotte Brontë's *Jane Eyre* (1847), and Thackeray's *Pendennis* (1848–1850) had all depicted the growth of a child through adolescence to adulthood. The development of the protagonists of these earlier novels was inevitably crowned with success: though initially at odds with society, each protagonist profited from the tests and

1. For a book-length study of the influence of Goethe's novel on English fiction see Susanne Howe, *Wilhelm Meister and his English Kinsmen* (New York, 1950).

"ordeals" to which he was exposed and eventually managed to win a place in society, even if, as in the case of Thackeray's Pendennis, his position might remain precarious. Meredith and George Eliot, however, depart from this practice. They impose on the form of the *Bildungsroman* a tragic outcome that is more in the vein of Goethe's *Sorrows of Young Werther*, in which the romantic aspirations of the young protagonist are cut short by his untimely death.

Richard Feverel and Tom and Maggie Tulliver are not allowed the social integration possible for Jane Eyre or David Copperfield. In denying their creations even the compromises possible for Thackeray's Pendennis or Dobbin, Meredith and George Eliot anticipate the bleak conditions faced by the protagonists of later *Bildungsromane*, such as Hardy's Jude Fawley and Butler's Ernest Pontifex (discussed in chapter seven of this study) or Lawrence's Paul Morel and Joyce's Stephen Dedalus. The orphaned Jane Eyre and the orphaned David Copperfield still follow in the path of those fatherless figures who, in eighteenth-century novels like *Tom Jones* or *Humphry Clinker*, could find their identity restored to them by a providential dispensation; Richard Feverel and Tom and Maggie, however, are wantonly destroyed by the mistakes of their parents. It is in the relentless portrayal of the breakdown of a family—that hallowed Victorian institution—that Meredith and George Eliot differ most significantly from their predecessors.

Usually written early in a novelist's career, the *Bildungsroman* allows the artist to objectify his private traumas and regrets. In creating Sir Austin Feverel and Richard, Maggie and Tom, their creators tried to mend deep personal wounds. It is undoubtedly relevant to Richard Feverel's fictional ordeal that Meredith should have lost his own mother as a small child and, more important, that he was faced with the bitterness of his wife's desertion and the task of raising an infant son while at work on his novel. Similarly, there is an unquestionable link between Marian Evans' despair over her brother's intransigence after her elopement with a married man and Maggie Tulliver's alienation from her brother, Tom ("George Eliot" was born in 1819, as is Maggie; her brother Isaac Evans in 1816, as is Tom).

Still, Meredith's *Ordeal* and George Eliot's *Mill* contain more than a private record of their creators' attempts to counter a deep personal disorientation. To an extent, any novel is shaped by the private experiences of its author. Thackeray's depiction of Georgy Osborne's precarious growth without a father can be attributed to his own fatherless childhood; Trollope's persistent characterization of weak men and domineering women, to his formidable mother. In *The Ordeal of Richard Feverel* and *The Mill on the Floss*, the disruption of the harmony of family life carries the same universal implications as in Emily Brontë's *Wuthering Heights*. By giving an even greater prominence to the clash between two generations than the novelists before them, Meredith and George Eliot brought to the fore the more acute severance between past and present felt by the mid-Victorians of the late 1850s.

## I

It is no coincidence that Meredith's *Ordeal* should have been published, and George Eliot's *Mill* composed, in 1859, a year commonly accepted as a turning point in Victorian sensibility.[2] The fathers of the mid-Victorians became to their children symbols for past solutions and past attempts at order which no longer seemed practicable in a present marked by the evolutionary theories of Spencer and Darwin, whose *Origin of Species* appeared in 1859. John Stuart Mill, whose *On Liberty* was published in 1859, had been molded by James Mill, who, like Sir Austin Feverel, relied on Reason and Locke. Matthew Arnold, who in 1859 ceased to be a despairing poet and wrote his first polemical essay, had been shaped by Thomas Arnold, the stern

2. See *1859: Entering An Age of Crisis,* ed. Philip Appleman, William Madden, and Michael Wolff (Bloomington, 1959), for a collection of essays dealing with that eventful year.

master of Rugby. James Mill was an atheist; Thomas Arnold, a Christian. Yet each man had a "system," and each son reacted against that system.

The differences between parents and children became to the Victorians a prime metaphor illustrating not only the artist's concern with his own threatened identity but also with the identity of all men in a world which more than ever seemed fortuitous and erratic. "This is a changing world," says Mrs. Deane in *The Mill on the Floss* to her sister Mrs. Tulliver, who soon proves to be utterly incapable of protecting her children from that changing world, "and we don't know today what may happen to-morrow. But it's right to be prepared for all things and if trouble's sent, to remember that it isn't sent without a cause."[3] This belief in a just providence belongs to the earlier generation; it is not shared by George Eliot's narrator, who, for all his desire to vindicate the "cause" for the troubles to be visited on the Tullivers, complains that Tom and Maggie have risen too rapidly "above the mental level of the generation before them" (Bk. IV, ch. 1). Their suffering, the narrator suggests, is that of "martyr or victim" and "belongs to every historical advance of mankind."

Increasingly insecure about the future, the mid-Victorians found a bittersweet delight in recording the breakdown of a heroic past. In 1859 Tennyson published the first four parts of his *Idylls of the King*, in which he portrayed the dissolution of an ideal order headed by the paternalistic King Arthur. The cohesion which, in an earlier generation, writers like Sir Walter Scott still sought in a wishful, feudal past was no longer possible. *The Mill* portrays the loss of an ancestral fief held by the descendants of Ralph Tulliver; *The Ordeal* depicts the decay of the family who pretend to hark back to the Norman Fiervarelles

3. *The Mill on the Floss*, ed. Gordon S. Haight (Boston, 1961), Bk. III, ch. 3. All future references are to this edition; they will include citations to each of the seven "books" into which the novel is divided, since George Eliot did not number her chapters consecutively but rather made each book begin with chapter one.

(the chivalric elements in Meredith's novel are treated with devastating irony).

In varying degrees, history to the mid-Victorians seemed a record of struggles and failures. George Eliot's narrator uncovers the layers of historical strata on which the present of St. Ogg's is built to show that the intermittent floods have merely separated one age of strife from another. The present warehouses of Guest & Co. rest on the site where Roman legions were displaced by Vikings, where Danes and Normans slaughtered Saxon settlers, and where Puritans and Cavaliers butchered each other. Though less explicit, Meredith's narrator suggests ominously that the curse in the Feverel blood, "Mrs. Malediction," has manifested itself again and again throughout the family's checkered history—in war, as well as in times of peace.

To elude the determinism of the past seemed an irresistible temptation. It was in 1859 also that Edward FitzGerald presented his translation of the *Rubáiyát of Omar Khayyám*, in which he refracted Victorian pessimism into an attitude of cynical escapism:

> "Ah, my beloved, fill the Cup that clears
>   Today of past Regrets and Future Fears
>   Tomorrow?—Why Tomorrow I may be
> Myself with Yesterday's seven thousand years."

FitzGerald's hedonistic speaker offers an escape route entertained by Richard Feverel as well as by Maggie Tulliver. Both Richard and Maggie try to escape a world of painful responsibilities. Both are prevented by their moralistic creators. Richard must reject the seductiveness of Bella as well as the self-indulgent attitude of his false tutor, Adrian Harley, "an Epicurean of our modern notions";[4] Maggie Tulliver must deny the blandishments offered by her specious lover, Stephen Guest, for whom "the inclination of the moment" is the only true "law." They must face, rather than avoid, the insecurities of past and future.

4. *The Ordeal of Richard Feverel,* ed. Charles J. Hill (New York, 1964), ch. 4.

These insecurities already existed in varying degrees of intensity in the three novels we have considered so far. Like Meredith and George Eliot, the earlier novelists availed themselves of the divisions separating parents and children; like them, they linked these divisions to the disruptions they saw in the world at large. The misunderstandings that alienate Eleanor Bold from her father in *Barchester Towers* were directly connected by Trollope to the disorder caused by the Londoners who disrupt Barchester's harmony. Thackeray likewise linked Osborne's ugly behavior toward his only son and Becky's rejection of little Rawdon to the misplaced values of the shifting Fair. And, in *Wuthering Heights*, as we saw, the rigidity of old Earnshaw—so like Sir Austin's own Puritanical severity—became emblematic of a world no longer bound by love.

Yet in *Barchester Towers* and in *Wuthering Heights* these conflicts ceased when the comic endings devised by each novelist allowed a return to sanity and order. Affinities that were threatened are restored; identities that seemed interrupted are continued. Far from remaining at odds with his daughter, Mr. Harding discovers that she has chosen to marry a man who is almost a double for himself; far from being disrupted by the excesses of Catherine and Heathcliff, the union of Hareton and the second Cathy blends the best of the Earnshaw and Linton lines and bypasses Heathcliff and his withered son. Even in *Vanity Fair*, where the Showman's pessimism survives, Thackeray manages to soften the abrasive quality of a world in which parents are inevitably pitted against their offspring: Dobbin's belated exaltation into fatherhood at least augurs a mildly better future for a Georgy and Janey who may grow up without the vanities that crippled two previous generations.

In the more tragic worlds devised by Meredith and George Eliot, such resolutions are impossible. The bond between parents and children becomes a destructive one. While Emily Brontë countered the tragic waste of Heathcliff and Catherine with a comic resolution, both of these novelists reverse the process by converting a childhood comedy into the tragedy of mature experience. Both works ostensibly begin in a comic vein. Meredith's aphoristic narrator matches witty epigrams with Sir Austin; George Eliot's ironic observer treats the insufficiencies of Mr. and Mrs. Tulliver with tongue-in-cheek. In *The Ordeal* the females who converge on Raynham Abbey to challenge Sir Austin's defiance of their sex—Miss Joy Blewins the blue-stocking, Mrs. Cashentire the banker's wife, the swift Camilla—are comic stereotypes similar to the Barchester ladies who engage in Trollope's version of the battle of the sexes. In *The Mill* the humorous clash between the proud Mr. Tulliver and his henlike Dodson wife is reminiscent of the confrontation between Mr. and Mrs. Bennet in the opening pages of Jane Austen's *Pride and Prejudice*. But the comic control exerted by each novelist vanishes. When reversals of fortune cut short the reader's expectations of a happy ending, Meredith and George Eliot obscure themselves. In the earlier novels, the tone established by Trollope's jovial narrator, by Thackeray's Showman, and by the cheerful Nelly Dean is maintained to the very end. Meredith, however, deliberately relies on Lady Blandish's despairing letter to inform the reader of the aftermath of Richard's duel and Lucy's pathetic derangement and death. George Eliot likewise dispenses with the stable voice of the narrator who had acted as the reader's guide and alternates between bursts of indignation and pauses of helpless silence as she documents Maggie's final trials and melodramatic drowning.

In both novels the gap between past and present proves to be impassable; the potentially paradisial Raynham Abbey and Dorlcote Mill are irrevocably lost. Moreover, the tragic conclusions augur no better future for those who remain behind. At the end of *The Ordeal*, Richard, himself now a father, is totally uninterested in the future of his infant son. Drained of all purpose, he can only look backwards at the vitality and love that he has wasted. Austin Wentworth, the Dobbin-like exile whose interventions in Richard's behalf were blocked by Sir Austin, is called to intervene once more to protect Richard's infant. In *Vanity Fair*, Georgy Osborne was released from his grandfather's grasp and entrusted to Dobbin; in *The Ordeal*, where Sir Austin is hatching a new foolproof system of education, it is doubtful that the baronet will release his grandson to a new surrogate father. The new Feverel heir seems destined to face a tortured future.

The ending of *The Mill on the Floss* also depicts a future that has been blocked. In the novel's "Conclusion" the wharves on the Floss are busy again "with echoes of eager voices, with hopeful lading and unlading." But the reader, like the small band visiting the tombs of Tom and Maggie, cannot participate in this hopefulness. The emphasis on the busy traffic on the river forces us to return in circular fashion to the book's opening paragraphs, in which the narrator who surveys the laden "black ships" was led to recollect the tiny child who stood absorbed by the churning mill wheel, so unconscious of her future. Lost in his reverie, the narrator managed to escape the weight of time, only to discover that his transcendence was short-lived. Like the widowed Richard Feverel, desperately "striving to image" Lucy "on his brain" (*ORF*, ch. 49), this time-burdened narrator sadly concludes even then that he was merely "dreaming" of an irrecoverable past.

*The Ordeal of Richard Feverel* and *The Mill on the Floss* represent their respective creators' attempts to master a temporal reality which had become even more intractable by the end of the 1850s than it had seemed to Thackeray in 1848. Both novelists try to prepare the reader for the tragic conclusions they deem irresistible; both narrators make sure to hint that mistakes in childhood can prefigure the catastrophes of adult life. Meredith's narrator warns the reader that Austin Wentworth could have prevented Richard's downfall: "very different for young Richard would it have been, had Austin taken his right place in the Baronet's favor" (ch. 4). George Eliot's narrator counters Mr. Tulliver's plan for Tom's education by stressing the miller's hopeless ignorance of "the world": "Nature," the narrator informs us, "has the deep cunning which hides itself under the appearance of openness" (Bk. I, ch. 5).

Childhood pranks are revealed to be far from trivialities. Richard's vengeful burning of Farmer Blaize's hay-rick foreshadows his disastrous duel with Mountfalcon; Maggie's impulsive dunking of her cousin Lucy and her consequent flight foreshadow her later escape by water with Lucy's fiancé. Fire in *The Ordeal* and water in *The Mill* provide a symbolic patterning for novelists who, in the words of George Eliot's narrator, always prove themselves eager to connect "the smallest things with the greatest" (Bk. IV, ch. 1).

In their efforts to interpret the larger reality that thwarts the education of Richard, Tom, and Maggie, Meredith and George Eliot meet with difficulties not experienced by the comic novelists before them. As novelists of a more "philosophical" cast of mind, they are forced to explain, as well as to illustrate—they are burdened with the task of educating the reader in the ways of that "Nature" which is ignored in the educations devised by Sir Austin and Mr. Tulliver. George Eliot's description of her heroine's plight thus acts as an apt description of the novelist's own predicament: rejecting the "absorbing fancies" of the romances of Scott and Byron as well as refusing to make "dream worlds of her own," Maggie demands "some explanation of this hard, real life: the unhappy-looking father, seated at the dull breakfast-table; the childish, bewildered mother; the little sordid tasks that filled the hours" (Bk. IV, ch. 3).

By using the novel in a far more exploratory fashion, by seeking, like Maggie, "some key that would enable" them "to understand," George Eliot and Meredith no longer possess the artistic self-assurance and self-sufficiency of their predecessors. Trollope, Brontë, and Thackeray managed to generate an internal logic in the invented worlds of their novels. We do not ask what power it is that restores order to Barchester or pause to question whether it was heredity or environment which led Catherine Earnshaw to prefer Edgar over Heathcliff. Yet, alerted by the novelists' own desperate search for "some explanation," we do wonder whether the fates of Richard Feverel and Maggie Tulliver could have been reversed and do want to know who is to blame for their destinies. Determinism and free will, chance and design, environment and heredity—terms so dear to the intellectual circles to which Meredith and George Eliot belonged —are far more relevant to their own brand of fiction than to the earlier novels.

Like the three novelists we have considered, Meredith and George Eliot are moralists eager to fight off despair by denying the logic of a totally anarchic universe. Resisting the nihilism of a Hardy, both are therefore led to extract a moral order from the "hard, real life" they find so intractable. Both try to suggest how a true understanding of the world might have prevented the tragedy to which their creations succumb. But although Meredith's "explanations" do not considerably vary from George Eliot's own, the two writers differ markedly in their method. The covertly romantic Meredith can ultimately avoid the need for explanations by falling back on the myth of the cursed Feverel blood; the overtly realistic George Eliot, however, finds it far more difficult to accommodate reason and hope, explanation and yearning. While the shift from comedy to tragedy in *The Ordeal* is by no means flawless, it is smoother and far more consistent than George Eliot's more incongruous shift from her realistic presentation of a miller's downfall to the contrived device of the apocalyptic flood which claims his children.

## 2

One of the contemporary reviewers of *The Ordeal of Richard Feverel* complained that the novel was itself a painful "ordeal" for the reader. Indeed, Meredith's self-conscious mixture of literary modes must have been almost as disconcerting to its Victorian audience as Emily Brontë's, a decade before. Few readers of the opening of *Wuthering Heights* could have suspected that Lockwood's witty tone would soon give way to Heathcliff's impassioned demands to see a ghostly apparition; likewise, few readers of the opening of *The Ordeal* can suspect that the aphorisms of Sir Austin the Jilted Sentimentalist are replaced by the powerful descriptive passage in which the baronet, silenced and impotent, watches Richard's intoxication with the flames of evil. The ominous fire challenges Sir Austin's ordered beliefs. Richard devours the flames with his eyes; his friend Ripton, with his mouth. Sententiousness and wit yield to description:

> Opaque and statuesque stood the figure of the Baronet behind them. The wind was low. Dense masses of smoke hung amid the darting snakes of fire, and a red malign light was on the neighbouring leafage. No figures could be seen. Apparently the flames had nothing to contend against, for they were making terrible strides into the darkness. (ch. 7)

The narrator who started in the vein of Thackeray has vanished. Meredith the humorist has become a cousin of Emily Brontë. Instead of commenting on the implications of the scene, he lets it gather its own meaning. Symbols rather than epigrams do the explaining.

It is Meredith's ability to maintain both the refined stance of the sardonic ironist and the lyrical quality of the romancer that makes possible the movement from comedy to tragedy on which his book ultimately relies. Meredith is both Sir Austin the intellectualizer and Richard the emotionalist, and he is able to play these polarities against each other. The novel is as much punctuated by Sir Austin's ever-present notebook, containing crisp and cynical observations worthy of Thackeray's Showman, as it is punctuated by the symbolic trials of fire and water that act as roadmarks in Richard's pilgrimage.

*The Ordeal* is structured by the tests that Richard undergoes, which increase in intensity and in duration. God placed Man in Paradise before the seventh day. Sir Austin wants Richard to emerge into a "Manhood worthy of Paradise" (ch. 4) after a career divided into three seven-year segments. Richard's seventh, fourteenth, and twenty-first birthdays thus pattern the novel. On Richard's seventh birthday, depicted in chapter two, "Mrs. Malediction" plagues both father and son. Richard hurts his father by reminding the baronet of the "beautiful lady" he assumes to be a dream; Richard, in turn, is hurt when his father's "Reason" steps forward and asks him "to withstand his inclinations" for ice and cake.

The ordeals surrounding Richard's fourteenth birthday, which take up ten full chapters, are no longer as negligible. "Mrs. Malediction" now manifests herself in more harmful ways. The intoxicated Richard becomes more self-indulgent, and Sir Austin, more self-pitying and prohibitive. The events which follow the rick-burning are potentially anarchic, threatening to make a mockery out of Sir Austin's belief in justice and perfection. Richard almost causes the death of Farmer Blaize and his cattle; moreover, the boy, by refusing to admit his guilt, almost causes the branding of Tom Bakewell, his innocent accomplice. Meredith imposes a deliberately inconclusive happy ending on these events in chapter fourteen, "In Which the Last Act of the Bakewell Comedy Is Closed in a Letter." Father and son become reconciled to each other, but the frowning Austin Wentworth, their moral conscience, is banished from Raynham. For Austin knows that the reconciliation is tenuous, achieved only through Sir Austin's need to convince himself that his system is flawless and Richard's need to maintain an unbroken self-esteem. The discordant elements smoothed over in the last act of the Bakewell Comedy thus merely remain dormant. They rise again in the final seven-year segment of Richard's career, when Sir Austin's denials no longer are centered around ice and cakes, and the passions that flare up in Richard are no longer those of a whipped boy.

The remainder of the book takes up this last seven-year period, which Sir Austin and the novelist have methodically divided into further stages: the Magnetic Age, the Age of Probation, and finally, the expected Age of Manhood and perfection. In the first of these stages, Richard falls in love with, is separated from, and finally elopes with Lucy, who, in Austin Wentworth's absence, now takes the place of his good angel. Yet, as was not the case in the Bakewell Comedy, the newly disappointed Sir Austin refuses to become reconciled to his son. Richard must remain apart from his father. Forced to go through the period of probation that Sir Austin insists on, Richard soon becomes separated also from his good angel, Lucy, and from the benign Mrs. Berry. When the baronet finally condescends to meet him in London, it is too late. A reconciliation is now impossible, for Richard is no longer reconciled to his own self. Full of self-loathing for having let himself be seduced by Bella, his Hell-Star (so unlike his Hesper, Lucy), and full of self-pity for his treatment of his cousin Clare, Richard escapes again. He has failed his father's probationary period.

Meredith goes through great pains at this point in the novel to suggest that all of Richard's difficulties can be resolved. The final phase of Manhood awaits Richard, despite his father's and his own mistakes. Thus, Meredith creates a countermovement by uniting the forces of good: Austin Wentworth returns and sides with Lucy and Mrs. Berry. Austin's directness is in contrast to the temporizing of Adrian and the Olympian detachment of Sir Austin; he and Mrs. Berry bring Sir Austin face to face with his daughter-in-law and grandchild. Lucy triumphs. The gap Richard has been moaning about no longer exists. Harmony is possible once again (even Mrs. Berry, the faithful Penelope, now finds her husband in Sir Austin's household). The ground is cleared for Richard's return to Raynham, to his wife, father, son, to the overjoyed Lady Blandish, and to Austin Wentworth his rightful tutor, who now follows Richard to Germany to inform him of this new and permanent reconciliation. Once again, plot is supported by symbolism. In the chapter entitled "Nature Speaks," amidst the rainstorm of the German forest, Richard feels purged of his fever and guilt. He is touched by his contact with the "Spirit of Life." Miraculously, by the agency of a force as beneficent as that which restores harmony in the wasted household at Wuthering Heights, a romantic idyll promises to enfold all characters and to dispel the disappointments and collisions that forced them apart.

Meredith's novel could easily have ended here. All the conflicts have been resolved: Sir Austin has mellowed, and to Lady Blandish's great satisfaction, he is even willing to admit that his system was fallible by acknowledging that his science could never have lighted on a better mate for Richard. The forces of evil have been exorcised: Adrian the false tutor is banished and Benson the misogynist butler has been fired. The other characters have been chastened by their experience: Mrs. Berry has forgiven her delinquent husband; Clare's mother, made wiser by her daughter's death, has become a true friend to Lucy; Lucy herself has benefited from Austin's schooling. Most important, Richard himself, the center of these ordeals, seems ready to assume his full manhood. Only his return is needed to complete the last act of the comedy. But when Richard does return to Lucy in the chapter called "The Last Scene," it turns out that this last scene ends in a new flight and separation. The expected Feverel comedy unexpectedly turns into tragedy, with Richard's duelling, his wound, and the maddened Lucy's sudden death of "cerebral fever—brain-fever"—that mysterious illness so prominent in Victorian novels.

The carefully built-up movement of the last third of Meredith's novel is thus destroyed by a quirk of fortune. Richard has grown. In the rainstorm he has come to a realization about himself and his place in the universe, a realization brought about by his love for Lucy. He tells her that she, and not Sir Austin, has made him a man, but his entry into manhood is made meaningless by her death. He has not been purged by the rainstorm, for by choosing the element of fire still raging in his hectic blood he finds himself extinguished at the very threshold of maturity (Maggie Tulliver, too, will perish before her twenty-first birthday). Mountfalcon's bullet, Lady Blandish informs us, injures no "vital part." But the vitality represented by Lucy and by that life spirit recognized in the German forest is consumed. When Lucy dies, she screams, according to Lady Blandish, "that she was 'drowning in the fire,' and her husband would not come to save her" (ch. 49).

Meredith's superimposition of a tragic ending on a novel that has so firmly been moving toward a happy conclusion seems, at first glance, even more arbitrary than George Eliot's immolation of Maggie Tulliver after the girl has expiated her breach of conduct. Maggie's tragedy follows in the path of her father's fall; Richard's occurs after his father has ceased to strew obstacles in the path of his son. Who is to blame for Lucy's death? Why does Meredith calculatingly destroy the anticipations of his readers? To answer these questions we have to look at the "explanations" he seeds throughout the novel, to understand how "Nature," that power which spoke to Richard, is denied both by Sir Austin and his son.

Lucy's death of brain fever, a nervous disorder, can only indirectly be caused by her anguish over Richard's departure and possible death. Taken literally, this death seems improbable. Meredith has stressed throughout that Lucy—like the vital heroines of his later comedies—is a strong and resolute creature. Unlike the morbid Clare, who takes iron to stay healthy, Lucy seems incapable of yielding to a death wish. She bore Richard's first flight with equanimity, strengthened by her impending maternity. There is no reason to suppose that her love for her child should now have abated. In his conclusion, however, Meredith consciously eschews the literal, scientific logic which measures events in terms of causes and effects; instead, he avails himself of a symbolic logic by which Lucy must die simply because Richard's last self-imposed ordeal reveals his failure in achieving manhood.

Lucy's strength, as Richard himself realized before, stems from a kind of moral instinct, the same fervor which drives both Austin Wentworth and Mrs. Berry, her allies, to Raynham Abbey. The force represented by these characters is nonintellectual (Lucy's death of a "cerebral" disorder is therefore all the more ironic). Austin Wentworth, though eloquent, hardly possesses the keen wit of Adrian Harley; Mrs. Berry's inarticulateness provokes Sir Austin the aphorist to smile in silence. Yet both Austin Wentworth and Mrs. Berry possess intuitions denied to the novel's intellectualizers. Lady Blandish sadly concludes about

Mrs. Berry: "I really believe she has twice the sense of any of us—Science and all" (ch. 49).

Like Austin Wentworth, who married unfortunately, and like Mrs. Berry, whose husband deserted her, Lucy suffers unjustly by Richard's absence. But like them, and unlike Sir Austin, she does not demand absolute perfection. When Richard returns to her, she does not reproach him for having been unfaithful, but rather makes it clear to him that if he still loves her and has loved her in the past he can amply repair his faults by accepting his responsibilities as her husband. Richard admits that he, and not Lucy, has been a coward; he acknowledges that she has made him a man. He fails to recognize, however, that his manhood demands that he risk the imputation of cowardice by rejecting his "devilish pledge" to fight Mountfalcon. By falling back on his notions of heroism and honor, he escapes the harder task of reconciling himself to his own faults. Deeming himself "base and spotted to the darling of his love," he derives a "mad pleasure in wreaking vengeance on the villain," Mountfalcon, and thus throws "the burden on Fate" (ch. 49). Like his father, Richard needs an external scapegoat to exorcise one of the two natures that war in him. By escaping, he shows himself to be his father's son, for, like Sir Austin's system, his chivalric notions stem from a fear of confronting man's potential for evil.

Sir Austin's "System" is predicated on the same principles illustrated in his *Pilgrim's Scrip* (the title of which, like *Vanity Fair*, is taken from Bunyan). In charting out the progress of his son's pilgrimage, Sir Austin tries to immunize Richard against the Apple Disease. Aware of the imperfections of the world, he tries to combat imperfection by creating a sinless human being. Though Sir Austin's ostensible purpose is his son's happiness, he is, in effect, as monomaniacal as Heathcliff in his efforts to strike back at the world. His wife's desertion has caused him to magnify sexual lust into the one sin from which Richard must at all cost be protected. He denies his son the sight of girls and surrounds himself with men like Adrian or Benson, that "taciturn

Hater of women," and with a physician who is acceptable only because he has been "jilted by a naughty damsel."

Sir Austin's system is predicated on reason, but his Popean belief that this world is "well-designed" only conceals his irrational fear of the Devil. His inability to account for injustice leads him to gloss over the imperfections that Richard develops before his very eyes. When the boy, gripped by his "birthday devil," becomes an arsonist, Sir Austin does nothing. He retires, hurt and wounded over the failure of the Adam he has produced. Eventually, when Richard confesses, his father is soothed and once again eulogizes the beneficent scheme of nature, his son's innate goodness, and the efficacy of the system. But Richard has not been good. Justice is not restored. Tom Bakewell is acquitted of arson not because of a public admission by Richard but because a witness has been bribed by Adrian. Throughout the trial Sir Austin presses his son's hand. Richard's lawlessness not only has gone unpunished but also is rewarded by the gift of a river yacht.

If Sir Austin's desire to play God is deeply flawed, so are the rationalizations Richard himself uses to explain away the rashness of his infected Feverel blood. Richard clings to his chivalric notions of "honor" just as tenaciously as his father clings to his "Science." Both men are uneasy; their smug self-satisfaction merely disguises deep doubts about the rationalizations they have erected. Unwilling to discard these rationalizations, both fall back on the device of blaming others for their own disappointments and failures.

Sir Austin is shattered upon Richard's elopement. To salvage his pride he aggrandizes his son's defiance of the system into the offense of human nature. Before, he declared the world to be well designed and man to be innately good. Now, he lapses into the opposite extreme: "A Manichaean tendency, from which the sententious eulogist of Nature had been struggling for years (and which was partly at the bottom of the System), now began to cloud and usurp dominion of his mind. As he sat alone in the forlorn dead-hush of his library, he saw the Devil" (ch. 37). Like George Eliot's uneducated Mr. Tulliver who, in his "rampant Manichaeism," blames his own failures on a world ruled by the devil, this philosophical system-maker is guilty of a gross exaggeration. Before, Sir Austin convinced himself that the universe was managed by a benevolent God, whose earthly agent he considered himself to be; now, to nurse his disappointments, he must invent a malevolent, Gnostic deity.

Richard also jumps from one extreme to the other. The "two natures" warring "in his bosom" (ch. 48) make him every bit as divided as the father who harbors "two voices in a brain" (ch. 37). Like Sir Austin, the impulsive youth who magnifies himself into a scourge for the evil of others is incapable of admitting his own shortcomings to himself. Sir Austin first blames Woman and then the Adam who has failed him; he concludes by indicting mankind for failing to come up to his expectations. With monstrous vanity he laments that "it is useless to base any System on a human being" (ch. 37). For his part, Richard successively blames Farmer Blaize, Bella, Clare, his father, and finally, Mountfalcon; he professes to be disappointed in the cowardice of his two squires (Ripton and Tom Bakewell) and of his wife. Yet the young man's self-righteousness masks self-doubts that are far deeper than his father's. By challenging Mountfalcon at the end, Richard merely lashes out against his own trespasses. He simply cannot accept Lucy's willingness to regard him—and, by inference, all humanity—as being compounded of good and evil.

The Richard who poached on the pheasants on Farmer Blaize's grounds was "happily oblivious of the laws and conditions of trespass" (ch. 4). It was his sudden confrontation with guilt that made the farmer's stinging whip, coiled like a "relentless serpent," so hateful to the fourteen-year old who had been taught to consider himself perfect. It is Richard's trespass as an adult, his poaching on Mountfalcon's seductive mistress, whose hairs have stung him like "little snakes," which makes Mountfalcon's interest in Lucy seem so unforgivable to him. In each case, the imagined affront and the planned revenge are disproportionate.

Richard discovered that the farmer who is Lucy's uncle was not at all the fiendish figure his imagination had concocted. Nor, for all his rascality is Lord Mountfalcon a totally depraved figure, a libertine like Thackeray's Lord Steyne. Mountfalcon has not seduced Lucy. Quite to the contrary, he becomes domesticated by her and tamely reads history books to her and to her unborn child. Richard, on the other hand, has been untamed by Bella. While Mountfalcon has read to Lucy about Julian the Apostate, Richard has turned apostate to his father's system and his own codes by playing games with the seductive "Sir Julius." His inability to admit that he is at least as guilty as Mountfalcon compels him to destroy the man whose alter ego he refuses to be. Mountfalcon tells Ripton that he would be satisfied by an apology, but the Richard who could not bear to apologize to Farmer Blaize is as devoid of humility as his father. Unable to extend charity to others, he fails to see that only by mortifying his pride can he regain his self-respect. Instead of starving that pride, he fans it by his inflated desire for revenge. And so the Feverel pride leads him to destroy that better self who is Lucy.

Read in this fashion, Lucy's death, capricious as it is, is integral to Meredith's purpose. Its swiftness and unexpectedness are necessary. For had the novel ended happily with the reconciliation of Sir Austin, Richard and Lucy, it would have validated both the father's and son's underestimation of man's "ordeal" in a world no longer offering the moral guidelines provided by belief in an omnipotent and just God. Richard's tragedy consists in his misjudgment of that world, in his failure to recognize that it need not thwart man's aspirations. Although Meredith rejects the comic conclusion which Emily Brontë imposed on *Wuthering Heights*, his novel still conveys his own need to affirm a belief in a potentially beneficent order. By exposing the deficiencies of Richard and Sir Austin, Meredith can rid himself and his readers from the debilitating sense of despair he attributes to these two characters. In their total intransigence, their diseased pride, Richard and Sir Austin go against that "Spirit of Life" whose positive powers the novelist tries to render in the brief scene in the German forest. In later years Meredith would convert this redemptive counterforce into the kindly "Comic Spirit" which prevails in a work like *The Egoist* (1879). There, "honorable laughter" rather than the mere possibility of a happy outcome would purge characters and readers of the "modern malady" to which the incurable Feverels must succumb.

## 3

When Maggie Tulliver makes her first appearance in chapter two of *The Mill on the Floss*, her mother asks her to go on with her "pretty patchwork, to make a counterpane" for her aunt Glegg. Maggie contemptuously rejects Mrs. Tulliver's invitation to act "like a little lady" and refuses. " 'It's foolish work,' said Maggie with a toss of her mane,—'tearing things to pieces to sew 'em together again. And I don't want to do anything for my aunt Glegg—I don't like her.' " While Mrs. Tulliver is dumbfounded by her daughter's defiance, her husband "laughs audibly" at the little girl's sally.

The event, though seemingly inconsequential, contains all the ingredients for the later Tulliver tragedy. Maggie's asocial nature, her charm and intelligence, Mrs. Tulliver's impotence, and her husband's indulgence of the "little wench" he prefers to his Dodson son, are all incapsulated in this miniscule action. Maggie later defies conventional duties again when, after having lost her father and become alienated from Tom, she tries to escape the puerilities of St. Ogg's with Stephen Guest (to Maggie's surprise, it is the aunt she least likes, Mrs. Glegg, who stands by her after her disgrace). Moreover, although the child does not yet know this at the time, her words are rather prophetic. At this very moment, the father who laughs at her wit has already begun to "tear things apart." By trying to fight the "puzzling world" he finds so threatening, Mr. Tulliver will never be able to sew things "together again." The education he is about to bestow on Tom proves useless; the litigations he is about to enter cause his downfall.

The Tulliver children are unable to reverse the breakup begun by their father. Inheriting the miller's impulsiveness Maggie can only help to rend things apart. Although Tom unlearns his false "education," his efforts to mend the past prove fruitless. At the end of the novel, the river, that ominous embodiment of that "Nature" so often invoked by the narrator, swells. The waters of the flood both span the irreconcilably opposed worlds of St. Ogg's and Dorlcote Mill and unite the pragmatic Tom and the romantic Maggie. Their union is short-lived. The river which tears off the "huge fragments" that slay Tom and Maggie cannot sew things together again. In *The Ordeal of Richard Feverel* the sudden death of Lucy is designed to mock her husband's defiance of a potentially beneficent order. But in the *Mill on the Floss* Tom and Maggie's capricious drowning signifies their creator's secret despair over a temporal order in which unity can only be found through death.

In the novel's conclusion the narrator tells us: "Nature repairs her ravages—but not all. The uptorn trees are not rooted again; the parted hills are left scarred: if there is a new growth, the trees are not the same as the old, and the hills underneath their green vesture bear the marks of past rending. To the eyes that have dwelt on the past there is no thorough repair." Nature thus seems to confirm Maggie's initial statement: it is foolish, because impossible, to tear things to pieces to sew them together again. Still, this is exactly what George Eliot, like the novelists before her, sets out to do. By tearing a family to pieces she wants to direct the reader towards a "new growth," to leave us purged, through pity and fear, first, by Mr. Tulliver's death, and then, all the more by Maggie's immolation.

Like *The Ordeal*, George Eliot's novel is structured to make the reader anticipate the failures of the children in the failures of their parents. The book falls into two distinct movements: in the first Mr. Tulliver vainly tries to shore his present against the impending future; in the second, where that future becomes the present of his children, Tom and Maggie vainly try to recover the idyllic past of Dorlcote Mill amidst the hard reality of St. Ogg's. The novel is divided into seven books. Maggie's story is subordinated to her father's in the first book. By book five, which concludes the second volume and ends with the miller's death, her unsatisfied yearnings for fulfillment are given prominence. The last two books, in the third volume, are taken up entirely with her destiny.

Like Meredith, George Eliot pretends to be as critical of a father's faulty "system" as of his children's mistakes. Mr. Tulliver's distrust of "the world" he deems to be ruled by the devil resembles Sir Austin's own secret Manichaeism; Maggie's passionate excesses as a child are treated with the same irony devoted to the impulsive actions of Richard the rick-burner. In *The Ordeal* Sir Austin's selection of "a pale, languid, inexperienced woman" who is his distinct inferior proves to be as disastrous as Mr. Tulliver's own choice of a woman who "from the cradle upwards had been healthy, fair, plump, and dullwitted" (Bk. I, ch. 2). The calculating baronet's choice is his one concession to sentiment; the hot-headed miller, on the other hand, deliberately picks the least pugnacious of the Dodsons because "she wasn't o'er cute," like her sisters, but "a bit weak, like; for I wasn't agoin' to be told the rights o' things by my own fireside." Mr. Tulliver's experiment in natural selection misfires when his "cute" daughter inherits the genes of the fiery Tullivers and Tom the stolid practicality of the Dodsons. "It's like as if the world was turned topsy-turvy," Mr. Tulliver complains (Bk. I, ch. 3).

The miller contributes to his children's unfitness to cope with a topsy-turvy world by thwarting his son's development and by indulging Maggie's fantasies. George Eliot makes it clear that the classical education Mr. Tulliver imposes on Tom would have been ideal only for Maggie. Just as Meredith demonstrates that Richard, though an emotionalist, is very much his phlegmatic father's son, so does George Eliot stress that, despite her greater intellect, the imaginative Maggie is very much her father's daughter. Both novelists equate imagination with passion. The same imagination that Richard drew upon as a child flares up when he vows revenge for imagined indignities: the adoles-

cent who dreams of himself as the "chief of an Arab tribe," flying on his mare in the moonlight, soon finds his fancy rekindled
by the masquerading Bella. Maggie, too, is a dreamer who takes
refuge in fantasies. The child who wanted to be crowned as
queen of the gypsies, who invented a world in which her cousin
Lucy was queen, "though the queen was herself in Lucy's form"
(Bk. I, ch. 7), will try, unsuccessfully, to escape the prosaic
reality of St. Ogg's by fleeing with Lucy's Prince Charming.

In her treatment of the adult Maggie, however, George Eliot
loses the ironic detachment maintained in the earlier portions of
her book. Meredith indicted both son and father through the
unexpected catastrophe of Lucy's death. George Eliot, however,
becomes increasingly uneasy as she moves closer to the expected
tragedy so carefully built up from the beginning. Whereas her
characterization of Mr. Tulliver's imprudence and downfall, her
sympathy with the plight of an extraordinary child, and her insights into the differences that separate Maggie from Tom are
almost unmatched in Victorian fiction in their veracity and psychological penetration, George Eliot falters when she converts
the tiny malcontent of the first half into a noble victim of epic
proportions to reconcile herself to the girl's destiny.

In Meredith's scheme Richard's sexual entanglement with
Bella can be forgiven, even if Richard is incapable of forgiving
himself. The ideal is in Richard's grasp; Lucy, the "Angel"
whose ineffable beauty Lady Blandish describes in her letter, is
idealized, but she is wholly credible as Richard's better nature.
In George Eliot's scheme, however, Maggie's far more harmless
elopement with Stephen Guest is forgiven only by Philip
Wakem, who believes in Maggie's innocence and attributes her
lapse to "that partial, divided action of our nature which makes
half the tragedy of the human lot" (Bk. VII, ch. 3). Philip himself remains inactive. Whereas Austin Wentworth gives Richard
a chance to embrace his better self, Philip can merely pity Maggie's self-division. Maggie, too, becomes hopelessly paralyzed.
Unlike the impenitent Richard, she has returned to atone only
to find that expiation proves impossible. The fulfillment possible

for Richard is denied in the world of St. Ogg's. Richard refuses to reign at Raynham; the girl with the "queenly" coronet of black hair lacks even the subjects her father possessed. She is disenfranchised. The same Raynham Abbey which once curbed Richard's growth now offers him unbridled happiness; Maggie, however, can only yearn neurotically for her lost childhood at Dorlcote Mill. St. Ogg's refuses to shelter this sufferer "tossed by the waves." The wholesomeness available to Richard is represented by Austin and Lucy; in George Eliot's novel, however, neither the understanding Philip nor the benevolent Dr. Kenn can assist Maggie. In *The Ordeal*, the humorous point of view of Mrs. Berry remains intact even in the face of the final catastrophe; in *The Mill*, the comical tone of Bob Jakin jars with George Eliot's canonization of a martyr awaiting her last ordeal. The normally loquacious Bob finds "his tongue unmanageable in quite a new fashion" when he fathoms Maggie's despair. Awkwardly, he asks her to take his baby into her arms, "if you'd be so good. For we made free to name it after you, and it 'ud be better for your takin' a bit o' notice on it." As soon as Bob's tongue is "loosed from its unwonted bondage," however, he waxes "timid" again; for he has realized that his attempts at therapy have been of little use (Bk. VII, ch. 1).

Richard Feverel chooses to destroy his better self to avoid condemnation; Maggie Tulliver finds herself condemned, regardless of her choice. The moral which the shrewd little girl drew from *The History of the Devil* applies to her later history in St. Ogg's: "Oh, I'll tell you what that means. It's a dreadful picture, isn't it? But I can't help looking at it. That old woman in the water's a witch—they've put her in to find out whether she's a witch or no, and if she swims she's a witch, and if she's drowned—and killed, you know—she's innocent, and not a witch, but only a poor silly old woman. But what good would it do her then, you know, when she was drowned?" (Bk. I, ch. 3). The question is all the more poignant in light of the answer framed by the child herself: "Only, I suppose, she'd go to heaven, and God would make it up to her." As an adult, Maggie is denied even this consolation. Like Meredith, George Eliot no longer could believe in a providentially ordered world; but, unlike Meredith, she also found it impossible to romanticize "Nature." Thus she had to convert Maggie into a martyr, for only by doing so could she "make it up" to this choiceless victim in a godless world.

Both Meredith and George Eliot are guilty of inconsistencies in their efforts to vindicate and explain the ways of "Nature" denied by their characters. Meredith resolves these inconsistencies by relying on paradox: although Sir Austin is satirized for believing that the world is well designed, the novelist manages to suggest that a beneficent order does exist. The lyricism with which Meredith portrays landscape is Wordsworthian. Richard's encounter with Lucy on an island removed by water from the mists of Raynham and from the lucubrations of the Scientific Humanist implies—like the later scene in the rain—the presence "of something far more deeply interfused," "a motion and a spirit" akin to that force intuitively felt by Wordsworth in "Tintern Abbey." George Eliot, too, alternates between satire and lyricism, irony and symbol. Unlike Meredith, however, she finds herself unable to balance these extremes when she depicts Maggie's plight at St. Ogg's. Her Thackerayan satire of the society which spurns Maggie clashes with the last-minute exaltation of an idyllic, Wordsworthian childhood. Whereas Meredith's treatment of the rainstorm suggests the existence of a regenerative force, George Eliot's reliance on the flood as a deus ex machina remains a mechanical device to bring about a harmony that brother and sister never experienced while alive. Meredith's ending is tragic because it suggests that the Paradise lost by Richard was in his grasp; George Eliot's ending is at best pathetic, for it asks us to believe that the muddy waters of the Floss have briefly restored an Eden that never existed.

George Eliot is guilty of sentimentalizing Maggie's childhood by claiming that in death brother and sister are allowed to relive "the days when they had clasped their little hands in love, and roamed the daisied fields together" (Bk. VII, ch. 5). There were few instances when Maggie the child was allowed to hold her brother's hand. The little girl asked by Tom to choose between two halves of a muffin found then, as well as later, that any choice would make her unhappy. By forgetting that her heroine's ordeals began as a child, George Eliot conveniently glossed over the "realism" with which she had presented that childhood. The narrator was able to expose Mr. Tulliver's insufficiencies by showing that the miller's vision of the world as evil was merely the product of his evasions of reality. Yet, even though this narrator wants us to believe that Maggie possesses the same "soul untrained for inevitable struggles" that led to her father's ruin, he cannot bring himself to accept that explanation. Mr. Tulliver blamed "old Harry" for his misfortunes; the intelligent narrator who exposed the simplicity of such an explanation now resorts to a fiction of his own. He lashes out against "the world's wife," the abstraction that Dickens was to call "the voice of Society," and blames this imaginary figure for Maggie's suffering in order to exorcise the novelist's mounting revulsion over the "opressive narrowness" to which Maggie is condemned.

The concluding portions of *The Mill* reveal George Eliot's acute split between realism and romance. Eager to dispel her own Thackerayan insistence on the world as it is, she desperately tried to infuse the world with the higher emotions of sympathy and love. In her desperation the novelist denied herself an opportunity to make the symbolic flood seem a more plausible agent of justice. Had the flood made its appearance at the time of Maggie's and Stephen's escape, had it then prompted the girl's remorse and led her to honor her past ties by returning to the Mill and to Tom, a logical connection between her willfulness and her bondage to the past might at least have been established. But the author wanted Maggie to become a noble sufferer, whose ordeals in St. Ogg's would provide a true "Imitation of Christ." The break in continuity, though allowing the narrator to pour his satire on the "world's wife," unfortunately also has the effect of making Maggie seem all the more a victim of accident and chance.

George Eliot was forced to resort to Maggie's martyrdom to counter a Manichaeism which seemed to deny her trust in goodness and love. Meredith, too, sacrificed a heroine to vindicate such a trust. But Maggie the helpless victim of chance is unlike the blameless Lucy who must die to remind others of their mistakes. Meredith's description of Austin Wentworth applies to George Eliot's heroine: "For a fault in early youth, redeemed by him nobly, according to his light, he was condemned to undergo the world's harsh judgment: not for the fault—for its atonement" (ch. 4). Austin remained behind as an example of his creator's belief that the world can be remade; only by dying can Maggie escape the harsh judgment of St. Ogg's. Though meant to inspire its inhabitants, her death also signifies George Eliot's despair over the reality of that City of Destruction. Unlike Christiana in *The Pilgrim's Progress*, which Maggie read as a child, she is unable to ford the river.

Thus it is that George Eliot in *The Mill on the Floss* found that, her intentions notwithstanding, it was hard work to tear things to pieces to put them together again. Her Thackerayan emphasis on the world-as-is and her thwarted idealism ultimately found a compromise in her greatest novel, *Middlemarch* (discussed in chapter six). But it was Charles Dickens who, in his last complete work, was able to achieve what she could not do in *The Mill on the Floss*. By carrying the form of the romance beyond Meredith and even Emily Brontë, the Dickens of *Our Mutual Friend* methodically tears apart the world as he finds it and then proceeds to put it together again before the reader's startled eyes. George Eliot the realist was forced to sacrifice Maggie the dreamer, but Dickens the myth-maker destroys the logic of the actual world by defiantly superimposing on it the logic of the fairy tale. Out of the fragments of a sterile material existence he sews together a fantastic ideal order, and, through the force of his art, compels us to accept his patchwork in place of the reality he has displaced.

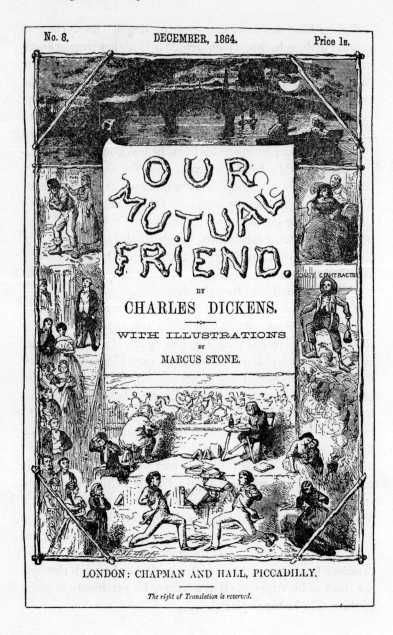

No. 8.      DECEMBER, 1864.      Price 1s.

OUR MUTUAL FRIEND.

BY

CHARLES DICKENS.

WITH ILLUSTRATIONS

BY

MARCUS STONE.

LONDON: CHAPMAN AND HALL, PICCADILLY.

*The right of Translation is reserved.*

# V  *Our Mutual Friend*: Fantasy as Affirmation

Published in nineteen parts from May 1864 to November 1865, *Our Mutual Friend* marks the culmination of Charles Dickens' thirty-year reign as the most prominent of the major Victorian novelists. Thackeray, Dickens' onetime rival, had died in 1863; Dickens himself was to die in 1870 without ever completing his *Edwin Drood*. *Our Mutual Friend* can thus be regarded as his final work. The vitality of his last complete novel was not appreciated by his contemporaries. In their failure to recognize that he had intentionally portrayed the debility of an age, they dismissed the work as that of a debilitated novelist. On the contrary, the novel is the product of a practiced and self-assured craftsman in total command of all the rhetorical skills developed throughout his career: although Dickens was personally exhausted, ill, and obsessed with death, his inventiveness and powers of imagination were never higher. *Our Mutual Friend* is idiosyncratic, difficult, and different. In it the novelist gives his earlier insights new emphasis and new expression; he reformulates the questions asked in his previous fiction: what is society? what is endurable? what is real? And he conducts this inquiry by boldly attacking reality itself.

The narrative method of *Our Mutual Friend* relies on a double process of decomposition and cohesion, of disjunction and con-solidation. Dickens first breaks up a crumbling order in which all experiences seem incoherent and all identities become uncer-tain. Going far beyond Thackeray's efforts to come to terms with the instability of Vanity Fair, Dickens mercilessly dissects a society that has become unaware of its own state of decom-position. Mr. Podsnap is Dickens' archenemy. He represents a mentality that Dickens tries to overcome with all the forces at his command. Podsnap's way of beholding reality is completely adverse to Dickens' own. The smug insurance banker believes in a cosmic order reflecting the mechanical regularity of his own existence; he extols a Providence which oils the machineries of politics, industry, and the British Constitution. Mr. Podsnap asks his French visitor whether the gentleman has seen "evidences" on the streets of London of the constitution so providentially bestowed on the English nation. The foreigner does not understand. Mr. Podsnap graciously rephrases the question:

> "I Was Inquiring," said Mr. Podsnap, resuming the thread of his discourse, "Whether You Have Observed in our Streets, as We should say, Upon our Pavvy, as You would say, any Tokens—"
> The foreign gentleman with patient courtesy entreated pardon; "But what was tokenz?"
> "Marks," said Mr. Podsnap; "Signs, you know, Appearances —Traces."
> "Ah! Of a Orse?" inquired the foreign gentleman.[1]

This scene contains, in miniature, both the theme of *Our Mutual Friend* and the difference that separates the novel from the more "realistic" productions of Thackeray and George Eliot. The order that Podsnap believes in is based on false "appearances." The reality that oppresses Dobbin the idealist and destroys the aspirations of Maggie Tulliver becomes in Dickens' handling a mere compound of dust and slime. To rend apart this dispiriting reality, Dickens at first pretends to give in to despair. In the opening installments of his novel, he confronts the reader with a gigantic jigsaw puzzle in which all individual fragments seem hopelessly mutilated and incomplete. Our initial reading experience thus mirrors the disorientation of the characters themselves. Connections seem impossible. Only by methodically destroying Podsnap's spurious "Providence" can Dickens replace it with a higher order of his own. The "reality" of this new order can be seen in signs, tokens, and appearances totally

1. *Our Mutual Friend*, ed. J. Hillis Miller (New York, 1964), ch. 11. Future references to this edition are given in the text.

foreign to Podsnap's mode of perception. By shivering Podsnappery into splinters and substituting for it the symbolic evidences of myth and fairy tale, Dickens manages to remove the reader into an entirely different realm of experience—a realm shaped by the wishfulness of laughter.

Dickens' disjunctive tactics are inherent in the opening chapters of the book. The ghastly scene in which Gaffer Hexam fishes out the faceless cadaver is directly followed by the ludicrous proceedings at the Veneerings' dinner party. Dickens thus invites the reader to yoke these two episodes. But what sort of links are we expected to make? Are the two scenes being presented in succession only for purposes of contrast? Or is there a plot line connecting them to each other? Only at the end of the second chapter do we discover that the Man from Somewhere so jocularly discussed at the dinner table can now be presumed to be the corpse on which the "wultur"-like Gaffer has already feasted. And even this surmise will eventually prove to be false.

Just as the reader of *Wuthering Heights* must share Lockwood's initial disorientation before he learns how to adapt himself to the strange "reality" that operates in Emily Brontë's fictional world, so does the reader of *Our Mutual Friend* quickly lose track of all those explicit signs or "tokenz" which would normally afford him the comfort of an ordered reading experience. In the opening pages of his novel Dickens continually deludes his reader and denies him the security he seeks. Our first instinct is to assume, with Gaffer Hexam, that the identity of the corpse is unimportant. To Gaffer the drowned man is already in "t'other world"; the money taken from the body is the only identification needed in Podsnap's material world. Hexam, sure of his own identity, remains unconfused, undisturbed by the fact that the ripples of water moving over the body's face seem "dreadfully like faint changes of expression on a sightless face." In our own eagerness to be oriented, we protect ourselves and instinctively adopt Hexam's grim self-assurance. But our assurance is short-lived. It is severely jolted as we move into the next chapter, where the reigning confusion and uncertainty again bring out our initial discomfort.

Whereas the reader was tempted into adopting Hexam's self-confidence, he is now led to identify himself with the confusion that besets that pathetic guest, little Twemlow. Twemlow's position at the Veneerings' party resembles the reader's own participation in events that seem maddening and incomprehensible. Poor Twemlow is in constant doubt about himself and his relation to the world of the Veneerings; the reader is in doubt about the relations he is expected to find in the world of the novel. Twemlow yearns for a friend; he wonders whether he is indeed a friend of the Veneerings—their first friend, their only friend, their oldest and dearest friend. The reader likewise yearns for a friendly narrator to order his experience; he feels threatened by a novelist who may be his and the characters' mutual enemy.

When Podsnap enters the room he only contributes to the reigning confusion by mistaking Twemlow for his host. Unlike Twemlow and like Gaffer Hexam, Podsnap is self-assured. He carelessly dismisses his mistake, since to him people are interchangeable. The party confirms Podsnap's belief. The guests prove to be interchangeable, indeed. The four men who are seated as "Buffers" between the more important guests speak in unison; Boots and Brewer, two of the guests, begin to coalesce into a "fusion" in the "looking-glass" that reflects this Mad Hatter's party (*Alice in Wonderland*, incidentally, appeared around the same time, in 1865). Only when one of the Buffers ceases to speak in unison and asserts "his individuality" is the monotony broken. Everyone is surprised. Individuality, a clearly defined identity of one's own, is truly startling in this chaotic world of faceless men.

Dickens puts the reader in the same position as Twemlow. He forces us to despair of finding order amidst a disjointed world which seems nothing more than an unstable heap of fractions as arbitrarily put together as the Dustman's garbage mounds. The novel's major plot lines, even after they finally

*The Bird of Prey*

become discernible, are constantly fractured, interrupted by seemingly unrelated chapters on the Veneerings, Podsnaps, and Lammles. New characters—Fledgby, Riah, Jenny Wren—appear just when we have begun to assemble the novel's major threads. These "buffers," by seemingly separating us from the fates of the important characters we are interested in, only contribute to the reader's general sense of disorientation. Gradually, however, this disjunction reveals Dickens' design. He takes things apart only to assemble them again. Some of the mixtures he has isolated are recombined into a new and stronger compound. As an alternative to Podsnap's dehumanized order begins to emerge, the reader eagerly clings to the cohesions that begin to take shape before his eyes. He may feel threatened again when, for a while, Boffin's unexpected malignity seems to jeopardize this countermovement of reintegration. At the end of the novel, however, the reader breathes easily again. Out of dust has come gold. Through Dickens' sleight-of-hand the oppressively mechanical order of Podsnappery and of the Veneerings has been blown away, displaced by an organic aggregation of mutual friends which even harbors the friendless Twemlow. The novelist himself, who seemed so unfriendly, has become all readers' Mutual Friend.

The following sections are designed to recreate some of the methods by which Dickens first dismembers and then reconstructs the world of *Our Mutual Friend*. The reader's initial alienation not only resembles Twemlow's but also is akin to that of Mr. Venus, the taxidermist, who moans that "the world that appeared so flowery" seems hopelessly sundered: "Cats. Articulated English baby. Dogs. Ducks. Glass eyes, warious. Mummied bird. Dried cuticle, warious. Oh, dear me! That's the general panoramic view" (ch. 7). But Dickens forces us into a more meaningful job of "articulation" and, by so doing, resists his anxieties and our own. Like Jenny Wren, the novel's other artificer, we learn to convert refuse and waste into new forms. Jenny skillfully fits together "certain pieces of cardboard and thin wood previously cut into various shapes" (ch. 18).

The reader, likewise, eventually learns to recombine the jagged pieces that Dickens has so meticulously cut asunder.

## I

In the course of *Our Mutual Friend* Dickens does his best to persuade the reader that the real is unreal and that the unreal is "real." Dickens had attempted to work out this paradox before, but never quite as consciously or as forcefully. He assaults the material world we ordinarily believe in and makes it seem so incongruous and implausible that we become convinced of its unreality. By dissolving before our eyes both the social organization and the physical world to which his characters belong, the novelist, like a magician, wants to condition us to accept the illusory fairy tale he offers as a substitute for our belief in the reality principle. And he succeeds. As we eventually shall see, we give our assent to fantasy only because Dickens the illusionist is so thoroughly capable of destroying our hold on ordinary reality.

In *The Mill on the Floss* the narrator who had held on to the reality of his armchair was at a loss to explain the ways of the temporal "Nature" to which Maggie must succumb. By challenging the logic of the material world to which both George Eliot and Thackeray so reluctantly surrendered, Dickens compels us to suspend our disbelief. He achieves this by pretending to rob his world of all the elementary devices by which, in actual life, men find the guarantees of stability and order. Dickens thus caters to the reader's insecurity. He threatens us with a universe emptied of the normal guidelines through which men can establish selfhood and identity. The security of names, relations, distinctions—all those means by which we individuate—seems impossible in the bizarre world of the Veneerings. By abolishing this security, however, Dickens merely clears the ground for the wish fulfillments he will eventually offer to placate the reader's need for order.

I have already suggested that poor Twemlow's doubts about himself and his relations to everybody else introduce a note repeated throughout the novel. In chapter ten we are parenthetically informed that the late Sir Thomas Tippins was "knighted in mistake for somebody else by His Majesty King George the Third, who, while performing the ceremony was graciously pleased to observe, 'What, what, what? Who, who, who? Why, why, why?' " The demented king's queries are echoed by reader and characters alike, beset by the maddening absurdities of the world Dickens has created. The reader asks, "What-who-why?"; the characters themselves seem more obsessed by, "Who-who-who?" Placed in a physical world of flux and in a social order of interchangeable nonpeople, they cannot even cling to the elementary security of their own being. Twemlow pathetically assures himself, "Then, there can be no more doubt . . . I AM." But the very repetition of this refrain expresses his fear of a world in which he is not.

Dickens' urban world wrecks identity far more thoroughly than do the Vanity Fairs and Cities of Destruction we have encountered so far. London and the river which has erased the features of the cadaver become emblematic of a world hostile to those few eccentrics—Boffin, Betty Higden, Lizzy Hexam—who refuse to compromise the integrity of self. By spilling all over the city, the older children of the Wilfers have surrendered their individuality and become faceless. When they revisit the parental household, their distracted father finds it difficult to tell them apart. "R. Wilfer generally seemed to say to himself . . . 'Oh! here's another of 'em!' before adding aloud, 'how de do John,' or Susan, as the case might be" (ch. 4). The city blunts the peculiarities by which men can be differentiated. Wilfer himself works for the house of Chicksey, Veneering, and Stobbles. But Chicksey and Stobbles no longer exist. They have "become absorbed" by the partner who acted as a buffer between their names. Veneering, the great absorber of spurious friends and ancestors, even manages to bring about a spurious marriage between Alfred and Sophronia Lammle. The couple who hoped to absorb each other's fortunes discover, after marriage has fused their surnames, their mutual identity as paupers.

To resist this anonymity men must rely on their powers of imagination. Throughout *Our Mutual Friend* runs the recurrent motif of characters who cling to a fiction. Unlike "realists" like Thackeray or George Eliot who puncture all the fictions by which men and women try to deny the reality principle, Dickens distinguishes between fiction as sham and fiction as a necessary, life-sustaining form of belief. He shows no pity toward the crass impostures of a Vanity Fair: the fraudulent Veneering crest, the Lammles' "mutual understanding" to act out the role of a devoted couple, Fledgby's imposition of the role of cruel moneylender on Riah the kindly Jew. But he is kinder to those pathetic lies which arise from a character's psychological need to escape a too repressive reality. Dickens sympathizes with Jenny Wren's myth about her future lover, the "Him" who will deliver her from misery and lovelessness. Even wrinkled Lady Tippins' "grisly fiction concerning her lovers" seems a permissible escape. Sir Thomas' widow records the names of these imaginary beings in a notebook called Cupidon and pretends that Eugene and Mortimer—who openly despise her—are entranced by her charms. To maintain their own sanity, the two young men cling to the pretense of a law practice; the Harmon case provides Mortimer with his first clients. Mortimer's clerk cannot live without this "fiction of an occupation." Thus, when Boffin comes to call, young Blight (appropriately named) pulls out an Appointment Book and a Callers Book and pretends to check an interminable list of names: "Mr. Aggs, Mr. Baggs, Mr. Caggs, Mr. Daggs, Mr. Faggs, Mr. Gaggs, Mr. Boffin. Yes, sir, quite right. You are a little before your time, sir" (ch. 8).

Silas Wegg, the peddler of fictions who adapts his ballads to suit any occasion, without concern for meaning or context and without any regard for the needs of his clients, is as bereft of imagination as Mr. Podsnap. Like Podsnap, Silas is shackled by the material world. This "literary man" who cannot even differentiate between the Roman and Rooshan Empires denies others their need for illusion. Still, he too is forced to resort to his feeble powers of fantasy to escape his surroundings. By concocting the fiction of "Our House" Wegg tries to possess the mansion he has seen only from the outside. Painstakingly, he strives to re-construct its interiors from "external appearances" and gives its inhabitants "names of his own invention" (ch. 5). When Boffin purchases the house and makes it his bower, Silas no longer nurses daydreams but schemes to possess it as a physical fact. By re-placing essence with matter, he forfeits whatever claim to our sympathies he might have.

Wegg's naming of the inhabitants of the house, like Lady Tippins' naming of imaginary lovers and young Blight's naming of imaginary clients, is related to another motif—that of the un-reliability or unreality of names. A name ordinarily acts as the token of one's identity, yet the characters in *Our Mutual Friend*, beset by uncertainty, either change their names or have them changed for them. Jenny Wren belongs to the first category: "Her real name was Miss Fanny Cleaver, but she had long ago chosen to bestow upon herself the appellation of Jenny Wren" (ch. 19). Reginald Wilfer, on the other hand, too shy to own to an aristocratic Christian name, finds that by using the initial "R." he has only exposed himself to the endless improvisations of others. Some, like Rusty, Retiring, Ruddy, Round, are more or less appropriate; others, like Raging, Rattling, Roaring, Raf-fish, derive "their point from want of application" (ch. 4). Nick-names help to impress some variety on an otherwise drab existence. By referring to his father only as "M.R.F." ("my respected father"), Eugene Wrayburn tries to laugh off that side of his own personality which is tied to the worn conven-tions of family and class, the inner self which is his superego.

If names are variable, they also prove detachable, for they have lost their oneness with the persons they are meant to designate. Georgiana Podsnap protests that "it is awful enough to *be* Miss Podsnap, without being called so." Veneering un-wittingly displays the completest separation between name and object when he asks Twemlow (whose own name he has already appropriated in sponsoring the wedding between the Lammles) for the support of Twemlow's aristocratic relative, Lord Snigsworth: "I don't go so far as to ask for his Lordship; I only ask for his name. Do you think he would give me his name?" (ch. 20).

Only Boffin is secure enough in his identity to challenge Wegg to disapprove of the "name of Boffin" and then of Nicodemus and the alternative nicknames of Nick and Noddy. But he imprudently decides to transfer John Harmon's identity to the orphan he intends to adopt. On seeing the names of the Harmon children scribbled on the wall, Boffin tells his wife: "We must take care of the names, old lady. . . . We must take care of the names" (ch. 15).[2] In their innocence the couple is delighted to find that Johnny the orphan only lacks the Harmon surname to be able to assume his role as their heir. Soon, they discover that the child cannot supplant the man they falsely presume to be dead. When Johnny dies, the Boffins realize the futility of their benevolent gesture. They allow Sloppy to retain his crude name (given to him because he was found on "a sloppy night") and be happy. Only after John Harmon, the son of the old jailer of Harmony Jail, openly reassumes his father's name, can order replace the disharmony reigning in the book.

This disharmony is based, above all, on fragmentation. Characters speak incompletely, without connectives or prepositions. Jenny's father whines, "best of children, object dearest affection, broken-hearted invalid," and Lightwood mumbles his appreciation of Boffin, "vigorous Saxon spirit—Mr. Boffin's ancestors—bowmen—Agincourt and Crecy." Lady Tippins catalogs wedding guests according to the cost of their cloth as if they were items on a laundry bill; the callers who visit the Golden Dustman leave cards which read like a "miscellaneous lot at an auction." Wegg's ballads are ready-made, prefabricated without rhyme or reason. Jagged pieces are strewn together as capriciously as the garbage on the dust mounds. Fractions

2. The scene bears comparison with the one in *Vanity Fair* where Georgy sees his father's initials on the windowpane at the Osborne house. Thackeray stresses the potential perpetuation of vanity; Dickens, the benevolence of those who wish to repair the errors of the past.

abound. Wedding guests "are overheard to whisper Thir-ty Thou-sand Pou-nds" (ch. 10). Wegg's placard displays a garbled message:

> Errands gone
> On with fi
> Delity By
> Ladies and Gentlemen       (ch. 5)

And the novelist himself mercilessly chops up the continuity of narrative, description, chapter titles, words.

One of the most startling devices by which Dickens manages to suggest the mutilation of all identities and relations is his sur-realistic fragmentation of the very anatomy of his characters. Throughout the novel he dissects human beings and reduces them into isolated bodily components. The novel begins with Gaffer Hexam pulling out "the upper half" of a man. The scene almost works in purely allegorical terms: Gaffer is concerned with the material half of man; Lizzie with "t'other world" her father denies. The half-body thus introduces the novel's entire contrast between two alternate realities—between the erosion of waste and the reconstitution of the true gold that cannot corrupt. It ushers in the persistent use of doubles—Radfoot and John Harmon, Eugene and Bradley Headstone, Headstone and Riderhood—as well as the dual aspects of characters actually or seemingly self-divided: Bella the egotist and Bella the beautiful, Riah the Bad Wolf and Riah the Godmother, Boffin the Bear and Boffin the Benefactor.

More specifically, however, the half-body fished out of the river's slime introduces Dickens' anatomy of a society threatened to become soulless because it is composed of hopelessly mangled people. Mr. Venus at one point admires one of the bodies in his shop: "A Beauty—one leg Belgian, one leg English." The taxidermist who is a victim of love can at best patch together disparate limbs in his efforts to "articulate a whole human being." By portraying a Daliesque landscape of separate hands, arms, eyes, noses, legs, Dickens suggests that the larger framework of society—the body politic—must likewise remain a mere patchwork until the animating spirit of love can once again knit its components into a single and homogeneous identity. Dickens therefore breaks up this old body before "articulating" the new body formed by his band of mutual friends. And, to stress each character's incompleteness, he repeatedly designates human beings by a single member of their mechanical selves.

Even in death, Gaffer Hexam's rigid "clenched right hand" holds the silver that killed him (ch. 14). The caretaker at the church where the marriage service for the Lammles is held, sticks out "a left hand" which appears to be "in a state of rheumatism, but is in fact voluntarily doubled up as a money-box" (ch. 10). Moving from hands to arms, we find Mr. Podsnap, who has "acquired a peculiar flourish of his right arm in often clearing the world of its most difficult problems" (ch. 11). Miss Peecher's star pupil, whose piecemeal sentences are the product of Headstone's utilitarian education, has developed the classroom habit of mechanically stretching out an arm, "as if to hail a cab or omnibus"; she must hook her right arm behind her before she can even speak. Miss Peecher herself, who waters her flowers amidst the dust, is woefully incomplete. Thinking about her unreciprocated love for Headstone (whose own passion for Lizzie does not fit into the rigid, unemotional pattern he has created for himself), Miss Peecher looks at a "brown-paper pattern" of a dress she is making. With a sigh, she transfixes "that part of her dress where her heart would have been if she had had the dress on with a sharp, sharp needle" (ch. 18).

What is wanting in all these fragmented bits of humanity is a heart such as that possessed by the elect few who will later form the nucleus for a new body. Lady Tippins, who stares at the world through a large golden eyeglass that props up one of her drooping eyelids, is so padded and stuffed that "you might scalp her, and scrape her, yet not penetrate the genuine article." The genuine article is also missing in Rogue Riderhood, who goes through puppetlike motions on drinking wine, tilting it from left cheek to right cheek and jerking it into his stomach, as if asking each of these bodily parts, "What do you think of it?" (ch. 12). The heart is missing in Fledgby, whose nose is almost twisted off by Lammle; it is missing in Lammle himself whose own nose displays "ominous finger marks." It is missing, most of all, in Silas Wegg, the false servant who hoped to put his master's nose to the grindstone.

Dickens describes Silas Wegg by claiming that "he was so wooden a man that he seemed to have taken his wooden leg naturally, and rather suggested to the fanciful observer that he might be expected—if his development received no untimely check—to be completely set up with a pair of wooden legs in about six months" (ch. 5). Like Emily Brontë's Lockwood, the wooden rationalist who indulged in a castle-building as sterile as Wegg's, this "knotty man" epitomizes the inertness of a dehumanized world. Wegg's amputated leg is kept in Mr. Venus' shop; yet the taxidermist cannot work it into one of those "miscellaneous" skeletons he is so proud of. "You can't be got to fit," he tells Wegg. The statement recalls Jenny's later complaint about the dolls she stuffs with wooden shavings. She, too, finds it "very difficult to fit" them; their figures are too "uncertain." We have yet to see how Dickens manages to dispel uncertainty by fitting his band of mutual friends into a more hospitable world; but it is noteworthy that when he has done so he will signal this feat by declaring Wegg—and all those puppets like him—to be unfit to live in the substitute reality he has created. At the end of the novel, when John Harmon threatens to twist off Silas' head, the reader, amply conditioned by now by the prevailing aura of unreality, almost expects a cloud of sawdust to burst out of this "close-grained" nutcracker-man. Wegg wanted to furnish the insides of "Our House," but he has become a discarded piece of furniture.[3] He is thrown on the refuse

3. Humans have been treated as pieces of furniture earlier in the novel; Veneering rolls Twemlow in and out on "castors"; when Rokesmith offers his services as a "secretary," Boffin tells him that he already owns a desk.

van and hauled away. With him, Dickens can throw out the remnants of a defective order. The world can seem "flowery" again.

## 2

We have so far looked at some of the devices by which Dickens manages to unsettle our credulity. The uncertainty of names, the need for fictions, the anatomical fragmentation of dehumanized beings, all undermine our sense of what is stable and impress on us a deranged and scattered existence in which dislocation seems the only norm. These devices, however, merely support Dickens' reliance on the most basic fictional means of depicting disorder: the broken relationships among the characters themselves. The "buffers" separating the central figures in *Our Mutual Friend* are so strong that they prevent the characters from interacting or even communicating with each other. These barriers affect all basic human relationships: fathers are at odds with their children; husbands with their wives; masters with their servants. And, even more strongly than in the novels we have so far considered, potential lovers face obstacles which conspire against their fulfillment.

To reinstitute order into his world, Dickens must break down some of the seemingly insurmountable obstacles he has created. He must rely on plot, as well as on symbol, to restore to his chief "mutual friends"—John Harmon, Bella Wilfer, Eugene Wrayburn—the identities they seem unable to adopt. Eventually, he can provide them with the ordinary relationships and functions denied to them at the outset of the novel. Only by reapportioning their roles and by assigning them the parts of sons, masters, husbands, lovers, can he settle and solidify the threatened identities of characters who seemed destined to a life as incomplete as that which maims Richard Feverel, kills Maggie Tulliver, and leads Heathcliff to escape into a mythical world.

In the earlier parts of the novel the various plot lines only appear to confirm the dominant impression of incompleteness. Just as in *Richard Feverel, The Mill on the Floss*, or *Wuthering*

*Heights* disorder is introduced through the figure of a father, so in this novel the shadow of old Harmon, dead before the action begins, appears to determine irrevocably the fate of others. Old Harmon is guilty not only of having stunted his son and killed his daughter; but also of settling on Bella as a future mate for his son out of sheer perversity: seeing a nasty girl who stamps and screams, the old man decides, "that's a very nice girl; a promising girl." His irrational decision is of a piece with the demented world in which he has ruled. Boffin speaks of his master as the "diseased governor." He means "deceased," of course, but his error is revealing. Old Harmon is guilty of a disease which son and servant seem unable to cure. The reader has no way of anticipating that, in Dickens' handling, such disease will become essential to health and that the girl who seemed so selfish and mercenary will indeed become "promising" and "nice."

The specter of parental guilt informs the novel's second plot line as well. Lizzie Hexam also wants to amend a father's mistakes. Like John Harmon, she finds her identity to be predetermined; yet to undo Gaffer Hexam's faults she chooses to remain loyal to his name and station and rejects her brother Charley's demands that she better herself by embracing a new future. Eugene Wrayburn, on the other hand, who ought to embrace a different future, is rendered impotent by the voice of "M.R.F." The other parent-children relations are equally perverted: Pleasant Riderhood and Georgiana Podsnap are shackled by their fathers; Jenny Wren castigates her whimpering father in an inversion of roles. Only the Boffins, who have maintained a childlike innocence of their own, decidedly act as "the children's friend" (unlike the Lammles, whose friendliness toward Georgiana Podsnap is feigned). When Boffin tells Mortimer Lightwood the moving story in which his wife vainly tried to shelter John Harmon from the exile commanded by old Harmon, the lawyer counters with an unfeeling remark: "My dear Mr. Boffin, everything wears to rags" (ch. 8).

At this point of the book, Mortimer's cynicism seems justified: the only solid relationship between two people of the opposite sex, Mr. and Mrs. Boffin, has produced no offspring. On witnessing old Harmon's destruction of his daughter, the Boffins decided to remain childless. Though sentimental and good, the old couple also seem hopelessly unfit for the world which has made Lightwood and Eugene Wrayburn so sarcastic and disillusioned. Their relationship is an anomaly in a world of false friendships and of marriages as severely flawed as those of the Lammles, the Wilfers, or Fledgby's parents. Though the Boffins have been able to maintain their own integrity by firmly standing against "the old man," their master, they have also acted as honest stewards, faithfully serving his interests. Elsewhere, however, even this relationship is corrupted: Riah compromises his integrity by secretly bearing the vituperations of his true master Fledgby; Boffin's interests are threatened by the machinations of his presumed servant, Silas Wegg.

On the surface, these corrupted relationships seem to add up to a panorama of perversity, a Thackerayan Vanity Fair in which the Boffins cut a figure that is even more incongruous and out of place than that of "honest" Dobbin, the Christian man. Good men, it would appear, simply cannot survive in their own identity. The benevolent Riah, though a mere servant, is forced to play out the role of cruel master and to pretend that he, the Jew, and not the Christian Fledgby, is "Pubsey & Co." Riah's dilemma is no different from that of John Harmon. Riah's ancestors have permitted the pressures of Christian society to force on them a role essentially opposed to their true being. As Riah eventually comes to understand, his acquiescence to such a role is equivalent to perpetuating the dishonor and shame of the past. The past weighs on all characters. To be true to it, the novel's two Elizabeths—Lizzie Hexam and Betty Hidgen—must escape. To avoid its stigma, John Harmon must annul his identity by wearing the mask of Boffin's servant. Though dead, the old jailer of Harmony Jail still hovers over a present that seems blocked and frozen. The world of matter over which he presided may wear into rags; yet it also seems to imprison those who want to believe in a spiritual riches.

Dickens forces the reader to side with those few characters who crave for some way to counter the disheartening world which confronts them. In straining for order the reader identifies particularly with the Man From Somewhere, John Harmon. We soon penetrate the identity of Boffin's mysterious secretary. As we begin to sense his motives and recognize that this archetypal figure yearns, as we do, for order and meaning, we willingly embrace his cause. Rokesmith-Harmon arranges Boffin's papers into "orderly heaps," and his ludicrous master is delighted by this "apple-pie order." But the reader is soon thwarted by Harmon's own disappointments. Though well-intentioned, this active man, too, is impotent, incapacitated by his mask.

Bella's egotism only seems to confirm the vision that John Harmon has come to dispel. His identity hinges on her love and on the money that Boffin has inherited. He wants the love, but despairs of getting it; he could get the money, but does not want its taint. Eventually, of course, he will get both Bella and his father's fortune. At the novel's midpoint, however, Harmon concludes abjectly that he has failed in his role of moral conscience. Thinking Bella's regeneration impossible, he decides to remain another man by disguising his true being for the remainder of his life. His own resurrection has been in vain. The death of Radfoot, he concludes, has killed him as well—on revisiting the churchyard by the river, he alludes to "the scene of my death." He thinks of himself hopelessly crippled by the reality of the world he wanted to change: "I no more hold a place among the living than these dead do" (ch. 30).

John Harmon's despondency marks the low point in the reader's own expectations. There seems to be no alternative to this grim reality of living dead. Lizzie and Betty Higden must escape; Eugene Wrayburn is condemned to a perpetual mask of indifference; Riah and Jenny can live only in their make-believe world above the roofs of the city; Twemlow shuffles back and

forth. And, just as our hopes are slightly raised by Bella's transformation, Boffin himself—the grotesque but lovable man whose
Bower acted as a refuge from the inconstancy of his surroundings—suddenly seems to become infected by Old Harmon's
cancerous disease. This instability is, of course, feigned. Dickens
has merely moved us into a precarious position in order to
command our assent to the regeneration he now begins to under-
take. Death leads to resurrection. John Harmon's despair proves
to be unjustified. The river fragments, divides, and kills; but it
can also deposit, add, and renovate. The ebbing plot lines of
the novel now flow again. A countermovement of accretion and
integration has begun. The unreal Bower the pair has erected
as a haven begins to expand and others can take refuge in similar
shelters. Symbol and plot weave a fairy tale to which we must
extend our belief. There is no other choice.

### 3

The fairy tale by which Dickens placates the reader's wishes
is presented through four separate plot lines: the story of Lizzie
Hexam's regeneration of Eugene, of Betty Higden's triumph
through death, of John Harmon's reformation of Bella, and of
Boffin's victory over Wegg. These four stories are enriched by
the subsidiary plot lines which involve the fates of Charley
Hexam and Bradley Headstone, Rogue Riderhood, Jenny and
Riah and Fledgby, and Mr. Venus and Pleasant Riderhood.
What is more, the four main plots can actually be resolved into
two: Betty Higden's story is integral to Lizzie's; the education
of Bella, though undertaken by John Harmon, is really brought
about by Boffin's adoption of the mask of a miser.

Seen in this fashion, *Our Mutual Friend* can be broken into
two narratives—the one centered around Lizzie Hexam and the
other only ostensibly centered around John Harmon. Both of
these narratives bring about the desired restitution of order,
but they are treated quite differently. The triumph of John
Harmon and Boffin is primarily effected through plot—an unexpected turn of events. The triumph of Lizzie Hexam, on the

other hand, is achieved largely through a consistently symbolic presentation. Dickens carefully works out the parallels between Lizzie and John Harmon: both are conscious of suffering, both have seen this suffering inflicted by a father, both try to make amends for past ills. Lizzie makes a new man out of Eugene; John Harmon and Boffin alter Bella's personality.

Yet Lizzie is less of a character than John Harmon. She is associated with the novel's main symbols: with the river that gives death and life and with the fire of the hearth. Lizzie witnesses both Betty Higden's dying belief in a new life and Jenny's curious reversal of life and death. She is present at two of the book's most crucial scenes: she remains passive when her father fishes out the body presumed to be John Harmon, but becomes active when she fishes out the reborn Eugene Wrayburn. Despite this one action, she is essentially static. The readers are invited to share John Harmon's long soliloquy; we are merely asked to behold this character who sees so much, but says so little. Lizzie is usually spoken to; Eugene admits that, "I never thought before that there was a woman in the world who could affect me so much by saying so little." John Harmon's doubts and uncertainties ("There was no such thing as I") are akin to the readers'. Lizzie, on the other hand, is remote from our immediate experience. We must accept her on faith, for she is herself is figure of faith. Like Meredith's Lucy, she exists primarily as a symbolic presence. It is through her that we are introduced to the alternate reality that her brother Charley cannot see.

The uneducated Lizzie possesses an intuitive understanding which her brother, corrupted by the mechanical system of Bradley Headstone, cannot fathom. She possesses imagination—which for Dickens is always equivalent to the possession of a heart. Lizzie shudders on seeing the changing expressions of the corpse in the river, even though her father is unmoved by such "fancies." Similarly, she reads into the fire at their home a meaning which Charley's understanding is no longer able to entertain. When her brother maintains that they should "turn our faces full in our new direction and keep straight on," she asks, "And never look back? Not even to try to make some amends?" (ch. 18). Charley dismisses her simple question as irrelevant:

> "You are such a dreamer," said the boy, with his former petulance. "It was all very well when we sat before the fire—when we looked into the hollow down by the flare—but we are looking into the real world, now."
> "Ah, we were looking into the real world then, Charley!"

The contrast between the perceptions of a dreaming sister and a pragmatic brother distinctly recalls the similar contrast between Maggie and Tom Tulliver. George Eliot could not bring herself to allow Maggie her dreamworld. To reunite brother and sister she was forced to submerge both into the swirling waters of the Floss and declare that their death marked a return to childhood oneness. Dickens, however, condemns Charley for rejecting the vision his older sister has been able to preserve. Ironically enough, in his haste to grow, Charley turns his back on the childhood faculties that allow Lizzie to see beyond him. There is no compromise. Only "the real world" recognized by this female seer is true. Like the two fellow-escapists and fellow-sufferers she is associated with—Betty Higden and Jenny Wren —Lizzie possesses the candor and faith of a child. Like them, she believes in the invisible and the intangible.

Charley's tutor, Bradley Headstone, wants to "educate" the girl who sees beyond him. But even Eugene Wrayburn, who resents the schoolmaster's interference and recognizes Lizzie's qualities, cannot free himself from the world in which Charley and Headstone are mired. Eugene's predicament dramatizes the conflict that lies at the core of Dickens' novel. He is suspended between two worlds, one dead and the other waiting to be born. Eugene cannot embrace the alternate reality offered by Lizzie. Skeptical of the dead world in which he wanders, he also extends his disbelief to his ability to animate it through faith and love. Eugene feels entrapped, volitionless. He hides his love for Lizzie from his best friend, fearful of being mocked. When

Charley and Headstone expose Eugene's attachment, Mortimer conducts a forensic inquiry:

> "Eugene, do you design to capture and desert this girl?"
> "My dear fellow, no."
> "Do you design to marry her?"
> "My dear fellow, no."
> "Do you design to pursue her?"
> "My dear fellow, I don't design anything. I have no design whatever. I am incapable of designs. If I conceived a design, I should speedily abandon it, exhausted by the operation." (ch. 22)

Eugene hates Lady Tippins' fiction of lovers, yet the grotesque lady at least provides him with an outlet for his own wit, reminiscent—in its defensiveness and sterility—of that of Meredith's Sir Austin. Incapable of yielding to illusion, he finds a mild comfort in satirizing the illusions of others. Sentiment is inadmissible. Thackeray's George Osborne, who briefly yielded to sentiment by marrying Amelia against the prohibition of his father, soon proved himself to be his father's son. Eugene, though ostensibly laughing at his respected father, also finds "M.R.F." to be an ineradicable influence. After Eugene has pursued Lizzie to the mouth of the river, he entertains once again the notion of marrying the penniless daughter of a bargeman. Conducting a dialogue with himself, he asks how "M.R.F." would "reason with the legal mind?" The answer is quick: "You wouldn't marry for some money and station, because you were frightfully likely to become bored. Are you less frightfully likely to become bored, marrying for no money and no station? Are you sure of yourself?' Legal mind, in spite of forensic protestations, must secretly admit, 'Good reasoning on the part of M.R.F. *Not* sure of myself'" (ch. 56).

Thus, at the very moment before he will be attacked, bruised, deformed, and beaten into a new shape, Eugene's "legal mind" still uses the false adult logic which makes him a skeptic. Just as Twemlow wonders whether the friendship of the Veneerings is "real," so does Eugene question whether his own love for

Lizzie is "a *real* sentiment on my part." Only by being taken to the threshold of death can he be reborn into a new reality. His "outer form" is crushed (ch. 60), but the self which is now liberated no longer is bound to a world of living dead. The crippled Eugene asks Jenny to dress his wounds. His request signifies his new understanding. He has ceased to be an indolent bystander and has joined the suffering visionaries, Jenny and Riah, whom he had previously judged only by their outer form. His transformation not only enables him to become Lizzie's husband but also impresses a different character on his relation with Mortimer Lightwood.

Before, the two men could speak only through indirections. Now, all ellipsis is dropped in favor of unvarnished emotion. It is Mortimer who begs Jenny to honor Eugene's request by blurting out, "I shall break down if I say more"; it is Mortimer who engineers Eugene's marriage and vows, "you will be blessed with a noble wife." Eugene, in turn, admits, "I love you, Mortimer" (ch. 60). These touches are sentimental, but the sentimentality is intentional. When the two men were "more than brothers" in the Veneering world, a show of emotion seemed unforgivable. Now that their relation threatens to be broken by death, feeling comes to the fore. It is Lizzie who has consecrated their mutual friendship. Mortimer's conversion is essential to Dickens' purpose. As Boffin's lawyer, Mortimer is related to the other nucleus of mutual friends forming around John Harmon. Moreover, as one who has belonged to the Veneering world, he can vindicate Lizzie's vision. The novel ends with his delight over Twemlow's unexpected show of feeling in defending Eugene's wife. Brightening into a smile, Mortimer ceases to be a light wood tossed by capricious waves. He shakes Twemlow's hands and goes to his quarters, "gaily." Even Twemlow may escape the Veneering's circle of false friendships and join the society of "mutual friends."

Lizzie Hexam thus acts as a regenerative force. It is Lizzie's river, and not her father's river, that gives life to Eugene. It is through her also that Eugene's rebirth is associated with the death of Betty Higden. This death is as final as that of Gaffer Hexam, Riderhood, and Headstone, yet Dickens also suggests that Betty is allowed a resurrection in afterlife akin to that which Eugene experiences in his own life. Shaped, like Lizzie, by a consciousness of past suffering, Betty also refuses to succumb to the mechanized world of London. She, too, is conscious of a higher reality: "There was abundant place for gentler fancies, too, in her untutored mind." Lizzie flees to the countryside so that she may live according to the dictates of the higher order she believes in; Betty flees so that she may die as she had lived. Her pilgrimage is blocked by the lock. In order to pass into a world of the imagination she must bribe the lock-keeper, Rogue Riderhood, the same man who betrayed Lizzie's father for silver. Once she has passed the lock, she is free. She can find Lizzie and die, unsundered.

Even the spot where Betty dies offers a kind of immateriality to the woman who had seen a funereal barge manned by her dead children and dead grandchildren. The physical setting seems to dissolve as she sees "beyond some intervening trees and branches, the lighted windows, both in their reality and their reflection in the water" (ch. 41). Convinced that the tree against which she is resting is the foot of the Cross, Betty faints next to her "orderly basket." When she awakes, Lizzie's face bends down on hers (as it will later bend down on the drowning Eugene's). To Betty, Lizzie's features blend with those of Bella. The fusion is almost prophetic; in the next chapter, Bella, summoned to Betty's burial, will be affected by Lizzie's exemplary goodness. Betty asks Lizzie to lift her up. The chapter ends laconically: "Lizzie Hexam very softly raised the weather-stained grey head and lifted her as high as Heaven."

The scene works in purely symbolic terms. Dickens derives his symbols from orthodox Christianity, yet renders them from the dying woman's point of view. Betty is confident of salvation; the "Heaven" to which she is transported seems more "real" to her than a world of lock-keepers and poorhouses. Still, her assurance does not depend on the tenets of an implied Christian belief that Dickens wants his readers to share; rather, it hinges on her peculiar visionary powers, on a capacity she shares with all those who, by becoming "as little children,"[4] are able to see beyond the physical world of matter. Christ, who took on a corporeal shape to vindicate a higher spiritual order, hovers as an imponderable presence throughout this novel of transformations and resurrections. He is suggested by Riah, the Jew who responds to Jenny's invitation to "come up and be dead" by seeming to rise from his grave. He is evoked by Jenny's puzzling words about her imaginary bridgegroom: "He is coming from somewhere or other, I suppose, and He is coming some day or other, I suppose. *I* don't know any more about Him, at present" (ch. 66). The Redeemer of the New Testament, whose second coming can dissolve the shackles of the material world, may even be one of the figures suggested by the novel's elusive title. Dickens associates Betty's death with the agony on the Cross and punctuates Lizzie's miraculous rescue of Eugene by inserting her prayer to the "wonderful workings" of a divinity capable of raising bodies above water. But these Christian overtones merely color his own belief in the power of the imaginative heart shared by Betty and Lizzie. And it is this purely personal myth which he wants the reader to share through Lizzie's and Betty's intimations of a higher order.

## 4

The symbolism of death and rebirth associated with Lizzie, Eugene, Betty Higden, Riah, and Jenny establishes a pattern by which all other characters in the novel can be measured. But symbols illuminate only; they make nothing happen. Lizzie, as I have already suggested, is but a walking emblem; Eugene's transformation and Betty's transcendence rely on the myth that death is life; Jenny and Riah fit into that same myth. To animate this fantasy, however, Dickens must use plot. Accordingly, he enlists the plot of John Harmon and the Boffins to persuade the reader of the truth of Lizzie's belief in a better

4. Matthew, 18:3.

world. The novel's symbols are startling and unusual; but it is the comic reversal Dickens springs on the reader which finally shocks us into accepting the improbable.

We have seen how the novelist tempts us into empathizing with the figure of John Harmon. We are attracted by the aura of mystery which surrounds the Man from Somewhere. This mystery, however, is a clever ruse. Dickens admits in the post-script to his novel that he intentionally deluded his readers into thinking that he was "at great pains to conceal exactly what [he] was at great pains to suggest: namely, that Mr. John Harmon was not slain and that Mr. John Rokesmith was he." Dickens wants us to identify "Rokesmith" early in the novel so that we will identify also with his motives. We are teased by the story of the good man who must mask himself to restore order; we fasten on this somewhat romantic figure because the only other "good" figures, the Boffins, strike us as being mere caricatures. The Boffins are children in a threatening adult world. We place our trust in their protector. Harmon–Rokesmith, we assume, is more believable than the impossible Dustman and his "Heneriet-ty." The plot developments, however, soon undercut this re-sponse. Only by unequivocally identifying himself with the grotesque and childish Boffin can the reader of *Our Mutual Friend* purge himself of the nightmare that threatens John Har-mon, the adult man.

When Dickens tricks us into believing that Boffin is, in Bella's words, "being spoilt by prosperity and is changing everyday," we realize, by our mounting insecurity, how important the Golden Dustman has been to our well-being. Though we may have identified with the aspirations of John Harmon, the Bof-fins have all along acted as our main bulwark against the dispirit-ing world of the Veneerings. We have witnessed John Harmon's deep despair and followed Lizzie's flight from London. The old couple, however, remained in the London world in their own identities; they alone imparted stability to the city's fluid motions. Their Bower, like the equally eccentric tavern of "The Jolly Porters," withstands the mutability of the dehumanized surroundings. We are therefore aghast at Boffin's presumed change. Desirous of reassurance, we at first refuse to believe it; but the Golden Dustman's harshness to our "mutual friend," John Harmon, is all too convincing. The symptoms of miserliness are everywhere. Boffin's innocence seemed impregnable when Wegg read the *Decline and Fall* to the couple who wanted to better themselves. Now that he models himself on a succession of misers, we fear that master and servant have indeed become one, that Boffin has declined and is rapidly falling.

Boffin's changed outlook comes precisely at the point at which John Harmon and the reader had hoped for changes of an opposite nature. Bella began to show a new comprehension; though she continues to rise, Boffin continues to decline. Bella's regeneration suddenly no longer seems as significant as it would have been under the old circumstances: if Boffin succumbs to the values of a Vanity Fair, then the efforts of the John Harmons and Lizzie Hexams of this world surely must go for nothing. Perhaps the Veneering world is, after all, the "real world," and Lizzie's notions are but an empty dream. Skillfully, Dickens proceeds to toy with our expectations by mingling hope with fear. We rejoice when Bella marries John Harmon; but we are sobered when we reflect that the husband she worships seems condemned to live under his assumed name. The bower the Rokesmiths have created strikes us as but a frail bubble; their talk of galleons and islands as feeble fantasies. Carefully, Dickens injects new hopes. The Golden Dustman rises a little to punish the Lammles; soon, however, he falls again. The intensity of our wishes begins to mount. A baby, like that once wished for by the Boffins in the manner of "the kings and queens in the fairytales" (ch. 9), is now granted to the Rokesmiths. Eugene's change, Riah's liberation, Fledgby's punishment, convince us that our wishes may be fulfilled, after all.

Dickens has moved the plot lines of his novel in such a way that its jagged pieces begin to cohere, but the largest piece in the jigsaw puzzle is still missing: Boffin. When Boffin reveals that his "change" was feigned, that he has actually been "playing a part," we are elated. Nicodemus Boffin has been as invariable as always. Our security is restored. Delighted, we yield to his nonsense, as he delivers "in the grisliest growling of the regular brown bear" his blessings on the John Harmons and their child: "A pretty and hopeful picter? Mew, Quack-quack, Bow-wow!" (ch. 63). In a novel full of allusions to Goldilocks, Jack Horner, Cinderella, Red Riding Hood, Beauty and the Beast, the Golden Dustman's return appeals to that same irrational need satisfied by the illogical logic of nursery rhymes and fairy tales. Far from lapsing into childishness, Dickens, the admirer of Hans Christian Andersen,[5] exploits the power of unreason by which the child can order a reality hostile to reasoning men.

Boffin is unvarying. His identity has not altered with his acquisition of wealth. His permanence is recognized by the enemy he now defeats with John Harmon's help, Silas Wegg: "and there was you, Mr. Boffin, as you *identically* are, with your *self-same* stick under your very *same* arm" (ch. 5, italics added). Though predicated on the fabrications of a fairy tale, Boffin's fixity allows us to dispel the doubts created by the shifting Veneering world. It is tempting to identify Boffin with Dickens himself: the old man's ability to fool Bella corresponds to the aging novelist's ability to throw dust in the eyes of his readers. Boffin triumphs over Wegg the maker of fictions through a fiction of his own devising. His wife "couldn't abear to make believe" (ch. 63), but this innocent and candid creature has realized that only through make-believe could he bear out his trust in goodness and harmony.

Boffin, the impossibly ridiculous man, thus replaces John Harmon as the reader's prime "mutual friend." He is the keystone in a new society which binds together all those characters who seemed so hopelessly divided. Lizzie, Eugene, and Mortimer join his group; Riah gets a better master; Sloppy may

5. Dickens and Andersen met in London in 1847 and again in 1857, when the Danish writer made the trip "not for London's sake," but "for you alone." They corresponded from 1847 to 1862. See Elias Bredsdorff, *H. C. Andersen og Charles Dickens* (Copenhagen, 1951).

become the "Him" that Jenny Wren is waiting for. This unexpected happiness corrects the melancholic "panoramic view" that Mr. Venus had bemoaned. Pleasant Riderhood, now freed from her father's tyranny, is willing to marry the taxidermist as long as he ceases to deal with fragments and bones. Wegg, soon to be cast out, comments jealously, "It would seem, Mr. Venus, that you are flush of friends." Mr. Venus and the reader joyfully agree.

Through this unexpected fairy tale conclusion Dickens gives a new vitality to the comic forms employed by Trollope, Emily Brontë, and Thackeray. Trollope very tentatively invites us to identify with an eccentric who plays on an imaginary violincello; Dickens peremptorily forces us to accept a preposterous childman who growls like a bear. Trollope and Emily Brontë eject their intruders from their imagined worlds; Dickens, however, concocts a whimsical Bower around his mutual friends and denies entrance to all those unwilling to accept illusion. While Emily Brontë carefully encases the myth of Heathcliff and Catherine within a comic shell, Dickens pits both Boffin's comedy and Lizzie's myth against all the veneers that would deny the fulfillments of romance. In *Our Mutual Friend* there is no need for an authorial voice to manipulate our responses. Dickens *is* everything he describes. The jerky motions of the characters convince us of their puppetlike nature. No Showman is needed to put them in and out of their boxes. Descriptions suggest in themselves the irrationality of Dickens' fictional world:

> The schools were newly built. . . . They were in a neighbourhood which looked like a toy neighbourhood taken in blocks out of a box by a child of particularly incoherent mind and set up anyhow; here, one side of a new street; there, a large solitary public-house facing nowhere; here another unfinished street already in ruins; there, a church; here, an immense new warehouse; there a dilapidated old country villa; then, a medley of black ditch, sparkling cucumber-frame, rank field, richly cultivated kitchen-garden, brisk viaduct, arch-spanned canal, and disorder of frowziness and fog. As if the child had given the table a kick and gone to sleep. (ch. 18)

Dickens the novelist becomes that child of particularly incoherent mind as he forces the reader to recognize the incoherence
of the world to which we are bound. Yet he enlists irrationality
to lend new coherence to man's existence amidst chaos. Dickens'
description of the "moral straightness" of the Boffins in chapter
nine of the novel is significant in two respects: first, because it
reminds us how seldom such authorial intrusions occur in this
work, and, second, because his implied belief in an "external law"
which rewards good and forces evil to "stop short at itself"
shows how far in outlook he is from the English novelists who
were his competitors and successors. Dickens admits that "ten
thousand weaknesses and absurdities might have been detected
in the breasts" of Mr. and Mrs. Boffin, and "ten thousand vanities
additional, possibly, in the breast of the woman" (ch. 9). George
Eliot would have exposed the weaknesses, Trollope would have
laughed at the absurdities, and Thackeray would have satirized
the vanities. In their hands, the Boffins would have best played
a subsidiary role like those played by the Thornes, the Gleggs,
or the O'Dowds. For Dickens, however, it is precisely Boffin's
absurdity which makes this character eligible for his leading
part. It is because he is so very outlandish that the Golden Dustman manages to withstand the despair of the City of Destruction
and thereby allow his creator to sustain his own wishful belief
in an "eternal law."

Dickens enthrones Boffin's absurdity and renders Podsnappery
foolish. To other Victorian novelists, as eager as he was to
counter a dehumanizing world, such a paradox seemed an impossible sleight of hand. In the next chapter, we shall see how
the George Eliot of *Middlemarch* managed, through infinite
gradations and balances, to tame the world of Vanity Fair in a
panoramic novel of her own. Dickens makes no such concessions
in countering the reality endorsed by the unsentimental business-
man whom Thackeray had represented by old Osborne and
George Eliot, by Mr. Deane. He divests Podsnap's world of all
meaning by converting him into an automaton. Podsnap uses
his "right arm flourish" to put "the rest of Europe and the whole

of Asia, Africa, and America nowhere" (ch. 11). Dickens reverses the process. With a flourish of his own right arm this
great artist declares Podsnap's world to be unreal and decides
that only the "nowhere" of symbol, myth, and fairy tale validates
his own faith in an "eternal law" based on the heart.

# VI  *Middlemarch*: Affirmation Through Compromise

While at work on *Middlemarch* (published in eight installments from December 1871 to December 1872),[1] George Eliot wrote, "I shudder to think what a long book it will be—not so long as Vanity Fair or Pendennis, however, according to my calculations.[2] It is more than a coincidence that George Eliot should have chosen Thackeray's work, and not that of Dickens (whose *Bleak House* and *Our Mutual Friend* are certainly as long as *Vanity Fair*), to serve as a yardstick for her novel. Although Dickens, unlike Thackeray, had been George Eliot's friend and early admirer,[3] the "realist" who claimed that her work could never be "ideal or eclectic" distrusted the irrational means through which Dickens managed to conquer a hostile and threatening world. As early as 1858 she decided that she would never exclude "disagreeable truths" from her art or sugarcoat "things as they have been or are" through idealization or evasion (*Letters*, II, 362). "In this respect," she maintained, "at least I may have some resemblance to Thackeray," whom she professed to regard, "as I suppose the majority of people with any intellect do, on the whole the most powerful of living novelists" (*Letters*, II, 349).

1. Books I–VI were published in intervals of two months from December 1871 to October 1872; Books VII and VIII were published in November and December of 1872.

2. *The George Eliot Letters*, ed. Gordon S. Haight (New Haven, 1954–1955), V, 297. Referred to as *Letters* in the text.

3. Dickens was one of the few readers who instantly recognized that George Eliot's *Scenes of Clerical Life* was the work of a woman; he admired her work and asked her to contribute to the periodicals under his editorship. Thackeray, on the other hand, assumed that her first work was written by a man; although he respected her as a novelist, he claimed that he could not fully appreciate her fiction.

George Eliot's identification with Thackeray is borne out by her practice: *Middlemarch* is indeed closer to *Vanity Fair* than to an "ideal or eclectic" fantasy like *Our Mutual Friend*. But, as we shall see, the resemblances between her and Thackeray's novel also reveal important differences which suggest that, like Dickens, she found it emotionally impossible to embrace Thackeray's unmitigated skepticism. Although her Thackerayan insistence on "intellect" prompted her to reject Dickens' wishful means of escaping "disagreeable truths," she also needed an outlet for her intense idealism. The intricate form of *Middlemarch* allowed George Eliot to blend conflicting impulses. By balancing reason and yearning, she could expose human vanity while affirming at the same time the sustaining power of great illusions. The novelist who had wept while describing the death of Maggie Tulliver was able to devise, in her greatest novel, a construct against despair through which she could preserve Maggie's idealism amidst a prosaic world composed of "things as they have been or are."

## I

Like *Vanity Fair*, *Middlemarch* exposes the misconceptions of characters who are inevitably limited in their perceptions and just as inevitably buffeted by time and change. In George Eliot's handling of what she calls the "irony of events," destiny always "stands by sarcastic with our *dramatis personae* folded in her hand."[4] The slow motions of provincial life depicted in her novel are almost as unsettling as the more rapid shifts of Thackeray's mobile city world:

> Old provincial society had its share of this subtle movement: had not only its striking downfalls, its brilliant young professional dandies who ended by living up an entry with a drab and six children for their establishment, but also those less marked vicissitudes which are constantly shifting the boundaries of social intercourse, and begetting new consciousness

4. *Middlemarch*, ed. Gordon S. Haight (Boston, 1956), Riverside Edition, ch. 11. Future references in the text are to this edition.

of interdependence. Some slipped a little downward, some got higher footing; some were caught in political currents, some in ecclesiastical, and perhaps found themselves surprisingly grouped in consequence; while a few personages or families that stood with rocky firmness amidst all this fluctuation, were slowly presenting new aspects in spite of solidity, and altering with the double change of self and beholder. (ch. 11)

In a novel like *Our Mutual Friend*, Dickens resists such fluctuations by imposing the timeless dimensions of myth and fairy tale on the world from which his characters escape. By inviting us to identify with figures like Betty Higden or the Golden Dustman, he encourages the reader to reacquire the trustfulness of a child. George Eliot, on the other hand, examines the mechanics of change from the superior vantage point of a saddened and mature consciousness which has carefully studied "the varying experiments of Time" ("Prelude"). She challenges her reader to share the understanding of her omniscient narrator, a commentator whose psychological shrewdness and awareness allows him to unravel the webs which enmesh all human endeavors. Just as *Vanity Fair* retreats three decades to the times of Waterloo, so *Middlemarch* goes back forty years to another watershed in English history, the era of the Reform Bill. The historical vantage point allows the novelist to scan the comparative failures and achievements of characters still unaware of their future. Their failures are many; their achievements are small. In the epilogue called "Finale," we are informed that "Will [Ladislaw] became an ardent public man, working well in those times when reforms were begun with a *young* hopefulness of *immediate* good which has been much checked in our days" (italics added). The look here is retrospective, mildly elegiac, far closer to that taken by Dobbin at the end of *Vanity Fair* than it is to our delight in the bastion of mutual friends formed at the end of *Our Mutual Friend*. "Immediate good" has not yet been attained; we must resign ourselves to small gains. Of the novel's three "ardent" reformers, the ideals of Dorothea and Ladislaw have been "much checked," while the ambitions of

Lydgate have been completely thwarted. The world which George Eliot and Thackeray deem to be "real" has asserted its ways.

*Middlemarch* is a novel without a hero. Its salient character is Dorothea Brooke, a "foundress of nothing." Although the reader is irresistibly drawn to this idealist's "self-forgetful ardor," Dorothea cannot triumph over the ways of the world. In *Our Mutual Friend*, our unexpected identification with the characters grouped around Boffin, the child-man who steps out of a fairy tale, allows us to believe in a better world ruled by the golden, golden heart. In *Middlemarch*, however, the sober narrator tempers our overeagerness to identify with Dorothea's ardent heart by twice calling her "childlike" in the scene of her greatest victory. This comes when she defies the fallible world around her by stoutly refusing to believe in Lydgate's guilt: "I believe that people are almost always better than their neighbours think they are," are the words by which this enthusiast challenges the opinions of Middlemarch (ch. 72). All of Lydgate's neighbors, including the physician's own wife, are convinced of his culpability. Even the compassionate Mr. Farebrother, conscious of his own shortcomings, is ready to indict his friend. But Dorothea is unflinching in her idealism. Her intuition proves correct; Middlemarch is wrong. By listening to Lydgate's confession, by promising to vindicate him in the eyes of others, and by freeing him from his financial debts, the unique Dorothea rises above the Middlemarchers and becomes Lydgate's and the reader's mutual friend. She has become a healer, and Lydgate the physician, her grateful patient. Still, George Eliot's "realism" severely circumscribes Dorothea's triumph. Whereas Dickens' uneducated Lizzie Hexam is able to redeem Eugene Wrayburn, Dorothea's ability to help Lydgate is sorely limited by her ignorance of the world. She cannot persuade the doctor to remain in Middlemarch, for, in her innocence, she underestimates the extent to which his ideals have been broken. Lydgate smiles sadly as he listens to her speech. He finds that her "childlike grave-eyed earnestness" and her "ready understanding of high experience" blend into "an adorable whole"; but the narrator pointedly interrupts to inform us that of "lower experience such as plays a great part in the world, poor Mrs. Casaubon had a very blurred shortsighted knowledge, little helped by her imagination" (ch. 76).

The sympathetic and intuitive power of imagination possessed by Dorothea, though an asset which separates her from most other characters in the novel, thus hardly carries the significance it would hold in Dickens' fictional world. Dorothea's shortsightedness must still be corrected; indeed, her scanty knowledge of "the world" is soon brought to a test. Earlier, she was pained to discover that her idealization of Casaubon did not correspond to his actual self; now, as she enters Lydgate's house, she finds Will Ladislaw, the man she had exalted in Casaubon's place, bending over Rosamond Lydgate. The "irony of events" forces her and the reader into another reconsideration. Her "ardent faith in efforts of justice and mercy" had, at the time, seemed superior to Mr. Farebrother's "cautious weighing of consequences" (ch. 72). Now, however, both Dorothea and the reader are compelled to admit the minister's better knowledge of the world: "character," Farebrother had warned her, "is not cut in marble—it is not something solid and unalterable" (ch. 72). The words were meant to apply to Lydgate; they now apply to Ladislaw. The young man is not a paragon; although in his independence and insights he is free from the impulses which degrade other men, he is not immune to weakness. By marrying the fallible Ladislaw, Dorothea admits her own needs as a woman, yet admits also the insufficiency of her abstracted ideals. Like Thackeray's Dobbin, she conforms to the motions of an imperfect world.[5]

At first glance, then, *Middlemarch* resembles *Vanity Fair* in its relentless exposition of the mistakes and misjudgments by

5. In *Vanity Fair*, it is the frankly selfish Becky Sharp who enables Dobbin to marry Amelia by puncturing Amelia's illusions; in *Middlemarch*, it is Rosamond the egotist who paves the way for Dorothea's union with the imperfect Ladislaw.

which human beings invariably frustrate their ambitions for fulfillment. Bound by their narrow illusions, the novel's characters engage in faulty alliances, faulty speculations, faulty anticipations, oblivious to the "subtle movement" of events which affect their lives in ways they could not have suspected. Dorothea and Mr. Casaubon, like Lydgate and Rosamond, marry without an adequate knowledge of each other's wants. Fred Vincy's expectations of a legacy are quashed by Mary Garth's refusal to burn Featherstone's will; Featherstone's desire to control Stone Court beyond the grave is annulled by the action of his heir, Joshua Rigg, who, against all expectations, sells the land to Featherstone's archenemy, Bulstrode. Bulstrode's own bid for power misfires when the past he had tried to conceal comes to the fore and forces his banishment from Middlemarch. The "irony of events" constantly blocks the outcome of all predictions and produces effects exactly opposite to those eagerly anticipated by the characters. Casaubon assumes that the codicil in his testament will prevent Dorothea from marrying Will; Lydgate is confident that Raffles will not die; Fred is sure that he can repay the sum he owes to Caleb Garth by engaging in an advantageous horse trade. Even the most inconsequential obstacles can reverse the results foreseen by a given character: "a second glass of sherry" makes a shambles of Mr. Brooke's preconceived electoral speech (ch. 52); a change in weather ruins Ladislaw's "stratagem" to meet Dorothea out of doors (ch. 37).

The expectations of the Middlemarchers are thwarted primarily because they are too obdurate, too firmly rooted in the tracks they choose in their quest for self-fulfillment. Their obduracy makes them prone to error and disappointment. With the exception of the illusionless Mary Garth and the malleable Will Ladislaw, each character is wrapped up in the pursuit of goals that will have to be modified or abandoned. These goals are manifold; they range from Raffles' greed to Dorothea's and Lydgate's efforts to improve the lot of others. In their unwillingness to adapt themselves to a reality which gives the lie to their aspirations, the characters fall back on self-deception. Rationalizations abound: Rosamond disguises her increasing discontent with the role of a provincial doctor's wife by arguing that Lydgate would be better recognized in London; Casaubon hides his insufficiencies from himself by clinging to the notion that his scholarly work will have momentous repercussions; Bulstrode denies the inconsistencies between his temporal ambitions and spiritual professions by pretending that his exercise of worldly power serves the interest of a divine Providence.

Even Dorothea and Lydgate are not exempt from such self-rationalizations: in the first chapter of the novel, the puritanical Dodo tries to excuse her sensual delight over an emerald ring by arguing that "gems are used as spiritual emblems in the Revelation of St. John"; in his first action in Middlemarch, Lydgate likewise glosses over an inconsistency in his behavior by telling himself that he is voting against Farebrother on Bulstrode's side only because of reservations about Mr. Farebrother's gambling habits. Dorothea absurdly insists that by marrying Casaubon she will become the helpmeet of another Milton; Lydgate weakly assures himself that Rosamond's companionship will actually help to further his researches. George Eliot implies that even the reforming impulses of these two characters are slightly tainted: Dorothea is disappointed to find that Mr. Casaubon's parishioners are not as hopelessly needy as she had expected; Lydgate subordinates his willingness to do "good small work for Middlemarch" to his ambition to do "great work for the world" as a scientific pioneer (ch. 15).

In their self-absorption most of the characters lose sight of the inner life of their fellow man. Only the detached narrator can detect "the stealthy convergence of human lots" and point to the "slow preparation of effects from one life to another, which tells like a calculated irony on the indifference or the frozen stare with which we look at our unintroduced neighbour" (ch. 11). When Dorothea and Lydgate first meet, she is engaged to Casaubon and he is attracted to Rosamond: "nothing at present could seem much less important to Lydgate than the turn of Miss Brooke's mind, or to Miss Brooke the qualities of the woman who had attracted this young surgeon" (ch. 11). The narrator's interjection alerts the reader. We are prevented from sharing each character's indifference toward the other and sense that somehow their destinies will converge. The "irony of events" confirms our premonition. Whereas Lydgate on first seeing Dorothea patronizes her as an ignorant woman who has to fall back on her "moral sense" to settle questions better re- solved by reason (ch. 10), he will, five-hundred pages later, gratefully recline on this uncompromising moral sense. On meeting her in chapter ten, he declares the "good creature" to be a "little too earnest" for his taste; in chapter seventy-two, it is her "simple earnestness" which conquers his "proud reserve" and allows Rosamond's husband partially to regain his self- esteem.

It is through such interrelations, through its careful re-creation of "the stealthy convergence of human lots," that *Middlemarch* most markedly departs from Thackeray's narrative method. The reader of *Vanity Fair* is amazed to discover that a bowl of rack punch has indeed possessed all the significance attributed to it by the jocular Showman; the reader of *Middlemarch*, however, never doubts that the narrator who constantly forces us to un- ravel human lots and see "how they were woven and inter- woven" is capable of finding a larger design (ch. 15). Like Thackeray, George Eliot demonstrates how, in an imperfect world, "noble impulse" and "great feelings will often take the aspect of error, and great faith the aspect of illusion" ("Finale"). But by enabling the reader to disentangle the strands in which the characters are bound, the novel's ironic method also allows us to incorporate these individual experiences into a larger, comprehensive view. Like Dickens—though in an entirely dif- ferent manner—George Eliot dissects only to connect. Her novel asks us to assemble each and every strand of which it is composed. Though Lydgate may, at first, care little about Dorothea, though Fred Vincy "knew little and cared less about Ladislaw" (ch. 59), though Dorothea and Mary Garth never meet face to face, the reader is constantly compelled to join their stories through analogy and differentiation. The Providence that Bulstrode and other Middlemarchers invoke with such confidence may not exist; but the novelist who dispenses rewards and punishments through the "irony of events" binds all characters into a just and comprehensible whole.

Gradation and balance are all in *Middlemarch*. In *Vanity Fair*, the Showman pares down all human efforts to the same common denominator; egotists and altruists, realists and idealists are fitted into an identical panorama of universal vanity. In *Middlemarch*, however, the narrator resists all efforts to provide a simplified perspective: "Our vanities differ as our noses do: all conceit is not the same conceit, but varies in correspondence with the minutiae of mental make in which one of us differs from another" (ch. 15). The panoramic form of the novel allows George Eliot to calibrate a vast number of separate experiences; she constructs a network in which the qualities and destiny of any one figure are set off against the qualities and destinies of all others. In *The Mill on the Floss* the narrator lashes out against a prosaic world that would deny epic fulfillment to the unique Maggie. The collision between the ideal and the actual informs *Middlemarch* as well: Dorothea's "passionate desire to know and think" (ch. 4) greatly resembles Maggie's own thirst for a larger life; the town of Middlemarch is as retrograde and stultifying as St. Ogg's. But by counterbalancing Dorothea's story with those of Lydgate, Bulstrode, Fred Vincy, and the Garths, George Eliot resisted the temptation of creating another female martyr immolated to a hostile world. Though Dorothea fails to find her *epos*, she is granted a fulfillment denied to either Lydgate or Bulstrode, the other two exiles from Middlemarch. At the same time, however, the fulfillment of this rare but impulsive creature is not as complete as that of the sensible Mary Garth, the provincial ugly duckling who finds happiness in Middlemarch itself.

George Eliot's insertion of the plot surrounding Fred Vincy and the Garth family best illustrates her refusal to cast "the blight of irony over all higher effort" (ch. 58). The story of

Mary's love for and regeneration of Fred is an idyll, akin to Emily Brontë's story of Hareton's deliverance by the second Catherine. But *Middlemarch* is not a romance; it purports to be the work of a "realist" eager to depict the world as it is. In the hands of a lesser writer, Fred's redemption by Mary and her honest father could easily have degenerated into a mawkish homily on the powers of true love and of practical, hard work; in the hands of Dickens, this idyll would have been transformed into Eugene Wrayburn's melodramatic resurrection into the new life offered by a bargeman's daughter. It is a tribute to George Eliot's integrity and artistic skill that this idyll is neither homily nor overdramatized wishfulfillment; though it encases her own idealism, it remains perfectly compatible with the reality of a novel in which the lives of most other characters are not crowned by a happy ending.

*Middlemarch*, then, contains a compromise. In it, George Eliot avoids Dickens' escapism through fantasy, but, at the same time, resists a Thackerayan pessimism that would blight all "higher effort." Her idealism qualifies her realism; the reality principle checks her Dorothea-like ardor. To achieve this reconciliation of opposites she created a form that is likewise a compromise between convention and innovation. By and large, *Middlemarch* relies on the same traditional elements that Trollope drew on in his picture of provincial life. Like Trollope, the George Eliot of *Middlemarch* remains in the tradition of the eighteenth-century novel. The interaction between the points of view of the characters and of the narrator is as integral to her novel as to *Barchester Towers*. George Eliot also follows the example of Trollope and Thackeray by adopting Fielding's pose of a novelist-historian and by enlisting the epic as an ironic correlative for actions which are prosaic and unheroic.[6] Still, as we shall see in the section that follows, these fictional

6. See pp. 17–18 and 51–54, above. While at work on *Middlemarch* George Eliot read Trollope's *The Vicar of Bullhampton* (1870) and the first installments of *The Eustace Diamonds* (serialized in the *Fortnightly Review* from July 1871 to February 1873).

elements are subservient to a design far grander than Trollope's. Whereas Trollope adopts the role of historian with tongue-in-cheek, George Eliot actually writes a novel about history that celebrates "unhistoric" acts; whereas he occasionally uses the epic vein to mock the blunders of his characters, she creates an epic which mourns the impossibility of an epic life. In explaining the novelist's objectives in chapter fifteen of *Middlemarch*, George Eliot's narrator places himself in the school of Fielding, but stresses, at the same time, the more momentous task of the novelist who must find a design in the confusing and potentially tragic web of modern existence. Though indebted to the humorists before her, George Eliot's masterpiece also sets—in Henry James' words—a limit to the "development of the old-fashioned English novel."[7]

## 2

In *Middlemarch* George Eliot greatly expands and perfects the convention of an omniscient narrative voice which both Trollope and Thackeray had so effectively used in their efforts to exert an artistic control over their unruly fictional worlds. Like Trollope's narrator and Thackeray's Showman, the narrator of *Middlemarch* interjects his own point of view and complicates our responses to the positions taken by the characters. His tone, like that of his predecessors, is ironic. He is capable of a sense of fun and self-depreciation, as shown in his jocular identification with "older Herodotus," another historian who "thought it well to take a woman's lot for his starting-point; though Io, as a maiden apparently beguiled by attractive merchandise, was the reverse of Miss Brooke" (ch. 11). Like Thackeray's and Trollope's narrators, this figure deliberately calls attention to the "make-believe" of his craft ("These things are a parable. . ."; "This fine comparison has reference to . . ." [chs. 27, 59]). He often bursts out in seemingly uncontrolled exclamations: "but, dear me! has it not by this time ceased to

7. Henry James, "George Eliot's *Middlemarch*," reprinted in *Nineteenth-Century Fiction*, VIII (December 1953), 170.

be remarkable—is it not rather what we expect in men, that they should have numerous strands of experience lying side by side and never compare them with each other?" (ch. 58).

It is precisely in his command of "numerous strands of experience" and in his willingness to bring them together that this narrator differs from the intentionally limited narrators who acted as spokesmen for Trollope and Thackeray. The narrator in *Middlemarch* is a synthesizer, as capable of laughter as of interpreting the sum total of the experiences of his characters. His method resembles that of Lydgate's master, the French physician Bichat, who saw that only by connecting the separate "materials" of a living body could he estimate "the entire structure or its parts—what are its frailties and what its repairs" (ch. 15). George Eliot's narrator is equally cognizant of the need for connections. He dissects human frailties with uncanny precision; but in his efforts to interpret and repair them he always moves from the particular to the general.[8] It is "a narrow mind," he informs us, "which cannot look at a subject from various points of view" (ch. 7). This concern with universals, like his superior erudition, gives weight and consequence to the narrator's utterances. He is as much a kinsman of the mock-heroic jesters of the English comic novel as he is a cousin of the grave epic poet who interprets human existence in *Paradise Lost*.

The narrative voice that George Eliot creates in *Middlemarch* is thus both more complex than those devised by Thackeray and Trollope and more effective than the one she herself used in *The Mill on the Floss*.[9] In that novel, too, the narrator pro-

8. See, in this connection, the exchange between Mary and Fred in chapter fourteen. When Mary implies that Fred, of all people, has no right to be critical of others, the young man asks: "Do you mean anything particular—just now?" Mary responds: "No, I mean something general—always." In a novel in which all other characters are inevitably enmeshed in particulars, Mary's disinterestedness is unique. Just as the girl's father resembles Robert Evans, so does Mary resemble the Mary Ann Evans who speaks primarily through the omniscient narrator's voice.

9. For an excellent discussion of George Eliot's evolution of her narrative personae, see the third chapter in the late W. J. Harvey's *The Art of George Eliot* (London, 1961).

fessed that "there is nothing petty to the mind that has a large vision of relations."[10] But the comical, bookish gentleman who was forced to hold on to his armchair in his study in the first chapter of *The Mill*, became a helpless observer of Maggie's agonies in the novel's tragic conclusion. In *Middlemarch*, however, the narrator maintains absolute control from beginning to end. In this novel of balances and compromises, this figure combines a scientific with a literary and religious culture. Although his qualifications are those of a scholarly searcher for historical truth, his sympathy is always extended to small, ordinary, and unhistoric acts. His credentials are evident in the very first sentence of the novel: "Who that cares much to know the history of man, and how the mysterious mixture behaves under the varying experiments of Time, has not dwelt, at least briefly, on the life of Saint Theresa, has not smiled with some gentleness at the thought of the little girl walking forth hand-in-hand with her still smaller brother . . . ?" ("Prelude").

The narrator thus combines head and heart; he possesses the knowledge sought by the poorly educated but highly compassionate Dorothea, as well as the sympathy for weakness lacking in the highly knowledgeable but intolerant Lydgate. His scientific preparation allows the narrator to look at human motivations in a far more penetrating fashion than the shortsighted Dorothea or the weak-eyed Mr. Casaubon: "Even with a microscope directed on a water-drop we find ourselves making interpretations which turn out to be rather coarse; for whereas under a weak lens you may seem to see a creature exhibiting a certain voracity . . . , a stronger lens reveals to you certain tiniest hairlets which make vortices for these victims" (ch. 6). Despite his superiority over all the characters, the narrator is never condescending. Nor does he ever misuse his rank or authority as the Middlemarchers frequently do. Rosamond, for instance, deems herself superior to all other townspeople; her proud husband dismisses Dorothea in an ironic sentence and

10. *The Mill on the Floss*, ed. Gordon S. Haight (Boston, 1961), Bk. IV, ch. 1.

fails to take notice of the plain Mary Garth. The narrator, on the other hand, always makes his ironies self-inclusive: "We are all of us born in moral stupidity, taking the world as an udder to feed our supreme selves. Dorothea had early begun to emerge from that stupidity" (ch. 21). Humane and tolerant, he pauses to consider the contradictions in Bulstrode's behavior and refuses to stereotype the banker as a hypocrite; though unsentimental, he can find endearing qualities in the droll personal habits of Mary's father: "pardon these details for once— you would have learned to love them if you had known Caleb Garth" (ch. 23).

In connecting the various narrative strands of the novel the narrator constantly complicates our experience by forcing us to evaluate opposing points of view. The reader, he implies, cannot assess the total movement of the novel without such changes in perspective: "In watching effects, if only of an electric battery, it is often necessary to change our place and examine a particular mixture or group at some distance from the point where the movement we are interested in was set up" (ch. 40). Only by seeing a character or an event from a variety of angles can the reader avoid the narrow vistas to which the characters themselves succumb. Rosamond and Lydgate—like Dorothea and Casaubon before them—completely miss "each other's mental track" (ch. 58); Dorothea and Ladislaw are frustrated by their inability to fathom each other's feelings; the Middlemarchers, in their blindness, are as willing to defame Ladislaw as to extol the unscrupulous Raffles. By giving full play to a multitude of outlooks, the narrator gradually enables us to see beyond the characters in the novel. Only after we have fully sifted their discrepant attitudes does he intervene to integrate these opinions and to guide us in forming a judgment of our own.

Nearly all of the characters in *Middlemarch* are highly opinionated. Indeed, "opinion"—like "point of view"—is one of the words most frequently repeated in the novel. Each opinion, we discover, possesses some truth; yet each opinion is also one-sided. In the first ten chapters of the novel Dorothea's hasty idealization of Mr. Casaubon is counterbalanced by the opinions of those who see the clergyman in a totally different light. Dorothea aggrandizes the scholar into a figure as "instructive as Milton's 'affable archangel' " simply because he has understood her religious views and supported them by drawing on "historical examples before unknown to her" (ch. 3). But the girl who is complimented by the unwitting Sir James for her "power of forming an opinion" about abstract principles, cannot, like Sir James or Celia, resort to tangible signs in forming "an opinion of persons" (ch. 3). Dorothea's contention that Casaubon is "one of the most distinguished-looking men" she ever saw, "remarkably like the portrait of Locke" (ch. 2), is immediately challenged by a Celia who has already announced that she will no longer "be bound by Dorothea's opinions" (ch. 1). Dorothea finds Casaubon's "deep eye-sockets" to correspond to Locke's, but Celia tartly retorts, "Had Locke those two white moles with hairs on them?" Like Celia's later allusion to Casaubon's annoying habit of scraping with his spoon, this information comes as a surprise; such physical details could not have been perceived by Dorothea. The reader is slightly baffled. Whose point of view is he to adopt? The soulful Dorothea's or the sensual Celia's? In introducing the Reverend Edward Casaubon to the reader the narrator has been guarded, repeating only through hearsay that the scholar is "noted in the county" as a man of profound learning who has been "understood" to be engaged in some important work. We are likewise given to understand that Mr. Casaubon is wealthy, that he possesses "views of his own" which are expected to become clearer upon publication of his book. Even the allusion to the "impressiveness" of his name remains uncomfortably ambiguous (ch. 1). Finding the narrator to be of little help, the reader is thus thrust on his own devices. We have, by the end of chapter two, overheard Mr. Casaubon's rather chilling speech about his spent eyesight and his loneliness; yet his words are also dignified and rather melancholic. His self-description can simultaneously inspire feelings of revulsion and of deep pity; Celia's view is as possible as Dorothea's: "My mind is something like the ghost of an ancient, wandering about the world and trying mentally to construct it as it used to be, in spite of ruin and confusing changes" (ch. 2). Sensing that this man's aims are, after all, not unlike those of the learned novelist who is also engaged in reconstructing an irrevocably altered past, we remain unsure of the attitude we are expected to adopt. The chapter containing the opposing views of Dorothea and Celia is headed by an epigraph contrasting the perceptions of Don Quixote and Sancho Panza. Are we to share Dorothea's quixotism or are we to adopt the "carnally-minded" pragmatism of her sister? At the end of the chapter the omniscient narrator merely offers a glimpse into Sir James' condescending view of Casaubon: "it never occured to him that a girl to whom he was meditating an offer could care for a dried bookworm towards fifty" (ch. 2). Sir James' estimate corroborates Celia's, yet it is presented as an indictment of his limited perspective rather than as a view endorsed by the narrator.

By the beginning of chapter three, when Dorothea has magnified Casaubon into "a living Bossuet" and "a modern Augustine," we expect the narrator to break his detachment and expose not only her extravagance but also Casaubon's inconsequence. But once again the narrator remains noncommittal. In commenting on Dorothea's impressions, he still refuses to assert that her view of Casaubon is false: "Signs are small immeasurable things, but interpretations are illimitable." Although the signs Dorothea has gone by may be as faulty as those chosen by Celia and Sir James, her interpretations may nonetheless be correct: "Because Miss Brooke was hasty in her trust, it is not therefore clear that Mr. Casaubon was unworthy of it." Checked in our eagerness to judge Mr. Casaubon, we must wait for the evidence of further signs.

In the chapters which follow, these signs begin to mount

against both Casaubon and the girl who gratefully accepts his offer of marriage after her uncle discloses her suitor's "very high opinion" of her qualities. Casaubon's letter of proposal is an ironic masterpiece, comparable to Jane Austen's rendition of the marriage proposal made by the pompous clergyman Mr. Collins. Moreover, we are now introduced to a new batch of opinions. Sir James, Celia, and Mrs. Cadwallader are more vehement in their condemnation of Casaubon than the indecisive Mr. Brooke who consoles himself that the man whose reserve he finds so disturbing may some day become a bishop. The judgments made by these characters confirm the reader's own uneasiness about Casaubon's eligibility as Dorothea's husband. And yet these judgments are still superficial, made from rather selfish vantage points. When Sir James, the most vocal of the objectors, declares Casaubon to be "no better than a mummy," the narrator tells us that the baronet's "point of view has to be allowed for, as that of a blooming and disappointed rival" (ch. 6); Sir James' disparagement of Casaubon's weak legs is dismissed by Mr. Cadwallader for the same reason.

Only after briefly considering still another point of view, that of Will Ladislaw, does the narrator sum up the indictments made against Casaubon:

> If to Dorothea Mr. Casaubon had been the mere occasion which had set alight the fine inflammable material of her youthful illusions, does it follow that he was fairly represented in the minds of those less impassioned personages who have hitherto delivered their judgments concerning him? I protest against any absolute conclusion, any prejudice derived from Mrs. Cadwallader's contempt for a neighbouring clergyman's alleged greatness of soul, or Sir James Chettam's poor opinion of his rival's legs,—from Mr. Brooke's failure to elicit a companion's ideas, or from Celia's criticism of his personal appearance. I am not sure that the greatest man of his age, if ever that solitary superlative existed, could escape these unfavourable reflections of himself in various small mirrors; and even Milton, looking for his portrait in a spoon, must submit to have the facial angle of a bumpkin. (ch. 10)

This protestation is not an equivocation, akin to those made by Thackeray's Showman or Trollope's slippery narrator. As a moralist, George Eliot definitely wants us to judge both Casaubon's egotism and Dorothea's illusion; but she also wants this judgment to be absolutely thorough and complete, to be made on the widest possible spectrum of "opinion." The narrator thus emphasizes that the very selfishness that Casaubon and, to a lesser extent, Dorothea, are guilty of is inherent in the distortions made by their accusers: "Mr. Casaubon, too, was the centre of his own world; if he was liable to think that others were providentially made for him, and especially to consider them in the light of their fitness for the author of a 'Key to all Mythologies,' this trait is not quite alien to us, and, like the other mendicant hopes of mortals, claims some of our pity" (ch. 10).

It is at this point that the novelist begins to change her perspective. For the first time she allows us to enter Casaubon's own point of view of the marriage we have so far seen only through the eyes of others. The shift is dramatic. From external caricature and distortion we move to the inner fears of a lonely and insecure human being. Not only Dorothea is guilty of illusion; as his marriage approaches, Casaubon begins to sense that his anticipations of happiness will turn out to be illusory. He is incapable of giving and of receiving affection: a "certain blankness of sensibility" comes over him precisely at the moment "when his expectant gladness should have been most lively." When we see the couple again, in chapter twenty, Dorothea has experienced the disappointments her husband dreaded. Although she has been led through "the best galleries" and been taken to "the chief points of view" of Rome, her perspective has altered. Previously her view of Casaubon was too heroic; now it is too petty, for she is "as blind to his inward troubles as he to hers." We observe Casaubon through her disenchanted eyes until in chapter twenty-nine George Eliot once again reverses the process and forces us to commiserate, not with Dorothea, but with Casaubon's own anguish: "One morning, some weeks after her arrival at Lowick, Dorothea—but why always Dorothea? Was her point of view the only possible one with regard to this marriage? . . . Mr. Casaubon had an intense consciousness within him, and was spiritually a-hungered like the rest of us" (ch. 29).

Dorothea can never break down her husband's distrust and reserve; she cannot "in the least divine the subtle sources" of his behavior (ch. 29). Only after his testament is made known to her, does she fathom the full extent of his egotism; while he is alive, she ministers to his frailties and is grateful for any small tokens of appreciation. The omniscient narrator, however, probes into the fears, ambitions, and frustrations of this pitifully self-defensive man. Just as Lydgate diagnoses Casaubon's illness as a "fatty degeneration of the heart," so does the narrator's probe detect the deficiencies of a "proud narrow sensitiveness which has not mass enough to spare for transformation into sympathy" (ch. 29). The narrator thus finally confirms Sir James' earlier opinion that Casaubon has no heart (ch. 8). And, in addition, by forcing us to see the plight of this cardiac scholar, the narrator at the same time vindicates Dorothea's devotion—a devotion that is incomprehensible to the likes of Sir James.

Dorothea's devotion reveals the positive side of the very same quixotism that had led her to marry Casaubon against the opposition of her friends. The reader who sided with those who censured her delusions must now readjust his views. Dorothea has finally come to sense that "the once 'affable archangel' " is but a poor fallen creature, as repugnant in soul as he is repulsive in his sexual role. Nonetheless, she is willing to extend to him her pity even after Will Ladislaw breaks her last illusion by apprising her of the futility of her husband's investigations. The cosmopolitan Ladislaw possesses a "mind made flexible with constant comparison" (ch. 22); in this, he resembles not only the narrator's own habits of mind but also those habits which the narrator wants to inculcate in the reader. On the other hand, Ladislaw is also quite selfish. He wants to discredit Casaubon's scholarship. It is his jealousy of Dorothea's devotion to his cousin that impels Ladislaw to tell her that an unfamiliarity with

German writers makes Casaubon's inquiries outdated and worthless, as if he were "groping about in woods with a pocket-compass while they have made good roads" (ch. 21). The narrator quickly turns on Will: "Young Mr. Ladislaw was not at all deep himself in German writers; but very little achievement is required to pity another man's shortcomings" (ch. 21). In his own, more scrupulous look at Casaubon's mythological researches, the narrator confirms Ladislaw's findings: the scholarly "march" which Casaubon undertakes is not only far from "monumental," but totally objectless (ch. 29); at the same time, however, the narrator makes us see that Casaubon actually suspects the fruitlessness of his labors. The picture given by Ladislaw is thus considerably altered: instead of a scholar who proudly persists in folly and wrong-headedness, we see an aging man pitifully clinging to twenty-five years of labor to protect himself from the suspicion that his life has been misspent. Unlike Ladislaw, therefore, and very much like Dorothea, the narrator refuses to deny sympathy to this inadequate human being. The world of *Middlemarch* is full of other marchers propelled toward futile goals:

> For my part I am very sorry for him. It is an uneasy lot at best, to be what we call highly taught and yet not to enjoy: to be present at this great spectacle of life and never to be liberated from a small hungry shivering self—never to be fully possessed by the glory we behold, never to have our consciousness rapturously transformed into the vividness of a thought, the ardor of a passion, the energy of an action, but always to be scholarly and uninspired, ambitious and timid, scrupulous and dimsighted. Becoming a dean or even a bishop would make little difference, I fear, to Mr. Casaubon's uneasiness. Doubtless some ancient Greek has observed that behind the mask and the speaking-trumpet, there must always be our poor little eyes peeping out as usual and our timorous lips more and less under anxious control. (ch. 29)

I have dwelt so long on the presentation of Mr. Casaubon to demonstrate how the narrator appropriates yet redirects the opinions of the various characters to widen our understanding and our sympathy. The narrator modulates our responses through accumulation. His effects are additive, incremental. As we progress in the narrative and move from one plot to the other, we constantly must take new stock of all that has gone before. Words like "opinion," "ardor," "Providence" gain new shades of meaning, while retaining their former connotations; metaphors appear in new contexts, creating unexpected links to their earlier usage. This continuous process of reassessment is produced, on the narrative level, by changes in perspective such as the ones I have discussed. These changes force the reader to reconsider and redistribute earlier judgments and opinions: if, in the early portions of the book, Celia's disparagement of Casaubon's appearance seemed a wholesome corrective for Dorothea's idol-worship, this process is reversed when, in later chapters, the widowed Dorothea seems far superior to the child-worshiping wife who persists in berating a dead man ("I never did like him, and James never did. I think the corners of his mouth were dreadfully spiteful" [ch. 50]). The reader who laughs at Ladislaw's estimate of Casaubon as a "dried-up pedant" and "Bat of erudition" must nonetheless admit the validity of Casaubon's own estimate of his cousin as a "Sciolist." Truth is multisided.

## 3

What is *Middlemarch* about? To reduce the novel into a single thematic statement or motif is to deny the very essence of the narrative method we have been describing. One of the principal word clusters in *Middlemarch* is centered around the idea of motion and exploration: the progress of the individual characters, their strides forward, their halts, indecisions, and detours, are contrasted with each other and assessed against the larger movements of historical change. The novel's own shuttlelike motions encourage this continuous process of contrast and assessment by weaving separate strands into an evergrowing tissue of relations and connections. Like most other Victorian novelists, George Eliot is obsessed by variability and change. Her novel is deliberately set in an era of transition. The world it depicts is, as the narrator incessantly reminds us, protean and versatile; the impulses propelling any one character form but a feeble "current" running through a single filament in a vast network of multiple pulsations. By carefully relating each of these fibers to the larger network to which they belong, George Eliot orders an existence that would otherwise remain inexplicable in its diversity. Although the novelist refuses to impose an artificial fixity on a fluid and multiform world in which no absolutes are possible, the infinitely adjustable web she creates is founded on her recognition of sameness in variety and of continuity in change. This recognition, gradually shared by the reader, proves sufficient in conferring permanence on the impermanence of temporal life.

In *Middlemarch* each individual strand intersects with four larger circles or orbits of experience. These four concentric circles are graduated in proportion to their comprehensiveness and universality. Thus, the outermost circle consists of general allusions: to history, science, literature, and myth; the second circle is made up of more specific references to the events of the 1830's: the death of George IV, the threat of a cholera epidemic, the state of law and medicine, the initial rejection and final passage of the Reform Bill. The third circle incorporates the attitudes and manners of the Middlemarch community; and the innermost circle focuses on the particular events that make up the stories of Dorothea's two marriages, of Lydgate's defeat, of Bulstrode's crime and exile, and of Fred Vincy's regeneration by the Garths. As we shall see, these four circles frame the experiences or motivations of each individual character.

The allusions in the outmost circle of the novel's web are primarily metaphoric; they are contained in the epigraphs that act as chapter headings,[11] in the comments made by the cultured narrator, and in the identifications with prominent historical or fictional figures often made by the characters themselves and

11. Whenever these epigraphs do not give a source, they are George Elliot's own handiwork.

sometimes merely suggested by their names and surnames. The associations thus created act as rich, though usually ironic, cross-references; through them, the reader may link Dorothea to Antigone as well as to Don Quixote; he may view Casaubon as a mediocre namesake of a famous Renaissance theologian and also see the clergyman as a caricature of the "angelic doctor" Thomas Aquinas; he may learn to distinguish between the objectives of Fielding and those of modern novelist-historians. The associations are transhistorical; they render essences, establish continuities and discrepancies, provide meanings that are disengaged from time and space.

The ironies introduced by this outer ring of allusions are additive: the epigraphs taken from Elizabethan drama and sonnet cycles, like the narrator's own copious allusions to the richness of the Elizabethan age, are enlisted as a running background against which we must measure the poverty of a modern age epitomized by the mediocrity of the Middlemarchers in general and by Mr. Brooke's confused references to famous contemporaries like Wordsworth or Romilly. Mr. Brooke's continuous name-dropping only accentuates his inability to synthesize the strains of the present or the past (at one point, he is even tempted to claim Virgil as a friend, but recollects in time "that he had not had the personal acquaintance of the Augustan poet" [ch. 6]). However, as always in *Middlemarch*, this ironic frame of reference works in both ways. Although George Eliot exposes the unheroic nature of the present, she also dismisses any undue idealization of the past. Casaubon's stilted professions of love may hardly resemble the sentiments voiced in Renaissance poetry, yet the narrator reminds us that even "those sonnets to Delia which strike us as the thin music of a mandolin" might have proceeded from genuine human emotions (ch. 5). Again, the irony inherent in Dorothea's resolve to read Latin and Greek to Casaubon, "as Milton's daughters did to their father" (ch. 7), revolves around her failure to recognize that a father is not a husband and that Mr. Casaubon is no Milton; but the narrator also wants us to see that a similitude lurks in what seems so incongruously different. Milton's mythographic knowledge and sublime egotism may have resulted in a far greater work than the paltry "Key to All Mythologies"; yet that egotism does nonetheless link Milton the man to the human being who tries to exploit Dorothea as a secretary.

The associations created by these allusions are sometimes explicit, as in Lydgate's identification with the anatomist Andreas Vesalius, and sometimes playfully obscured: Elinor and Humphrey Cadwallader bear the Christian names of a duke and a duchess in Shakespeare's *Henry VI*, Part II; their surname is that of a famous Welsh king, as well as that of a misanthrope in one of Smollett's novels. Whether explicit or suggestive, these associations are always double-edged. Thus, for instance, when the ironic narrator takes the persecution of Faithful in Vanity Fair as the epigraph for chapter eighty-five of the novel, he soon goes beyond "immortal Bunyan" in his ensuing commentary by applying the incident to the degradation of Bulstrode. To understand the twist the narrator gives to Bunyan's fable we must first appreciate the difference between the guilty Puritan banker and the spotless hero of the Puritan fable, and then recognize that, at the very same time, there is both a difference and yet an analogy between their detractors. Faithful's torture at the hand of the "persecuting passions" requires no pity, for he knows himself to be above his torturers. Bulstrode's plight, however, is of a different nature, for he is accused by beings as fallible as himself: "The pitiable lot is that of the man who could not call himself a martyr even though he were to persuade himself that the men who stoned him were but ugly passions incarnate" (ch. 85). George Eliot thus appropriates Bunyan's parable, yet gives it a new moral dimension by making both victim and victimizers members of Vanity Fair.

The references to contemporary political and social events in the novel's second circle are less wide-ranging, confined as they are to the three-year period that elapses between Dorothea's first encounter with Casaubon in the late summer of 1829 and her marriage to Will Ladislaw in June of 1832. It is here that

George Eliot most approximates the role of "a diligent historian" (ch. 71). From the notebooks she kept it is clear that she wanted all of the novel's fictional events to be most carefully interspliced with the actual events alluded to in the course of her book.[12] The allusions to the spreading cholera plague—like the allusions to Burke and Hare, two criminals who sold the bodies of their victims to medical schools, and to St. John Long, a quack physician tried for manslaughter—not only gives us a concrete background for Lydgate's attempts to improve the state of medical science "in those days" (ch. 45) but also allow us to establish the dates of purely fictional occurrences like Lydgate's creation of the New Fever Hospital. Similarly, the many references to the country's agitation over the Reform Bill and to the consequent rise and fall of ministries and legislatures, which punctuate the entire novel, are far more precise than Trollope's similar attempts to connect the oscillations of Tory and Whig governments to the fates of his Barchesterians.

Despite their precision, however, these historical references are still metaphoric. *Middlemarch* is no more a social document than is *Barchester Towers*. The agitation that takes place in the outer world again acts as a correlative that allows us to measure the changes that take place in the lives of fictional characters. The scandal concerning Lydgate and Bulstrode gathers, for the Middlemarchers, "a zest which could not be won from the question whether the Lords would throw out the Reform Bill" (ch. 71). Although the town is concerned that the cholera epidemic has spread from Danzig to southern England and prepares itself for a "quarantine," the "Sanitary Meeting" convoked for that purpose addresses itself to the prevention of moral sickness: the "diseased state" that halted Raffles has infected Bulstrode and contaminated Lydgate, his unwilling accomplice, as well as their more than willing accusers.

12. See the list of historical and "private" (i.e. fictional) dates recorded in Quarry Two, one of George Eliot's notebooks, reprinted in *Quarry for Middlemarch*, ed. Anna Theresa Kitchel (Berkeley and Los Angeles, 1950), pp. 43, 45–46.

History blends with fiction, but fiction remains the novelist's prime vehicle for truth. It is no coincidence that Dorothea should reject "all the obstructions which had kept her silent" by choosing to marry Will Ladislaw precisely at the moment in which the House of Lords has, in a last-ditch effort at obstruction, thrown out the Reform Bill for the third time (ch. 83). Mr. Brooke, the unsuccessful Reformist candidate, is for once far less dejected "by the state of politics" than by the decision of his niece. Although he admits that the Lords may be "going too far," to Mr. Brooke, the "sad news" is "here—at home" (ch. 84). To the characters, their actions seem unrelated to the larger movements of history around them. But as always the novelist exploits analogy in contrast. The emancipated Dorothea renounces fortune and status in favor of a more purposeful life with Ladislaw; the English nation is about to liberate new sources of power by curtailing the privileges of a few. Dorothea marries Ladislaw in June; it is in June likewise that the Reform Bill is finally passed. Dorothea's "full nature" will spend itself "in channels which had no great name on the earth"; yet her diffusive effect on others proves that "the growing good of the world is partly dependent on unhistoric acts" ("Finale").

Whereas the novel's second circle creates the restrictions as well as the correspondences which arise from its historical setting, its third circle introduces the limitations and relations that arise from its geographical setting. Middlemarch is a mythical community in the Midlands. Its location in the "north-east corner of Loamshire" (ch. 1) makes it as imaginary as Trollope's Barchester. To be sure, George Eliot's careful attention to geographical detail (such as her placement of Middlemarch in relation to neighboring towns like Brassing, a railroad center to the South, and to Bilkeley, forty miles "in the North") lends a greater verisimilitude to her almost sociological dissection of the narrow provincial life which challenges the aspirations of Lydgate, Dorothea, Ladislaw, and Bulstrode. Having either come from or been educated far outside the town, these four characters are regarded with suspicion. Distrustful of all that is foreign to their experience, the clannish Middlemarchers resist change; like Trollope's Barchesterians, they regard "London as a centre of hostility to the country" (ch. 58). The town's doctors and pharmacists dislike Lydgate's innovations; its politicians and lawyers oppose social reform (to Lawyer Hawley, the "cursed alien blood" of the cosmopolitan Will Ladislaw is enough to indict him as a dangerous subversive "emissary"). The reactions of the Middlemarchers are enlisted by George Eliot in much the manner of a dramatist who relies on the fluctuating comments of a chorus. The subtle gradations and delicate ironies the novelist wants us to perceive are impossible for the provincial minds who prejudge Bulstrode and Lydgate and declare them to be equally guilty.

The Middlemarchers are thus treated far less sympathetically than Trollope's quaint Barchesterians. Their obstructionism is indirectly responsible for Lydgate's fall and Dorothea's exile. To them, "Pride must have a fall" (ch. 74), even if their own prejudices are warped by pride. The narrator satirizes their mentality: "To be candid, in Middlemarch phraseology, meant, to use an early opportunity of letting your friends know that you did not take a cheerful view of their capacity, their conduct, or their position; and a robust candor never waited to be asked for its opinion" (ch. 74). Yet George Eliot does not denounce the Middlemarchers as harshly as she attacked the society of St. Ogg's in *The Mill on the Floss*. Rather than indicting the town as a City of Destruction such as that which had suppressed Maggie, she regards it as a microcosm of the fallible world which characters and readers must learn to accept. Though imperfect, the Middlemarchers become—again, like a Greek chorus—the means for retribution and justice. It is through them that Lydgate comes to acknowledge the insufficiency of his belief in science, and Bulstrode realizes the insufficiency of his belief in a Providence that would erase his crime. As Bulstrode rides by the town's gathering rank and file, he feels secure and self-righteous, thinking that with the corpse of Raffles he has forever buried his past guilt. The gathering crowd, however, has come to listen to

Mr. Bambridge's account of his conversation with Raffles. The gossip about Bulstrode spreads "like the smell of fire," and men like Mr. Hawley are quick to draw their "inferences."

The inferences of Middlemarch, though still as one-sided as usual, prove correct. The town's opinions provide a further perspective on the novel's actions; its conservatism can be wholesome as well as destructive. Although their notions of justice are crude and imperfect, the Middlemarchers also possess an elementary righteousness. It is among them that Fred Vincy, the mayor's son, will find a new and better father in Caleb Garth, the traditionalist. Likewise, it is Mr. Vincy's sister who extends to Bulstrode the pity which he could not find in his conception of a legalistic God. Unlike the Swiss-educated Dorothea, Harriet Bulstrode is an "imperfectly-taught woman" (ch. 74). Vain of her husband's position, slightly petty in her delight in adornments, she hardly resembles the self-denying young idealist who married Mr. Casaubon; but Mrs. Bulstrode more than matches Dorothea's loyalty to her loveless mate when, in one of the novel's greatest scenes, she strips off her worldly vanities and silently shares her husband's degradation.

We have come to the novel's inner circle, to the plots surrounding Dorothea, Lydgate, Bulstrode, Fred, and the Garths. Just as these stories are enlarged by their relations to the outer three circles we have examined, so are they enlarged by their constant juxtaposition to each other. The links binding them are manifold. They are created through overt genealogical or professional ties, some of which are given at the outset, while others become apparent only as the novel proceeds. Through Featherstone's double kinship to the Vincys and the Garths, we are able to contrast Rosamond to Mary; through the ties between the Vincys and the Bulstrodes, we are able to appreciate the contest between Fred's two rival uncles, Featherstone and Bulstrode. The hidden family ties also invite comparisons, once they come to the fore: Featherstone acknowledges the existence of an illegitimate son, but his heir sells the lands the old miser expected him to keep; Bulstrode acknowledges the existence of his first wife's grandson, but Ladislaw rejects the money the banker expected him to take.

The various marriages in the novel furnish George Eliot with further opportunities for major counterpoints. Often mislabeled as a novel "about marriage" by readers who tend to forget that—from Chaucer to Lawrence—marriage has always been a prime metaphor for exploring the conditions of human existence, *Middlemarch* does nonetheless invite us to assess the marriages that take place at the outset and to scale them, at the end, against the delayed union of Mary and Fred. The marriages of the younger generation must be viewed not only in relation to each other but also to those of their elders. It is noteworthy that, with the exceptions of Celia's union to Sir James and Caleb Garth's happy existence with his school-teacher wife, all marriages are based on social or moral inequality. Thus, Mrs. Cadwallader will not let her husband forget that she stepped down the social ladder by marrying an impecunious and unaristocratic curate; Mrs. Vincy feels blessed that she has risen from an innkeeper's daughter to mayor's wife; Bulstrode the onetime city-clerk has married respectability by choosing a mate who belongs to one of Middlemarch's oldest families. This background creates a norm by which the progress of the younger characters can be measured. Rosamond, whose snobbery makes her disdainful of her mother's occasional vulgarity, aspires to marry above her station by choosing an outsider whose uncle is a baronet; her social pretensions only drag down Lydgate and lead to the eventual prostitution of his ideals as he becomes a fashionable doctor in a health spa. Rosamond's brother, however, chooses to marry beneath his social station, as does Dorothea by choosing Ladislaw; by so doing, both Fred and Dorothea rise in moral worth.

The connections afforded by the novel's plot lines are infinite. By gratefully accepting Bulstrode's financial aid, Lydgate invites comparison to both Will Ladislaw and Caleb Garth, who, for different reasons, have refused to be dependent on the banker. Mr. Brooke's unsuccessful attempt to address the unruly crowd who mocks his reformist speech is complemented by Caleb's success in calming the mob of laborers who threaten to destroy the railroad. As the novel moves into its last third, these connections mount: Ladislaw cannot communicate with Dorothea, despite their love for each other; Lydgate cannot communicate with Rosamond because their affection has waned. Ladislaw has previously tried opium as a casual experiment in "ecstasy"; Lydgate now tries opium as a desperate remedy to escape his present. Dorothea has given her mother's amethysts to Celia; Rosamond is reluctant to give up her "purple amethyst" necklace to Lydgate. Like the organisms examined by Bichat, this organic novel constantly reveals "new connections and hitherto hidden facts of structure," all of which "must be taken into account" (ch. 15).

We shall, however, account for only one more connecting device: the novel's imagery. Its threads are used ironically to interlink those three characters most desirous of finding connections of their own: Lydgate, Casaubon, and Dorothea. At first glance, Lydgate's clear-eyed search for a "primitive tissue" that would allow him to demonstrate "the more intimate relations of living structure" hardly seems to parallel either Mr. Casaubon's dim-sighted groping for the key that would allow him to demonstrate the intimate relations among dead mythologies or the myopic Dorothea's own eagerness "for a binding theory" which might bring her life into "strict connections" with the past (chs. 15, 10). Casaubon's researches are repeatedly described through allusions to fish and to water: the clergyman who possesses a "trout stream" in his estate is greatly interested in "the Philistine god Dagon and other fish-deities" (chs. 8, 20); his imaginary rivals bear the names of Carp, Pike, and Tench (ch. 29). It is hardly surprising that the witty Mrs. Cadwallader should deride this cold-blooded scholar by proclaiming that his family shield should bear three inky "cuttle-fish sable" (ch. 6). Dorothea is associated with water imagery. It is Miss Brooke's "stream of feeling" that encourages the lethargic Casaubon to grasp the fish which "rises to his bait" (chs. 7, 8). To Dorothea herself, his feelings and experience are like "a lake compared to my little pool" (ch. 3).

When this same imagery is suddenly applied to Lydgate, after his own investigations come to a halt as a result of his marital difficulties, it reinforces parallels we could not have foreseen. The Casaubon who has long been outdistanced by German writers and the Lydgate who derided the efforts of "plodding Germans" are now equally blocked in their explorations. Casaubon has slowed down Dorothea with him; "the full current of sympathetic motive in which her ideas and impulses" always flow is temporarily stagnated by the "shrimp-pool" of their marriage and by "the enclosed basin" of her husband's mind (chs. 10, 20). Lydgate, on the other hand, has been irrevocably slowed by the "water-nixie" he had hoped to domesticate; he has suddenly become conscious of "new elements in his life as noxious to him as an inlet of mud to a creature that has been used to breathe and bathe and dart after its illuminated prey in the clearest of waters" (ch. 58). The physician who delighted in the "melodious sea-breezes" emanating from his wife's piano (ch. 45) is now forced to sell his furniture and to try out less expensive habits, "for example, the substitution of cheap fish for dear" (ch. 56). His earlier identification with Andreas Vesalius was proleptic in ways he could not have foreseen. Lydgate told Rosamond that the Flemish physician "got shipwrecked just as he was coming from Jerusalem. . . . He died rather miserably" (ch. 45). The man who accuses Rosamond of wrecking his life will die before the age of fifty, after alternating, "according to the season, between London and a Continental bathing-place" ("Finale").

# 4

The contemporary reviewers of *Middlemarch* complained mildly about the book's lack of a happy ending. One critic deplored that the novel leaves the reader "sad and hungry"; another, though praising it as "the most remarkable work of the ablest of living novelists," likewise maintained that it would leave everyone "restless and distressed" and in a state of "profound despondency."[13] That George Eliot had foreseen such reactions is evident from her correspondence. To Alexander Main she wrote: "I need not tell you that my book will not present my own feeling about human life if it produces on readers whose minds are really receptive the impressions of blank melancholy and despair" (*Letters*, V, 261). While writing the concluding sections of the novel, she assured her publisher that there was to be "no unredeemed tragedy in the solution of the story" (*Letters*, V, 296).

The novel's "Finale" bears out the contentions of both the novelist and of her reviewers. When Lydgate sarcastically calls Rosamond his "basil plant" and tells her that "basil was a plant which had flourished wonderfully on a murdered man's brains," Rosamond responds in kind by reminding him that he had chosen to marry her: "Why then had he chosen her? It was a pity he had not had Mrs. Ladislaw, whom he was always praising and placing above her." The complaint is Rosamond's, but it is also made by the reader. Had Lydgate indeed married Dorothea! As in *Vanity Fair*—where Amelia's jealousy of her daughter resembles Rosamond's jealousy of Dorothea—we pause to take a retrospective look and consider what might have been. In *Middlemarch*, however, this feeling of incompleteness must be shared by the completeness achieved by Fred and Mary and must be balanced with the partial fulfillment of Dorothea. Moreover, whereas in *Vanity Fair* Amelia's persistent egotism can only be countered by the stoicism of a husband who "never said a word to Amelia, that was not kind and gentle,"[14] in *Middlemarch* even Rosamond's recrimination is softened by the narrator's addition that "she never uttered a word in depreciation of Dorothea, keeping in religious remembrance the generosity which had come to her aid in the sharpest crisis of her life" ("Finale"). In

13. Sidney Colvin, *Fortnightly Review*, XIX (1873), 142–147; *Quarterly Review*, CXXXIV (1873), 336–369.

14. *Vanity Fair*, ed. Geoffrey and Kathleen Tillotson (Boston, 1963), ch. 67.

George Eliot's less pessimistic outlook, generosity need not be a futile illusion.

*Middlemarch* is the work of a moralist. In it, George Eliot vindicated her belief in justice by resisting the temptation to yield to the logic of a grim and purposeless world. In *Vanity Fair* Becky is able to proclaim her "innocence," even though she may have been guilty of adultery and murder. In *Middlemarch*, where we witness Rosamond's flirtations and actually see Bulstrode produce Raffles' death, George Eliot can be true both to an actual and to an ideal world. She had failed to maintain this equipoise in the tragedy of Maggie Tulliver; she clung to it in *Middlemarch* by refusing to regard life as tragic:

> Some discouragement, some faintness of heart at the new real future which replaces the imaginary, is not unusual, and we do not expect people to be deeply moved by what is not unusual. That element of tragedy which lies in the very fact of frequency, has not yet wrought itself into the coarse emotion of mankind; and perhaps our frames could hardly bear much of it. (ch. 20)

The balances on which *Middlemarch* is built find a final expression in the novel's last sentence. George Eliot ends, as she had begun, with Dorothea's quest: "But the effect of her being on those around her was incalculably diffusive: for the growing good of the world is partly dependent on unhistoric acts; and that things are not so ill with you and me as they might have been, is half owing to the number who lived faithfully a hidden life, and rest in unvisited tombs." The sentence compresses the novelist's mixture of hope and despondency, acceptance and revulsion. Although George Eliot was unsatisfied with the standoff she had achieved and tried to magnify her yearnings in her last novel, *Daniel Deronda*, *Middlemarch* remains her masterpiece. The balances on which George Eliot's tragicomedy is based soon gave way to the unmitigated pessimism of Hardy's tragedies and to the equivocal comedy of Samuel Butler. To both of these writers, compromise was no longer possible. Only through destructive irony could they counter the ironies of existence itself. Thus *Middlemarch* stands as the last of the great Victorian efforts to find sanity in the motions of a disturbed and disquieting world.

# VII The End of Compromise: *Jude the Obscure* and *The Way of All Flesh*

In *Jude the Obscure* (1895) and *Ernest Pontifex, or The Way of All Flesh: A Story of English Domestic Life* (written from 1873 to 1884, but not published until 1903), Thomas Hardy and Samuel Butler tried to order, through tragedy and comedy respectively, the same irreconcilables faced by previous Victorian novelists. Hardy, who died in 1926 at the age of eighty-eight, insisted that *Jude* had been in advance of the times: accordingly in his 1912 "Postscript" to the novel he depicted himself as a herald of social progress whose views on marriage and education had been borne out by subsequent reforms. Samuel Butler, who died in 1902, also saw himself as an iconoclast ahead of his time who had been forced to adopt an "Ishmaelitish line" in order to maintain a precarious independence from the pressures of polite society.[1]

Although the differences that separate *Jude* and *The Way of All Flesh* from the works of earlier Victorian novelists are considerable, these differences cannot be attributed simply to Hardy's and Butler's more critical stance towards their age. The adjective "Victorian" has come to signify an undiscriminating acceptance of established social norms; yet the Victorian artist was in fact anything but a conformist. In *The Mill on the Floss* and *Middlemarch* George Eliot dwelt on the painful predicament of the idealist whose aspirations are thwarted by the material world with the same emotional intensity as the Hardy of *Tess of the D'Urbevilles* and *Jude*; in *Vanity Fair* Thackeray exposed the shams and self-delusions of a money-oriented so-

1. Henry Festing Jones, Samuel Butler, *Author of Erewhon: A Memoir in Two Volumes* (London, 1919), II, 39.

ciety that is Christian only in name with much of the same precision and forcefulness as Butler in *The Way of All Flesh*. Even Trollope, the most genial of the authors we have examined, directed his comedy against the values of the London world. By the time that Hardy and Butler came to write their novels the assault on false codes and value systems was hardly new. Steeped in the culture and assumptions of the Victorian era, both men basically remained within the track laid down by their predecessors.

Why, then, did both *Jude the Obscure* and *The Way of All Flesh* fail to gain the contemporary audiences which had once celebrated Dickens and George Eliot, Thackeray and Trollope? After the uproar following the publication of *Jude*, Hardy, cured of all "further interest in novel-writing,"[2] turned to lyrical poetry to express that deep personal sense of decay and hopelessness which he had allowed to surface in his last works of fiction. Butler, afraid that his contemporaries would not take him seriously, kept the manuscript of *The Way of All Flesh* hidden from all but his closest friends. Only after the posthumous publication of his novel, two years after Queen Victoria's death, did it gain a larger audience belonging to a new generation of readers now eagerly seizing on his indictment of the systems of religion, ethics, and education of their own Victorian forebears.

Hardy's and Butler's failure to capture a contemporary public for *Jude* and *The Way of All Flesh* can be attributed to their conscious breach of a compact still honored by their precursors. For all their pessimism, the earlier Victorian novelists refused to make negation the essence of their work. To resist despair became for them not only a deep personal need but also a kind of public task that was sure to be sanctioned by their readers. By

2. "Postscript," *Jude the Obscure*, ed. Robert B. Heilman, The Standard Edition: John Paterson, General Editor (New York, 1966), p. 48. Future references to his edition are given in the text; they will include citations to each of the six "parts" into which the novel is divided, since Hardy did not number his chapters consecutively but rather made each part begin with chapter one.

adopting the role of public moralists Dickens, George Eliot, Thackeray, Trollope, and even Meredith placed themselves in a position that was, by necessity, paradoxical: committed to uphold an idealism that was severely challenged by their skepticism, they were driven to exorcise a vision which all too often bordered on despair. The existence of a vast novel-reading public, as eager to be entertained as to be edified, afforded them a perfect opportunity for objectifying their personal doubts. To counter these doubts, however, the earlier Victorian novelists were also forced to compromise: their denials had to be tempered with the affirmation expected by their audience; in order to secure their reader's confidence they were led to mirror the values of the same society they found erratic and aimless.[3]

Finding their own idealism bruised beyond repair, Hardy and Butler refused to tailor their private vision to the expectations and emotional needs of their audience. As we shall see in greater detail in the section that follows, both men rejected the concessions by which earlier writers had managed to placate this shared need for affirmation and order. Although previous novelists had shown the strangulating effects that parents can have on their children, none of them would have portrayed the gruesome "triplet of little corpses" which Jude finds hanging in his closet or have endorsed Ernest Pontifex's caustic suggestion that men might emulate those respected insects, the ants and bees, who

3. It is noteworthy, in this connection, that the same public which found *Jude* distasteful had, twenty years before, celebrated George Eliot as its supreme spokesman. In her private life, George Eliot had denied the social conventions of her time: by choosing to live with a man legally married to someone else, she was, in fact, enacting a role quite similar to that played, in Hardy's novel, by Jude Fawley and Sue Bridehead. Initially, George Eliot's readers did not know the identity of the writer on whom they had bestowed their approval, but when her identity was revealed they readily accepted her unconventionality, as well as her agnosticism, for by then they had fully recognized that in her fiction she remained a moralist eager to uphold ethical standards. Although her readers were, by and large, orthodox Christians relying on the assurances of a Christian dispensation, they partook of her belief in altruism and love and derived a satisfaction from her efforts to order a potentially chaotic existence.

"sting their fathers to death as a matter of course."[4] George Eliot's suicidal Mr. Tulliver, who admits on his deathbed that "This world's been too many for me,"[5] at least is spared the troublesome sight of his dead children who perish in expiation for his mistakes; Jude, on the other hand, is not allowed to die until he has witnessed the extinction of all his offspring, "Done because we are too menny" (Pt. VI, ch. 2).

Positioned between Becky Sharp's frank egotism and Amelia's sentimental self-denials, Dobbin the idealist could still find a niche in life by becoming the hopeful father of a child; suspended between the Tulliver and Dodson approaches to life, Maggie could at least rise above both extremes by enacting the role of noble martyr. Jude Fawley, on the other hand, torn between the dualities represented by Arabella and Sue, becomes the victim of an idealism that proves futile and debilitating. Whereas George Eliot tries to use Maggie's death to fashion a purifying belief in duty, toleration, and love, Hardy uses the death of Jude and his children as a merciful release from an unbearable life of contradictions. He refuses to endow Jude's alienation and death with any kind of hopeful overtones or redemptive touches; his protagonist remains, in Sue Bridehead's words, a foolish "dreamer of dreams," a "tragic Don Quixote" (Pt. IV, ch. 1). Sue herself, who resembles Dorothea Brooke when she denies her passion by returning to an older and repulsive husband, is treated with devastating irony; whereas George Eliot guardedly endorses the "Quixotic" Dorothea, Hardy regards Sue's final renunciation as a meaningless gesture that merely confirms that she has become dead to life. Butler, too, mocks the "lofty Quixotism" that would be "content with virtue as her own reward" (ch. 19). In telling the story of Ernest Pontifex, he deliberately resists the temptation of making his young hero

---

4. *Ernest Pontifex, or The Way of All Flesh,* ed. Daniel F. Howard, Riverside Edition (Boston, 1964), ch. 24. Future references in the text are to this edition of the novel.

5. *The Mill on the Floss,* ed. Gordon S. Haight, Riverside Edition (Boston, 1961), Bk. V, ch. 7.

a martyr. If Jude dies as the victim of his own sentimentality, Ernest lives by dulling himself to all sentimental claims on his person. He survives, as Becky Sharp had done, by unashamedly enjoying his money and health and embracing the ways of Vanity Fair. To Butler, "Pleasure, after all, is a safer guide than either 'right' or 'duty,'" those sacrosanct Victorian abstractions (ch. 19).

Long before Hardy decided to give up novel-writing altogether and Butler decided to keep *The Way of All Flesh* shrouded from the public eye, both writers had met with considerable difficulties in obtaining a large audience for productions which were personal and idiosyncratic.[6] Hardy was furious at discovering that the success of *Far From the Madding Crowd*, which he had published anonymously, was caused by the public's assumption that the work had been written by George Eliot. For his part, Butler swore that he would never court readers by imitating the successful *Middlemarch*, a novel he denounced as a "long-winded piece of brag."[7]

What finally caused the uproar over *Jude the Obscure*, like the previous controversy over Hardy's *Tess of the D'Urbervilles* (1891), was the author's unwillingness to return anything for what he had taken away. Hardy's readers were appalled by his denial of the hopefulness that they had come to take for granted from the Victorian artist. As far back as 1853, Matthew

6. It is interesting that George Meredith, himself an unconventional writer without a large following and a reader for a Victorian publishing house noted for printing unusual works, should have rejected both the manuscript of Butler's satirical fantasy *Erewhon* and the manuscript of Hardy's first novel, *Desperate Remedies*. Although both works were eventually published, *Desperate Remedies* (1871) did not appeal to the public, while the mild popularity of *Erewhon* (1872) was largely attributable to the sudden taste for Utopian fiction brought about by the publication of Bulwer-Lytton's *The Coming Race* in the previous year.

7. Jones, I, 184. Still, Butler carefully read *Middlemarch* before embarking on the novel that was to become *The Way of All Flesh;* George Eliot's successful fiction was, after all, the work of one who, like Hardy and himself, was an agnostic and a believer in natural evolution.

Arnold had given his reasons for removing the pessimistic "Empedocles on Etna" from his volume of poems: the function of literature, he implied, was above all to inspire and to affirm, to hold out universal ideals which an author could share with his public. The artist's duty, therefore, called for a rejection of all those situations in which "the suffering finds no vent in action; in which a continuous state of mental distress is prolonged, unrelieved by incident, hope, or resistance; in which there is everything to be endured, nothing to be done."[8] Arnold's description fits the "state of mental distress" of the reader invited to share Jude's prolonged plight. In *The Ordeal of Richard Feverel*, Meredith at least permits the reader to hope that the combined efforts of Austin Wentworth, Lady Blandish, and Mrs. Berry might rescue Richard's son from the threat posed by Sir Austin; in *Jude*, however, no such sop is given to the reader—no forward look is possible. Even if one of Jude's children managed to survive its father, it could hope for no better future at the hands of the indifferent Arabella or the impotent widow Edlin. Hardy systematically undermines all the conventional means by which the Victorian reader had been conditioned to resist a "state of mental distress" such as that depicted in *Jude*. It was this deliberate contravention of his readers' wishes, his utterly uncompromising stance, which forever alienated the novelist from the public at large.

Butler, on the other hand, did not risk offending his readers. In his case, it is not his lack of resistance to despair but the idiosyncratic nature of that resistance which would have infuriated a public still nourished on Dickens and George Eliot. *The Way of all Flesh* is a private work, built on the eccentric evolutionary creed by which Samuel Butler had been able to reconcile himself to his parents and to the world at large. Although the novel is "Victorian" in its attack on false values and false institutions, Butler's introduction of his own inverted values betrays his un-

8. "Preface" (1853), *The Poetical Works of Matthew Arnold*, ed. C. B. Tinker and H. F. Lowry (London, 1957), p. xviii.

easiness as artist and thinker. Like Hardy, Butler rejects the compromises by which previous writers had balanced the claims of the head and the heart. But whereas Hardy's tragic novel is sustained by the emotional impact of a relentless pessimism which finds its only release through Jude's unheroic death, Butler's novel is marred by the tentativeness of its comic catharsis. The fable of Ernest Pontifex's rebirth through a conversion to the ways of Mammon and the flesh seems perversely artificial, built on Butler's tenuous belief in an unconscious memory, the ancestral will which restores to Ernest's children the vitality of his great-grandfather, John Pontifex. In *Our Mutual Friend* Dickens managed to vindicate an irrational fantasy through the persuasiveness of a comic fairy tale; the Butler who tries to vindicate his own fantasy of renovation is too self-conscious—a rationalist distrustful of the irrationality of his dream.

Writers like Dickens and George Eliot managed both to overcome their personal sense of alienation and to provide the Victorian reader with the means for a satisfying affirmation. The Hardy who despairs of all affirmation and the Butler who doubts his right to affirm were unable to continue this tradition. After *Jude*, Hardy the poet continued to be honored as a relic of Victorian pessimism; yet, like that other poet of despair, Matthew Arnold, he never could command as large an audience as that which had once listened to Tennyson. Butler, always more furtive, stored his novel in a drawer and devoted himself to bagatelles. Just as those self-projections, Ernest and his mentor Overton, delight in each other's company in the concluding chapters of *The Way of All Flesh*, so did Butler continue to amuse himself in the concluding days of his life by writing a book on Alpine art and a parody of a Handel cantata, by engaging in eccentric speculations about the identities of Homer and Shakespeare, and, just before his death, by revising his radical views in the mellow *Erewhon Revisited* (1901). By addressing himself, his best audience, he could at least privately become reconciled to an intractable world.

I

Like *The Mill on the Floss* and *The Ordeal of Richard Feverel*, *Jude the Obscure* and *The Way of All Flesh* are *Bildungsromane* structured around the ordeals of a young idealist who seeks to find a place in a world that proves hostile to his aspirations. In their pilgrimage through space and time Jude Fawley and Ernest Pontifex, like Richard and Maggie, are ironically linked by their creators to Bunyan's archetypal pilgrim Christian, who on his way to a more wholesome and redemptive life had escaped the City of Destruction and Vanity Fair.[9] Hardy's novel is divided into six parts; Butler's, into seven. Each of these divisions is associated with a distinct phase in the protagonist's development, as well as with a spatial locality related to that particular phase. In *Jude*, where the part divisions even take the name of localities, the progress of Jude and his fellow pilgrims, Sue and Phillotson, is circuitous. Only the initial movement is direct and linear. By moving from Marygreen to Christminster, Jude progresses, like Richard Feverel and Maggie Tulliver, from rural, childlike simplicity to urban, adult experience. Like Richard in London or Maggie in St. Ogg's, Jude is disappointed by his experiences in the city of Christminster, the university town to which he has been drawn; but unlike Richard and Maggie, who at least try to return to Raynham Abbey and Dorlcote Mill, Jude has no desire to retrace his steps by going back to his former existence in the country. Marygreen has hardly been a

9. Butler's original name for Ernest was "Christian"; Ernest's biographer Overton is a dramatist who has written a burlesque of *Pilgrim's Progress* and "made an important scene of Vanity Fair, with Mr. Greatheart, Apollyon, Christiana, Mercy, and Hopeful as the principal characters" (ch. 27). As a child, before he starts out on his journey, Jude thinks of "Apollyon lying in wait for Christian" (Pt. I, ch. 3); thereafter, he identifies Christminster, his goal, with Christian's own destination, the new Jerusalem. Like Christian, Jude will expire in this new Jerusalem; but his ignoble death from exhaustion only parodies the glorious new life granted to Bunyan's hero. For Meredith's and George Eliot's adaptations of *Pilgrim's Progress*, see pp. 124, 135, and 191, above.

paradise. Jude thus departs from Christminster in search of new outlets for his unabated idealism; but his displacement persists in Melchester, Shaston, and Aldrickham. The disappointed Jude discovers that for Sue and himself there is no one road, no straight and narrow way to the Ideal.

In Part V, chapter five, Hardy describes the road to Stoke-Barehills. The highway that connects the town to Aldbrickham branches into two separate byways: in the past, the narrator says, there were "endless questions of choice between the respective ways," but now, with the advent of the railroad, such choices have become meaningless: nobody travels on the "great western highway" any longer. As a modern pilgrim, Jude comes to discover that his choices of highways and byways have become equally futile. Marygreen is associated with the ways of Arabella and the flesh; Christminster, where Jude meets Sue the freethinker, represents "an intellectual track [rather] than a theological" (Pt. II, ch. 2). After both of these "tracks" are found wanting, Jude turns to Melchester, a locality which, in Hardy's overly explicit gloss, stands for "the ecclesiastical and altruistic life, as distinct from the intellectual and emulative life" (Pt. III, ch. 1). His passion for Sue also vitiates this mode of fulfillment. Jude the Hebraist turns into a skeptical agnostic, while Sue the Hellenist becomes a nunlike enthusiast who mortifies her flesh. Their wanderings have been circular, overlapping, objectless. The pilgrim who started out so hopefully, who had in his youthful enthusiasm incribed "THITHER J.F." on the bark of the signpost that pointed to Christminster, returns, shattered and disillusioned, to the onetime city of his dreams. Christminster has turned into a necropolis, the burial ground of dead illusions. Once back, the only road left for Jude to travel leads to the obscurity of the grave.

In *The Way of All Flesh* the stages in Ernest Pontifex's development also parallel the movements from place to place. As in *Jude*, the direction is away from agrarian simplicity (Paleham village) to the complexities of city life (London). The first part of Volume I depicts this movement in the person of Ernest's grandfather, George Pontifex, who deserts his strong rustic parents and gives birth to a debilitated city son, Theobald. The progress of Theobald's son will recapitulate the same movement: Ernest will march from childhood in the country at Battersby-on-the-Hill (Volume I, ii), to his education at Roughborough (II, i) and Cambridge (II, ii), on to his adult experience as a prisoner in the city jail (III, i), as a penurious family man living in "the neighbourhood of the Elephant and Castle" (III, ii), and, finally, as a wealthy bachelor able to settle, free from all family and financial obligations, in the most fashionable quarters of London (III, iii). Significantly enough, Ernest's movement is backwards as well as forwards. He and his children can recapture in the city the same instinctual vigor possessed in the country by his great-grandfather the carpenter. To counter a Hardy-like pessimism Butler thus resorts to a fantasy which, despite its more "scientific" trappings, distinctly resembles Emily Brontë's own eugenic myth about a family's instinct for survival. Just as the last of the Earnshaws and Lintons resist the death wish of a previous generation, so does Ernest resist the crippling handicaps imposed on him by his parents. Jude succumbs, like the first Catherine Earnshaw, because he is confounded by the conflicting ways that block his progress; Ernest, however, like the second Catherine, finds a thoroughfare binding past and future. He is, as his surname indicates, a bridge-builder, Butler's illustration of the beneficent powers of the way of all flesh.

Ernest the bridge-builder thus can revert to the strength of the original Pontifex. Although his parents have made him unfit for life, his re-education in the city and the education he provides there for his children allow his descendants to regain their original identity. Jude, on the other hand, is the victim of his ancestry. His aunt Drusilla has urged him not to marry his cousin Sue because such a union would only result in a "terrible intensification of unfitness—two bitters in a dish" (Pt. III, ch. 6). Jude's surname, "Fawley," not only betokens the folly of his endeavors (like Butler's narrator Overton, Hardy repeatedly stresses the foolishness of his protagonist[10]), but also his accursed, fallen stock. Jude and Sue discover that a "family curse" thwarts their aspirations; Sue complains that an ineluctable "tragic doom" overhangs their family, "as it did the house of Atreus" (Pt. V, ch. 4).

Both *Jude the Obscure* and *The Way of All Flesh* thus take up the dilemma of characters who discover that their identities are predetermined. For Jude and Sue, this discovery only accentuates their helplessness. Hardy bemoans the fact that a man's capacity for change does not match the motions of the fluctuating world into which he is placed; looking at her two children, Sue concludes that she and Jude are merely "beforehand" in their inability to adapt: "In fifty, a hundred, years, the descendants of these two will act and feel worse than we. They will . . . be afraid to reproduce" (Pt. V, ch. 4). Butler, on the other hand, suggests through Ernest's story that man can and must adapt himself to the mutations to which he is exposed. Ernest may not completely recover his great-grandfather's original grace, but he can find satisfaction in building a bridge for a saner race. By resorting to the theories he had developed in his bizarre writings on biological evolution,[11] Butler tried to arrest Hardy's dispiriting vision of a world in which the survival of the fittest failed to correspond to the survival of the best. Unlike Hardy, he equated goodness with a healthy instinct for survival; like D. H. Lawrence, though far more tentatively, he celebrated the power of the flesh. If Jude dies from the burden of an excessive

10. Jude is called a "tender-hearted fool" and "ridiculously affectionate fellow" (Pt. I, ch. 10; Pt. II, ch. 2); Overton repeatedly laments the "almost incredible foolishness" that Ernest is capable of (ch. 34).

11. Butler's *Life and Habit: An Essay After a Completer View of Evolution* (1877), the fullest exposition of his views, was written at the same time that he was working on his novel. It is directly referred to by Overton in chapter thirty-three of the novel and echoes some of the theories later expounded by the matured Ernest. For a fuller discussion of the relationship between Butler's evolutionary doctrines and *The Way of All Flesh*, see my *Religious Humanism and the Victorian Novel* (Princeton, 1965), pp. 244–256, *et passim*.

self-consciousness, Ernest survives when his unconscious self, the "dumb Ernest" who dwells "within him" (ch. 31), finally displaces the "conscious Ernest" that parents and teachers have tried to hammer into shape.

Even though Jude acts out his creator's despair while Ernest comes to typify his creator's tentative hopes, the careers of both characters are enlisted to deny the ideals by which the previous Victorian moralists had come to terms with the world. For Hardy as for Butler, the old gospels of love, disinterestedness, and renunciation have become invalid. The creeds of self-denial and duty which others try to impose on Jude and Ernest only elicit a "bitter laugh" (*Jude*, Pt. III, ch. 7). Like the sarcastic Overton, the embittered Jude discovers that "Everything seems to turn to satire" (Pt. III, ch. 7). Both novels exploit the glaring gap between practice and ideal; both are directed against any undue idealization of marriage and family, education, and religion.

The convention of a happy marriage, still relied on in *Our Mutual Friend* or *Middlemarch*, is as much denied in Hardy's tragic novel as it is in Butler's comic fantasy. Jude's marriage to Arabella and Sue's union to Phillotson prove disastrous; their children are destroyed and all the marriage partners but Arabella, maimed. Similarly, the union between Ernest's parents and his own union to Ellen are at least potentially destructive. Butler must resort to a quirk of fate to save Ernest from being tied to a coarse, alcoholic wife. In Hardy's book, Arabella returns from abroad to be remarried to Jude; in Butler's novel, however, Ellen is conveniently shipped off to allow the matured Ernest to become a happy bachelor like his godfather Overton. Jude's aunt Drusilla and Ernest's aunt Alethea, who utter each novelist's views on the proper behavior in the worlds they have created, are both spinsters who have deliberately avoided the marriage bond.

Hardy's and Butler's attacks on education and religion are equally relentless. Although Jude is prevented from entering the university, Hardy makes it clear that the education he would have received there would have been as worthless as Ernest's training at Roughborough and Cambridge. Both men must divest themselves of their religious hankering after a spiritual fulfillment based on self-renunciation and service to the poor. Jude abandons his theological pretensions when he finds that neither fasting nor reading in the "Ascetics of the second century" can dispel his mounting passion for Phillotson's wife. When Sue joins him, he takes his collection of religious books, cuts "the volumes into pieces as well as he could, and with a three-pronged fork [shakes] them over the flames" (Pt. III, ch. 9; Pt. IV, ch. 3). On finding his crusade among the poor to be a mockery, Ernest, too, gives in to his carnal desires; before his attempted rape of Miss Maitland, the young clergyman makes sure to kick his Bible into the farthest corner of his room (ch. 60).

*Jude the Obscure* is an elegy lamenting the death of nineteenth-century idealism. Walking through the streets of Christminster at night Jude recalls Matthew Arnold's words about the sweetness of medieval Oxford: "Beautiful city! so venerable, so lovely, so unravaged by the fierce intellectual life of our century, so serene! . . . Her ineffable charm keeps calling us to the true goal of all of us, to the ideal, to perfection" (Pt. II, ch. 1).[12] Jude hears other echoes from the past. He hears Browning, "the last of the optimists," speaking of a beneficent "general plan"; he hears the confident strains of Sir Robert Peel, the political reformer. Jude the dreamer has come to his New Jerusalem in pursuit of an absolute. That earlier pilgrim to the university town, Phillotson the schoolmaster, tells his former student how disenchanted he has become ("The idea was given up years ago"), but Jude refuses to give up his obsession with the ephemeral gleam that has drawn him to the city of his vision: "I have never forgotten it. It was that which brought me to this part of

12. The quotation is taken from the concluding paragraph of Arnold's preface to his *Essays in Criticism,* First Series (1865). Hardy refers to Arnold earlier in the chapter when he has Jude reflect about the succession of Oxford graduates "from the friend and eulogist of Shakespeare" (Ben Jonson) "down to him who has recently passed into silence" (Arnold, who died in 1888).

the country" (Pt. II, ch. 4). Like the Ernest Pontifex who becomes infected by the religious mania of his fellow students at Cambridge, Jude must be brought to discover that the realities of the modern world are inhospitable to the aspirations of a Victorian idealist. When daylight replaces night, Christminster seems appalling in its decay: "What at night had been perfect and ideal was by day the more or less defective real." But Jude persists; he tries to read into the crumbling Gothic walls "the original idea" to which he clings so avidly. Lest we miss his delusion, Hardy steps in in his own voice: "He did not at that time see that medievalism was as dead as fernleaf in a lump of coal; that other developments were shaping in the world around him, in which Gothic architecture and its associations had no place. The deadly animosity of contemporary logic and vision towards so much of what he held in reverence was not yet revealed to him" (Pt. II, ch. 2). Jude the stonemason cannot repair the ruins of an irretrievable past; his Ruskinian identification with the "dead handicraftsmen" of the Middle Ages is ironic, for it only betokens his own obsolescence.

At the end of the novel Jude, now reunited with Arabella, again looks yearningly at the Gothic walls of the Christminster colleges. The experiences he has undergone between his two visits have convinced him of the futility of all ideals. He is now Arabella's possession, and Arabella has become the voice of the "deadly" logic he has tried to stifle:

> "What are you looking at?"
> "Stupid fancies. I see, in a way, those spirits of the dead again, on this my last walk, that I saw when I first walked here!"
> "What a curious chap you are!"
> "I seem to see them, and almost hear them rustling. But I don't revere all of them as I did then. I don't believe in half of them. The theologians, the apologists, and their kin the metaphysicians, the high-handed statesmen, and others no longer interest me. All that has been spoilt for me by the grind of stern reality!" (Pt. VI, ch. 9)

*The Way of All Flesh*, too, depicts the predicament of one whose "sanguine trustfulness" leads him to believe in the pietisms and creeds invented by those who would deny the grind of a stern reality (ch. 35). Ernest is the victim of the sham "unworldliness" which some, like his parents, use to cover up their inadequacies as human beings, and which others, like his grandfather or Dr. Skinner, exploit in order to advance their own self-interests. Like Hardy, Butler deplores "that crop of earnest thinkers" sown, in a previous generation, by moralists like Dr. Arnold (ch. 6). Although Theobald proposes that his son be christened George, after his father the publisher of religious tracts, he is overruled by George Pontifex himself: "The word 'earnest' was just beginning to come into fashion, and he thought the possession of such a name might, like his having been baptised in water from the Jordan, have a permanent effect upon his character, and influence him for good during the more critical periods of his life" (ch. 18). The influence of the name, however, proves noxious. Like Jude, Butler's hero is gradually divested of his earnest trust in impracticable ideals. Instead, he learns to laugh and cease to look "so preternaturally grave" (ch. 37). He must reject all those false teachers who, under the guise of watching over "the development of [his] moral and spiritual nature" only undermine his instinctive capacity for survival (ch. 40).

Jude is seduced by those bodiless voices that emanate from the walls of Christminster; Ernest, by the appeal of parents whose so-called "moral influence" consists of impressing him with a deep sense of his inferiority and sinfulness (ch. 1), and of those false peddlers of spiritual truth who practice on the young man's desire to become a chosen vessel. Like Jude, Ernest finds these appeals to be spurious; but whereas Hardy shares Jude's yearnings after an impossible spiritual ideal, Butler, in the shape of Overton, laughs at Ernest's fumbles and declares all such urges to be a sham. Thus, while Jude finds the way of the flesh to be as unsatisfactory as the way of the spirit, Ernest becomes a convert to Butler's hedonism. After the painful process of cutting his ties, the young man learns what his mentor Overton has known all along, namely, that "All animals, except man, know that the principal business of life is to enjoy it" (ch. 19). Under Overton's supervision, Ernest studies the animals in a zoo and learns more from them than from his former teachers. According to the cynical Overton, "Young people have a marvelous faculty of either dying or adapting themselves to circumstances" (ch. 1). Jude dies; Ernest adapts. Butler makes sure that the "circumstances" for Ernest's adaption are propitious. By rescuing the young man from the life of poverty that crushes Jude, Butler prevents Ernest from succumbing to the fate of his "obscure" counterpart.

In his 1912 postscript to *Jude the Obscure* Hardy described the work as a novel of social protest modeled along the lines of a Greek tragedy. But neither *Jude* nor *The Way of All Flesh* can be regarded as works of social protest, for in both society has become totally meaningless. Both novels end with a withdrawal from all social interaction. The proletarian Jude withdraws by dying; the middle-class Ernest, by becoming, like Butler himself, a financially secure and self-satisfied writer of books unread by his contemporaries. The dignitary from Biblioll College (presumably Balliol College at Oxford) advises Jude: "I venture to think that you will have a much better chance of success in life by remaining in your own sphere" (Pt. II, ch. 6). The words are cruel. Through them, Hardy does more than indict the English class system; he signals the death of the stratified society which, in an earlier age, could have made room for Jude in one of its "spheres." There is no place for this constitutional misfit. Like the Ernest Pontifex who discovers that life among the poor is but a means to an end, Jude soon ceases to identify himself with his fellow workers. Hoping to find creatures as oppressed and obscure as himself, he is met only with incomprehension; neither the stonemasons nor the undergraduates in the tavern can understand his aims. He feels no more communion with the laborers who brag that books are unnecessary than with the students who pretend to learn from books. Jude's final alienation from society is more logical and meaningful than the reintegration that Sue, the other "Ishmaelite," forces herself to undergo.

For Butler, too, society has become a meaningless abstraction. Although he celebrates the earthy vitality of Mrs. Jupp, who belongs to the lower classes, and has Ernest ship out his children to be brought up by proletarian foster parents, Butler is equally disposed to celebrate the self-sufficiency of the aristocratic Towneley, Ernest's idol. Both novelists imply that man can be happy only if his heredity has provided him with the will to be happy. And happiness itself can be found best in isolation, away from involvement, away from the debilitating claims of marriage and family. For Dickens and George Eliot, Eugene Wrayburn and Dorothea Brooke can find fulfillment by marrying their social inferiors; for Hardy and Butler, creatures like Jude and Ernest are clearly better off not marrying at all.

To Hardy, Jude's contraventions of moral and social customs seemed, in retrospect, "a good foundation for the fable of a tragedy" ("Postscript"). Hardy hoped that England's obsolete marriage laws could, like the ancient religious observances binding the hero of a Greek tragedy, be used as "the tragic machinery of the tale." Confident that his readers would find "certain cathartic, Aristotelian qualities" in Jude's story, Hardy self-consciously tried to emulate the classic Greek tragedians. In what he evidently regarded as the climax of the novel's dramatic action, the scene in which Jude and Sue discover the bodies of the dead children, Hardy has Jude quote from Aeschylus:

> ". . . What can be done?" She stared at Jude, and tightly held his hand.
> "Nothing can be done," he replied. "Things are as they are, and will be brought to their destined issue."
> She paused. "Yes! Who said that?" she asked heavily.
> "It comes in the chorus of the *Agamemnon*. It has been in my mind continually since this happened." (Pt. VI, ch. 2)

It is noteworthy that *The Way of All Flesh* should contain an entire chapter devoted to a satirical attack on the "orthodox tragedians." In an essay presumably written during his undergraduate days at Cambridge, Ernest professes to be "repelled" by "those works of Aeschylus, Sophocles, and Euripides which are most generally admired." Against these, he opposes the comedies and parodies of Aristophanes, a "keen, witty, outspoken writer" who exposed the tragedians as a "fraud" (ch. 46). Overton, himself a wit and writer of stage burlesques, obviously approves of his godson's chosen target; he reprints the essay in its entirety, "re-edited" by the matured Ernest, now his collaborator.

As a novel of ideas, *The Way of All Flesh*, like Ernest's essay, is a polemic against a tragic view of existence. Nonetheless, Butler's novel comes perilously close to ending on the tragic note of *Jude the Obscure*. Ernest's final disengagement is artificial and contrived. The childless Jude dies yoked to Arabella while yearning for Sue the idealist; Ernest lives happily only because he has been so conveniently removed from the mate who gave birth to his vital children. Yet, had Ernest been deprived of the legacy which Overton withholds from him until the very end of the novel, he might easily have succumbed to the same despair which engulfs Hardy's protagonist. It is only a stroke of luck that allows Ernest to become the blissful companion of Overton the humorist. Butler created Overton (his contented older self) in order to be able to look at Ernest (his anguished younger self). He needed this detached comic persona to protect himself from self-pity, from indulging in the commiseration which Hardy shows toward his own self-projection. Overton dismisses such commiseration through laughter, but his laughter is unsure. His tone, at times, seems closer to that of one who, like Brontë's Lockwood, deliberately dulls himself to pain and involvement than it is to the more complicated voice of Thackeray's cheerfully "miserable" Showman. Hidden beneath Overton's fine witicisms and *bon mots* lies a negativism that is quite as bleak as Hardy's own: "Could any death be so horrible as birth? Or any decrepitude as awful as childhood in a happy united God-fearing family?" (ch. 6). The lines might well have been spoken by Jude and Sue at the highpoint of their embitterment.

As we shall see in the next section of this chapter, *Jude the Obscure* is not a tragedy in the classical sense—Hardy's efforts to make it so notwithstanding. But the intensity of the novel's pathos makes it superior to Butler's avoidance of tragedy through a laughter that has turned tentative and circumspect. In its unadulterated pessimism, *Jude* struck a deathblow at the idealism that had shaped a *Middlemarch* or *Our Mutual Friend*. In his efforts to purge himself of that pessimism, Samuel Butler, too, marked an end to the Victorian novel. Brilliant as it is, *The Way of All Flesh* shows, above all, how inadequate the comic conventions that had been used to counter despair had become by the conclusion of the nineteenth century.

2

In the first chapter of Part Six of *Jude the Obscure* Hardy sets the scene for the high point of his intended tragedy. Jude has returned to Christminster after his fruitless wanderings; he is accompanied by Sue and their two children and by Father Time, his son by Arabella. Mocked by old acquaintances who point out to him that he has not accomplished any of the "great things" he had set out to do on leaving the town, Jude harangues the crowd who gathers around him. Growing increasingly self-defensive, he heeds neither Sue's entreaties to stop indulging himself before his listeners nor Father Time's ominous mournfulness: Sue is "screened" from Jude's sight; the child stands "submerged and invisible in the crowd." Jude reviles the townspeople for ridiculing his failures and insists that they extend him sympathy, instead. He feels that the humanity congregated on the square should identify with his plight and apply his experience to their own:

> "I may do some good before I am dead—be a sort of frighful example of what not to do; and so illustrate a moral story," continued Jude, beginning to grow bitter, though he had opened serenely enough. "I was perhaps, after all, a victim to the spirit of mental and social restlessness that makes so many unhappy in these days!"

Jude's words are tinged with irony. He thinks of himself as being at the low point of his travails, but he is unaware of the full terror that still lies in store for him. The "self-command" he possesses in addressing the crowd vanishes when, in the next chapter, he must survey the gruesome spectacle of his dead children. Their deaths will be brought about by the two people he has ignored in his efforts to secure the sympathy of his audience. And yet, despite this dramatic irony, the emotions that Jude demands from his audience, pity and fear, are akin to those which Hardy demands from readers about to witness his hero's "frightful example." Hardy presumably wants us to learn "what not to do" from Jude's personal tragedy and eventual death. He expects his readers to undergo a catharsis, to emerge sadder and wiser by understanding the forces which conspire against Jude's fulfillment.

What, however, is "the frightful example" we are to derive from Jude's story? What are the causes that precipitate his downfall? Hardy's attempts to find a "tragic machinery" for his novel by blaming Jude's fate on social incomprehension and on external agents like Father Time and Sue Bridehead only reveal that, like Jude himself, Hardy clings to outward explanations for what remains an inward state of mental despair. Even though Hardy tries to cast Jude as a modern Oedipus or Lear, there is no "moral" to be drawn from his pain, no catharsis to be gained from a familiarity with his mistakes. Jude is a victim, not of the incomprehension of society or of obsolete marriage laws, but of his creator's dim view of an existence drained of all hope, an existence governed by natural forces that "obscure" all noble action and devastate men like pigs. It is the consistency of Hardy's despairing outlook, rather than his attempted explanations, that lend Jude's story its poignancy and emotional impact.

Hardy relies on Father Time as the agent for the novel's most painful scene. The child introduces himself by mutely proclaiming that "All laughter comes from misapprehension" (Pt. V, ch. 3). He is but a symbolic representation of a universal sadness that Hardy cannot really fit into the intellectual schemes or psychological explanations to which he resorts throughout the book—the "internal warfare between flesh and spirit" (Pt. III, ch. 10), the conflict between the claims of religion and intellect, the opposition between society and the individual. When Jude first sees the boy and asks him, "What's this round your neck," we almost expect this appearance to say, "An Albatross" and to introduce himself as a reincarnated Ancient Mariner who has come across "some great Atlantic of Time" (Pt. III, ch. 10). The child does not quite say that; the object around his neck is just a key—the key to his trunk. Yet we know why he is there, why Hardy has waited so long before introducing this tragic catalyst. The boy appears to shorten what would otherwise have been an unending process of self-division and torture. He has come to unlock the true nature of Hardy's universe, to end the impossible "two-in-oneness" that Sue and Jude have tried so long to maintain. He is Hardy's pessimism personified.

Though a child, Father Time is far more "ancient" than Sue and Jude who, as Arabella contemptuously remarks, still act like small children. He represents Experience. His features are stylized; as Sue notes, his face is like the distorted mask of Melpomene, the muse of Tragedy. If Jude and Sue are "horribly sensitive," this creature is so sensitive to pain that it interprets Sue's momentary disillusion as a mandate for carrying out her death wish ("all is trouble, adversity, suffering"). By killing himself and the other two children, Father Time merely epitomizes the masochism already inherent in Sue's and Jude's lives. Still, Jude refuses to identify himself with the dead boy as strongly as Sue, who blames herself for having been responsible for the slaughter. Jude sees Father Time as but a type, which he is. By denying this creature the motivations of an ordinary human being, Jude tries to assuage Sue's guilt feelings:

> "No," said Jude. "It was in his nature to do it. The doctor says there are such boys springing up amongst us—boys unknown in the last generation—the outcome of new views of life. They seem to see all its *terrors* before they are old enough

to have staying power to resist them." (Pt. VI, ch. 2, italics
added)

To Hardy, as well as to Jude, Father Time remains a type, an
allegorical representation of the terrors of a nihilistic view of
existence. In describing the dead boy's face, the narrator makes
it stand for "all the inauspiciousness and shadow which had
darkened the first union of Jude, and all the accidents, mistakes,
fears, errors of the last. He was their nodal point, their focus,
their expression in a single term" (Pt. VI, ch. 2). Father Time
thus remains, in death as in life, an abstraction. Bereft of all individuality, he is not, to use Hardy's terms in his "Postscript,"
a "particular," but rather exists only as a universal, as the expression of the novelist's belief in cosmic pain. With his death, the
universal despair that he stands for begins to spread to Sue and
Jude. Hitherto, the two lovers managed to curb their propensity
for despair. Now, as Sue's resistance erodes, her defeatism infects Jude's own will to live.

Sue has accidentally caused Father Time's action of killing
himself and the children; his action, in turn, prompts her to re-
nounce whatever joys she had been able to find in life. Sue has
hardly been buoyant before the accident. Her laughter and wit
have barely disguised a temperament that has consistently been
inclined to see the world negatively. Like Father Time, she is
called "tragic" throughout the novel. As a child, little Susanna
Florence Mary would recite Poe's poem "The Raven" and "knit
her little brows and glare round tragically" (Pt. II, ch. 6); as a
young woman, she delights in adopting a "contralto note of
tragedy" when she recalls how she broke the heart of a young
student whose death she ascribes to her cruelty: "That's how
men are—so much better than women!" (Pt. III, ch. 4). Even as
a mother, Sue remains disenchanted and aggrieved: "it seems
such a tragic thing to bring beings into the world," she complains (Pt. V, ch. 7). Although at times her negativism grates on
Jude, he also enjoys sharing her state of unhappiness and dissatis-
faction. He, too, is a self-tormentor who relishes mortification

in an almost perverse way. As Phillotson recognizes, Sue's dolorous nature is a part of Jude's own character. Like that other set of tragic lovers, Catherine and Heathcliff, they are like "one person split in two" (Pt. IV, ch. 4), as bound by their acute reaction to the painful world around them as by their equally acute ability to inflict pain on each other. Their response to the wounded rabbit's cry is identical; they are unable to bear the animal's suffering. After Jude kills the rabbit, Sue protests feebly: "They ought not to be allowed to set these steel traps, ought they!" (Pt. IV, ch. 2). Both she and Jude get caught in a steel trap which is only partially of their own making.

Jude honors Sue's refusal to marry him. His acquiescence presumably begins a causal sequence that ends in their mutual destruction: the lovers' life out of wedlock leads to their persecution by society; the embitterment over their persecution prompts Sue to utter her careless words to Father Time; her words stimulate the child to commit the murder; the murder results in Sue's guilty return to Phillotson; her absence hastens Jude's decline and death. Their roles have become reversed. She has become a religious fanatic and he, a cynical skeptic. But the reversal is not really an Aristotelian *peripateia* such as Dorothea's assumption of Lydgate's role as healer in *Middlemarch*. The lovers have merely exchanged places; they remain incomplete, equidistant, the separate halves of a single identity. Sundered, they must die —Jude, literally, and Sue, figuratively and spiritually.

In tracing this sequence Hardy makes it possible for the reader to put the blame for Jude's fall on society, on Sue's willfulness, or on Jude's own uxorious compliance to the capriciousness of his chosen Eve. In addition, Hardy creates another culprit, Nature. The narrator himself berates this indifferent deity for her scorn for "man's finer emotions, and her lack of interest in his aspirations" (Pt. III, ch. 8). The characters, too, try to find a source for their misfortunes, but their explanations are circuitous. Sue Bridehead claims that she cannot be held personally responsible for her desertion of Phillotson:

"I am very sorry. But it is not I altogether who am to blame!"

"Who is then? Am I?"

"No—I don't know! The universe, I suppose—things in general, because they are so horrid and cruel." (Pt. IV, ch. 3)

Sue is essentially correct: "things in general" are as much to blame as the characters themselves. Sue admits that when she told Father Time that adversity and suffering were a "law of nature" she was not merely projecting her own discontent but also presenting him with "the facts of life" (Pt. VI, ch. 2). She only regrets that she did not shield the boy from reality by telling him "pleasant untruths." In expiation, she chooses to cling to unpleasant truths herself. No longer believing that "Nature" sanctions and rewards the life of the instinct, she swings back into the opposite direction by an excessive belief in the restraints of civilized society: "I said it was Nature's intention, Nature's law and *raison d'être* that we should be joyful in what instincts she afforded us—instincts which civilization had taken upon itself to thwart. What dreadful things I said! And now Fate has given us this stab in the back for being such fools as to take Nature at her word" (Pt. VI, ch. 2).

"Society" and "Nature" may, as Sue holds, be at odds with each other; more often, however, they become interchangeable abstractions. On one occasion, Jude reacts against "wifedom"—marriage—as a "vast maw" which only aims to squash and digest a human being "as an atom which has no further individuality" (Pt. III, ch. 9). His rhetoric is powerful but empty: "Nature" or "society," instinct or civilization, could all have been substituted for "wifedom" without disturbing the meaning. "Things in general" are at fault; no single entity can be held accountable. Phillotson best sums up this state of affairs when he holds with "biting sadness" that "Cruelty is the law pervading all nature and society; and we can't get out of it if we would!" (Pt. V, ch. 8). Phillotson is a particularly apt spokesman. The cruelty of Nature has made him physically repulsive to his young bride;

the cruelty of the society which spurns him for giving Sue her freedom has made him an outcast. He is a victim of the only true "law" operating in Hardy's painful universe.

Hardy succeeds in *Jude the Obscure*, not because of his efforts to write a tragedy on the Greek model or to fashion a work of social protest, but because the cosmic cruelty he feels so intensely permeates the novel from beginning to end. The narrator calls himself "a chronicler of moods and deeds" (Pt. V, ch. 5); his strength lies in his orchestration of moods rather than in his ability to affect us through the frightful examples of his characters' deeds. Mood, rather than example, rounds out the novel's ending. Jude's death does not make us see more clearly or teach us "what not to do." The characters around him have learned nothing. Cruelty persists. When the widow Edlin comments on the dead man's beauty, Arabella answers brutally, but realistically: "Yes. He's a 'andsome corpse" (Pt. VI, ch. 11). We are denied a final sentimental indulgence. For Arabella, life goes on undisturbed—she has already been excited by Vilbert's arm stealing around her waist, already felt his body pressing against her in the crowd. She belongs to the "hot mass" of humanity that clamors outside Jude's room; though "statuesque," the figure inside is a cold corpse. Life is not for those "horribly sensitive" people like Sue and Jude who cannot bear its full brutality.

To D. H. Lawrence, Hardy's admirer and critic, the Arabella who refuses to adopt Sue's "tragic note" or to indulge in Jude's diatribes against society was by rights the most positive figure in the novel. In his essay on Hardy, Lawrence accordingly denounced his predecessor for his presumed harshness toward Arabella: "He insists that she is a pig-killer's daughter; he insists that she drag Jude into pig-killing; he lays stress on her false tail of hair."[13] This disgusts Lawrence. He would have Arabella as heroine, and Hardy thwarts him. And so he rewrites the story to fit his own perspective: Hardy's "bad art" leads him to debase Arabella, but his better instincts forced him to "make insignifi-

13. "Study of Thomas Hardy," *D. H. Lawrence: Selected Literary Criticism*, ed. Anthony Beal (New York, 1956), p. 199.

cant in her these pig-sticking, false-hair crudities" and to accord her the prominence she deserves.

Lawrence is right, of course, in seeing that Arabella is Sue's exact opposite—that Jude is torn between two women that represent his own self-division, just as Tess of the D'Urbervilles in Hardy's previous novel is torn between two men representing the incomplete opposites of flesh and spirit. Lawrence errs, however, in altering Hardy's aims. Though Hardy uses Arabella as the antithesis to Sue and to those elements in Jude's character which correspond to Sue, he makes her a creature attuned to the ways of his own cruel "Nature" and not the beneficent "Nature" extolled by Lawrence or by Butler. While Jude and Sue almost delight in their ability to torture themselves and others, Arabella always sidesteps pain. As Lawrence recognizes, she stands for the will to live, for instinct. Unintellectual, unconcerned with the philosophical questions that plague Sue and Jude, she grasps the "reality" of Hardy's Nature, just as Becky Sharp, more self-consciously, grasps the "reality" of Thackeray's *Vanity Fair*. Like Becky, she is vital, perennially youthful, self-renovating—her hedonism is like that of Chaucer's Wife of Bath or Shakespeare's Falstaff. While Sue regards herself to be as ancient as Hellenic civilization and Jude identifies himself with a medieval past, Arabella adapts herself to her shifting present. She endures because she accepts what is enduring: man's lower instincts. To her, death is as natural as sex—both are to be made little fuss over. When Jude meets her again it is in the same tavern where, years earlier, his ideals were so sorely thwarted. The tavern has been "renovated," refurbished in a "modern style." Arabella, too, has adapted herself to change. She is as attractive as before, totally at ease, teasing a customer who bears the significant name of "Mr. Cockman." To Jude, as to Thackeray's Dobbin, the changes in environment only remind him of "vanished dreams" (Pt. III, ch. 8); to Arabella, as to Becky Sharp, any environment can contain the selfsame "reality." Uncivilized, instinctual, Arabella represents the attitude which Jude or Sue or Phillotson with their conscience, their feeling, their intellect, their morbidity, cannot bring themselves to accept: she adapts herself to Hardy's "Nature" uncritically and acts according to its promptings. To her, moral questions have little bearing on the conduct of life; she says of Australia: "Crime! Pooh. They don't think much of such as that over there" (Pt. III, ch. 9).

Hardy neither exalts Arabella into a mother-earth figure, as D. H. Lawrence would have him do, nor does he convert her into a Clytemnestra capable of murder, as Thackeray would do. He contrasts her frank lustfulness with Sue's aversion to sex by comparing her "amplitudes" to her rival's "apple-like convexities." Despite these amplitudes, despite her "portly self" and "inflated bosom," Arabella is not motherly; just as Becky Sharp finds little Rawdy to be an obstacle in her relationship with Lord Steyne, so Arabella eagerly parts with Father Time to win a new suitor. But Hardy does not condemn Arabella for her frank selfishness in the way that Thackeray subtly forces us into condemning Becky. Arabella is merely acting in accordance with the cruelty that is the "law" in *Jude the Obscure*—an animal rejects its young when it is ready to mate again.

Arabella, then, best defines for us what Hardy means by both "tragedy" and "nature." She acts as a foil to Jude's inability to accept a cosmic cruelty. The opposition between them conveys Hardy's meaning far better than the strained intellectual terms which he superimposes on Jude's quest. Thus it is that Jude's "tragedy" is already prefigured in the very beginning of the novel, at the end of the first part. The almost unbearable description of the pig-sticking incident, which so revolted Hardy's contemporary reviewers as well as D. H. Lawrence, dramatizes even more effectively than the later death scenes the assumptions on which Hardy's pessimism is based. Though Lawrence rejected the "pig-sticking crudities" as being insignificant, the scene is crucial to Hardy's purpose.

Jude's extreme sensitivity has already been established before the pig-sticking scene. He pitied the rooks he was supposed to scare off Farmer Troutham's land and could not bear to step on earthworms; but now that he is married to the pig-sticker's daughter, Jude is forced to cut a pig's throat. The struggle is Darwinian: men, like animals, must kill to live. As the animal is drawn in, it gives out a "cry of despair; long-drawn, slow and hopeless" (Pt. I, ch. 10). As it dies, the pig's "glazing eyes" rivet themselves on Arabella with "the eloquently keen reproach of a creature recognizing at last the treachery of those who had seemed his only friends." Jude is appalled. He identifies himself with the animal and, as in the later scene in the Christminster square, demands pity. "It is a hateful business," he protests. "Pigs must be killed," is Arabella's laconic reply.

The implications of the scene should be obvious. The pig *is* Jude himself. His notions about the love between him and Arabella have also been murdered. He, too, has been betrayed by the one person who seemed to be his friend. He has been forced into the role of aggressor by the same woman who began their courtship by throwing the "characteristic part of a barrow pig" at him. He prefers to remain passive. He cannot fit into this Darwinian world of struggles. Jude looks at the dead animal with regret, but his regrets are primarily for himself:

> Jude felt dissatisfied with himself as a man at what he had done, though aware of his lack of common sense and that the deed would have amounted to the same thing if carried out by a deputy. The white snow, stained with the blood of his fellow-mortal, wore an illogical look to him as a lover of justice, not to say a Christian; but he could not see how the matter was to be mended. No doubt he was, as his wife had called him, a tender-hearted fool. (Pt. I, ch. 10)

Yet pigs must be killed. Jude's relief over the animal's death ("'Thank God!' Jude said. 'He's dead.'") prefigures our relief at his own extinction at the end of the novel. Jude's reaction toward the pig becomes the reader's reaction towards him. We sympathize with him, yet wish his agony to end. We thank God —or the godlike novelist who acts as "deputy"—that Jude is finally and irrevocably dead, that his glazed eyes are no longer accusing us for remaining in the world that he has left. As

pointed out before, the Hardy of *Jude* deliberately adopts the
role that Matthew Arnold had rejected. Arnold had refused
to portray those situations which "when they occur in actual
life . . . are painful, not tragic."[14] In *Jude the Obscure*, Hardy
wants to pain us—to unsettle our sentimental expectations far,
far beyond Thackeray's similar aim in *Vanity Fair.*

*Jude the Obscure* thus releases the same bitterness that Thackeray had checked through laughter almost five decades before.[15]
Unlike the Thackeray who mingled Satire and Sentiment by
balancing the melancholy of Dobbin with the defiant cheerfulness of Becky Sharp, Hardy prefers the "tragic note" struck by
Sue and Jude to the "humorous impudence" of Arabella. Yet
there is a dark kind of humor running through this last novel by
the man who was to write *Time's Laughingstocks* and *Satires of
Circumstance.* Sue's plea to Jude not to "satirize" her almost
seems to be directed at the novelist himself. Hardy's bruised
idealism at least found a grim satisfaction in exposing the ironies
in his characters' lives. Only by mocking the aspirations of Jude
and Sue, could he express his outrage at a world which seemed
to have nullified his own hopes.

## 3

In chapter fifty-seven of *The Way of All Flesh* Ernest Pontifex, now a London curate who lives among the poor in order to
"give up all for Christ," meets his antithesis, his former college
chum Towneley. Increasingly doubtful about his goals, Ernest
has become possessed "by a subtle, indefinable *malaise*" (ch. 56);
Towneley, on the other hand, remains as self-assured as always,
"looking as full of life and good spirits as ever, and if possible

14. "Preface" (1853), p. xviii.
15. Hardy recommended *Vanity Fair* to his sister Mary for the "very
truthfulness" that made others denounce the novel as being "unfitted for
young people" (19 December 1863); in an essay written in 1888, he
instanced the first thirty-three chapters of Thackeray's novel as "well-
nigh complete in artistic presentation, along with other magnificent
qualities" ("The Profitable Reading of Fiction," reprinted in *Thomas
Hardy's Personal Writings*, ed. Harold Orel [Lawrence, 1966], p. 121).

even handsomer than he had been at Cambridge" (ch. 57). At the university Ernest had worshiped Towneley from afar as one whose perfection was diametrically opposite to all of his own deeply felt deficiencies; now, however, "still confused and shy," Ernest feels an urge to justify himself before his onetime idol. He informs Towneley about his new creed, "his little threepenny bit about poor people being very nice," and, emboldened, asks him whether he, too, does not like poor people very much. Towneley gives his face "a comical but good-natured screw," says, "No, No, No," and beats a hasty retreat. Rebuffed, Ernest is forced to admit that Towneley's repudiation applies not only to his remark about poor people but also "to the whole scheme and scope of his own recently adopted ideas"—his notion that, to find personal salvation, he must "regenerate the universe" by reclaiming the souls of indifferent parishioners.

The scene corresponds to that in *Jude the Obscure* in which Jude implores the Christminster crowd to give him their approval and sympathy. Like Jude, Ernest desperately desires the approbation of others in his quest for self-definition. His need for affection and recognition, thwarted by his parents "each time that it had tried to spring" (ch. 63), caused him to cling to "spiritual thieves, or coiners" (ch. 57), men like the Rev. Mr. Hawke or his fellow-curate Pryer, who have cowed him into accepting their spurious ideals. After his encounter with Towneley, Ernest begins to suspect that his friend's ability "to get on comfortably in the world" might be infinitely more satisfying than his own uncomfortable self-denials, yet he rejects his "old dejection" and perseveres in his former course.

Ernest hopes to find some value in his own life by redoubling his efforts at bringing Christ to others: "perhaps a light would be shed upon his path" (ch. 58). He decides to convert the men and women who live in his dwelling at Ashpit Place and expects to counter his disappointment over Towneley's rejection by gaining their approval instead. Like Jude, however, Ernest has not yet hit the full bottom of his travails. His crusade quickly divests him of all the tenuous props by which he had previous-

ly shored up his self-confidence: the terrifying strength of Holt
the tailor forces him to recognize his own cowardice and physical weakness; the faith of the Methodist Baxters leads him to
admit his ignorance of other religions; the skepticism of tinker
Shaw compels him to see his inability to defend his own religious beliefs. Deprived of his spiritual armor, Ernest must now
recognize the powers of the flesh. The charms of Miss Snow,
who is visited by the ever-laughing Towneley, arouse the sexual
desires he has stifled; his inability to distinguish between a pros-
titute and a respectable girl causes him to affront Miss Maitland;
the girl's accidental encounter with a policeman leads to his
arrest and imprisonment. As in *Jude*, an accident has caused an
irreversible turn of events. A light has been shed on Ernest's path,
yet it is not the kindly light he had expected. As he staggers to
jail, Ernest recognizes the inadequacy of the ideals he has tried
to follow. His features now resemble those of Jude Fawley;
the paralyzed young man glances ahead "with staring eyes,
ghastly pale, and with despair branded upon every line of his
face" (ch. 60).

The description just quoted ends the second volume of Butler's novel. The despair that now engulfs Ernest is akin to that
which overpowers Jude at the end of *Jude the Obscure*. Like
Hardy's social outcast, Ernest is "irretrievably" cut off from the
society whose values he had tried to observe. If Jude condemns
himself as one of "that vast band of men shunned by the virtuous
—the men called seducers" (*Jude*, Pt. VI, ch. 2), so does Ernest
feel crushed by the weight of his "shame and sorrow" (*The
Way of All Flesh*, ch. 64). Hardy's hero dies when he is left
alone; Ernest, whose constitutional weakness had been noted by
his aunt and whose death has been predicted by Mrs. Jupp (chs.
34, 55), seems far more frail than his counterpart, far less able
to resist his changed environment. Indeed, in his one concession to melodrama, Butler has Ernest suffer from an "incipient
attack of brain fever" as soon as the young man is condemned
to six months of hard labor (ch. 64). For two months, Ernest
hovers between "life and death, never in full possession of his

reason" (ch. 64). Yet Butler counters his protagonist's potential tragedy by devoting the third volume of his novel to Ernest's deliverance from his old self. The prison, a symbol of death in so many nineteenth-century novels, becomes, for Ernest, a place of resurrection and rebirth. His will to live is kindled when a nurse in the prison infirmary jokes with the invalid: "he laughed, and as he did so she clapped her hands and told him he would be a man again" (ch. 64).

The comic story of Ernest's rebirth which takes up the third volume of *The Way of All Flesh* thus is in direct opposition to Jude's gradual acquiescence to his creator's death wish. The childless Jude, bereft of Sue and Arabella, dies when he is cut off from all his former ties. Ernest, on the other hand, can be "born into a new world" (ch. 71 [69][16]) when his isolation in prison teaches him that health and survival depend on his separation from all his former acquaintances. When Ernest's parents try to reassert their claims over their son, he insists that "they must think of me as one dead, for I am dead to them" (ch. 70 [68]). Whereas Hardy makes Jude and Sue orphans to accentuate their pathos, Butler has the imprisoned Ernest brood "over the bliss of Melchisedec who had been born an orphan—without father, without mother, and without descent." Later, Ernest, like Arabella in Hardy's novel, will rid himself of his children, but he will do so for their sake rather than for his own, unwilling to subject them to the same parental control he found so stifling. On receiving a letter from Theobald and Christina, the young man recognizes the need for a total break: " 'There are orphanages,' he exclaimed to himself, 'for children who have lost their parents—oh why, why, why, are there no harbours for grown men who have not yet lost them?' " (ch. 68 [67]).

Ernest's remark is supported by the view of that other pro-

---

16. The first editor of *The Way of All Flesh* ignored several of the chapter breaks in the later portions of Butler's manuscript; to facilitate references to the many texts modeled on his version of the novel, the numbers he assigned are given after the correct chapter numbers used in Daniel F. Howard's edition.

jection of Samuel Butler, Overton the narrator. Early in the novel, Overton asks: "Why should the generations overlap one another at all? Why cannot we be buried as eggs in neat little cells with ten or twenty thousands pounds each wrapped round us in Bank of England notes, and wake up, as the sphex wasp does, to find that its papa and mama have not only left ample provision at its elbow but have been eaten by sparrows some weeks before we began to live consciously on our own accounts?" (ch. 18). Overton's rhetorical question is more than a witty barb. It contains the assumptions on which Butler bases his entire fantasy about Ernest's recovery of strength and freedom and illustrates the key tenet of his belief that life "is nothing else" than an unending "process of accommodation" in which men are engaged in adapting their "changed and unchanged selves to changed and unchanged surroundings" (ch. 71 [69]). The changed surroundings provided by the prison allow Ernest to rid himself of the misshapen self that has been affected by "postnatal rather than congenital misfortunes" (ch. 63). The deformities introduced, since his birth, by his parents and teachers can be erased as he starts life anew again by being reborn "not only as a little child but as a little embryo, or rather as a little zoösperm" (ch. 63).

In ridding himself of his sullied, conscious self, Ernest can bypass the mistakes of his parents and revert to the unconscious congenital strength of John Pontifex the carpenter. Ernest's aunt Alethea had tried to revive this ancestral unconscious by making the boy engage in building an organ such as that constructed by his great-grandfather. Now, once again sensing "the power which he felt to be in him," Ernest remembers his aunt's earlier wisdom in wanting him to "kiss the soil"; though he is too old to learn Old Pontifex's profession, he senses that there are other ways "of kissing the soil besides becoming a carpenter" (chs. 69 [68], 68 [67]). His work as a tailor and his life with Ellen provide Ernest with all the schooling needed to correct his "postnatal misfortunes." Like a child who is "a year or two old," he "learns to walk" (ch. 78 [73]). Eventually, he discovers that, through his aunt's provision, he does not even have to remain an obscure craftsman. Like the hypothetical egg mentioned by Overton, Ernest has been provided with crisp Bank of England notes that now allow him to hatch into a life of complete freedom. The money which Alethea had inherited from George Pontifex and which Overton has kept away from his godson gives Ernest the identity of a gentleman. He gains this identity without his parents' preferred financial help and without relying on the useless training he received at Roughborough and Cambridge. "Embryo minds, like embryo bodies, pass through a number of strange metamorphoses before they adopt their final shape" (ch. 53). Theobald and Christina have merely created a "zoösperm" or embryo; Ernest's development after his rebirth in prison, made possible by his aunt's foresight and by Overton's nonintervention, has been his own.

Ernest's god-parents, Alethea and Overton, thus have created a self-reliant being who replaces the feeble son of Theobald and Christina Pontifex. Freed from the mistakes of the past, this new Ernest steers his descendants toward a better future. The "drowning man" who picked himself "out of the water" (ch. 61) and regained "his own power to swim" (ch. 84 [78]) wants his children to learn instinctively what he has had to teach himself laboriously, painfully, and late in life. Dickens' Eugene Wrayburn is reborn by marrying a bargeman's daughter after being plunged into the river and hammered into a new shape. In Butler's more conservative fantasy, it is Ernest's children or even their children's children, rather than Ernest himself, who will be baptized into a better life. Ernest wants his children to model themselves after the set of foster parents he provides them with rather than have them follow his own example. His son Georgie becomes a bargeman, while his daughter Alice decides to live as "a bargeman's wife" (ch. 91 [84]). As Overton observes Georgie on his steamer, he notices the resemblances as well as the differences between the young man and Ernest: "He is a good deal like his father, in the face, but without a spark—so far as I have been able to observe—of any literary ability; he has a fair sense of humour and an abundance of common sense, but his instinct is clearly a practical one—I am not sure that he does not put me in mind almost more of what Theobald would have been if he had been a sailor, than of Ernest" (ch. 93 [86]).

Overton's reverie is revealing, for it suggests the extent to which *The Way of All Flesh* represents Samuel Butler's own private search for a more satisfactory identity than that which he had inherited from his father, the Reverend Thomas Butler, whose Christianity and parental influence he excoriated in the novel. By parceling out his identity among the chief characters in the novel, Butler-Overton (born the same year as Theobald) could look at Butler-Ernest (born the same year as Butler himself). Butler's self-divisions and wishful projections are even carried beyond these two figures. Georgie Pontifex, like the young George in his last work, *Erewhon Revisited*, is the creation of a "literary" man speculating on whether he might not have been happier if his own father had been a sailor.

Butler's attitude toward Ernest remains ambivalent. He magnifies Ernest, on the one hand, as the deliverer of a new and better race, yet, on the other hand, he also deplores Ernest's (and his own) inability to rid himself completely of his acute self-consciousness, his awareness of pain. Although Butler converts Ernest into Overton's coauthor by having the young man provide his laughing biographer with further instances of his former follies, this laughter at times seems too defensive, almost perverse in its delight in paradox for its own sake.

Butler's biological fantasy thus lacks the apocalyptic overtones of a D. H. Lawrence, another celebrant of the powers of the flesh. Though cured, Ernest is hardly a Lawrentian Superman. He merely lapses into an "amiable indifferentism" (ch. 69 [68]) such as underlies Overton's own noninvolvement. Though full of witty paradoxes, his "quietistic, comforting" writings are, again like Overton's, above all designed to quiet and comfort himself (ch. 92 [85]). Towneley remains Ernest's true ideal of perfection. He looks up to his friend in the same reverential way that he and Overton regard the music of Handel. Overton hints that Handel's harmony is attributable to the fact "that he lost his own father when he was six years old" and became totally "independent at the age of fifteen" (ch. 38). Similarly, Ernest regards Towneley's early independence as the source of an inward grace toward which he can never aspire in his own lifetime. Whereas Handel and Ernest's wife, whose father drowned "when she was a child" (ch. 38), have lost only one parent, Towneley has been more "handsomely" rewarded by fortune when he inherited a vast estate after both of his parents drowned in a boating accident "when he was only two years old" (ch. 48).

To Butler as to Ernest, Towneley thus represents a totally untroubled life of the instinct which the intellectual Ernest, still smarting from the painful aftereffects of his postnatal misfortunes, can never hope to lead. Before Ernest receives the legacy that at least allows Towneley to feel "as though Ernest was more one of his own class" (ch. 61), he disparages himself by comparing himself with his counterpart: "The people like Towneley are the only ones who know anything that is worth knowing, and like that of course I can never be. But to make Towneleys possible there must be hewers of wood and drawers of water—men in fact through whom conscious knowledge must pass before it can reach those who can apply it gracefully and instinctively like the Towneleys can" (ch. 78 [73]).

Ernest's words suggest the rather dismal underpinnings of Butler's avowedly joyous celebration of the powers of the flesh. In the world of *Jude the Obscure* there are no exemplary characters; as we saw, Arabella's instinctive adaptation to life is hardly presented as an ideal. In *The Way of All Flesh*, however, the unquestioning cheerfulness of a Towneley, so like Arabella's in Hardy's novel, is exalted for its avoidance of both emotion and thought. Samuel Butler was able to counter Hardy's dispiriting world only by devising an intellectual construct that also denied the pained awareness he shared with Hardy. If Hardy's overemotional narrator prefers sentiment to satire, Overton and the matured Ernest who resembles his godfather use satire to eradicate sentiment. William Butler Yeats' indictment of Samuel Butler seems to the point. To Yeats, Butler paid too high a price for his achievements: he eliminated "from the mind all emotional implications" and thus preferred "plain water to every vintage."[17]

Butler's creation of Overton, though necessary to the success of his book and integral to his belief in the value of parental disengagement, illustrates Yeats' point. Overton is a descendant of the Showman who laughed in public yet remained miserable in private, but he refuses to acknowledge these private miseries by his deliberate disengagement from Ernest's misfortunes: "I was glad to get away from him, for I could do nothing for him, or chose to say that I could not, and the sight of so much suffering was painful to me" (ch. 23). Overton accepts his godson only after Ernest has been remade in his own image as a jester dulled to feeling.

Butler's and Overton's tendency to dispel tragedy by regarding life as a burlesque grates on the reader. Towneley welcomes Overton as an ally when he discovers his profession:

> "Writes for the stage does he?" said Towneley, "Does he write comedy?" Ernest thought that Towneley meant that I ought to write tragedy, and said he was afraid I wrote burlesque. "Oh come, come," said Towneley, "that will do famously. I will go and see him at once." (ch. 61)

In one of his few active interventions in Ernest's behalf, Overton takes the young man fresh from prison to see a burlesque of *Macbeth*. The antics on the stage so fascinate Ernest that he "laughed till he cried: 'What rot,' he exclaimed involuntarily, 'Shakespeare is after this'" (ch. 72 [70]). Overton is satisfied with his disciple's progress; he clearly regards Ernest's experience as a cathartic one. Laughter has displaced pity and fear; it has purged Ernest of self-pity. Yet the quality of that laughter remains strained; its curative powers, highly dubious.

Overton's noninvolvement, his repeated excuses for not in-

17. "The Tragic Generation," *The Trembling of the Veil* in *The Autobiography of William Butler Yeats* (New York, 1958), p. 188.

tervening more actively in Ernest's education, though illustrative of Butler's theories also show Butler's own studious repression of all that is disturbing and painful in life. Analyzing a photograph of the writer, P. N. Furbank describes it as revealing "a resolute refusal of tragedy by a character naturally inclined to it."[18] The description seems apt. Thomas Hardy's overindulgence in a pessimistic gloom seems more genuine than Butler's resource to an optimism that is ingenious, but artificially contrived. In *Jude the Obscure* Hardy wrote a tragedy that is not a tragedy; in *The Way of All Flesh* Butler wrote a comedy that fails to be comical in its affirmation. Satire and sentiment, laughter and despair, intellect and feeling had split asunder. The English novel demanded a new form that would once again combine these opposites, that would, like the Victorian masterpieces of the past, again mingle denial with hope. This new combination was to be achieved in the form of Joseph Conrad's *Secret Agent*, a work fusing intellectual detachment with emotional intensity. In this modern novel, subtitled, significantly enough, "A Simple Tale of the Nineteenth Century," Conrad managed to maintain Butler's ironic distance while at the same time arousing the tragic emotions of pity and fear that Hardy had tried to generate.

18. *Samuel Butler (1835–1902)* (Cambridge, 1948), p. 113.

# VIII  *The Secret Agent*: The Irony of the Absurd

Joseph Conrad's *The Secret Agent, A Simple Tale* (1907) is prefaced by an "Author's Note" written in 1920 at a time when the innovations of James Joyce, Virginia Woolf, and Ford Madox Ford were beginning to introduce fresh standards for judging fiction. Like Hardy in his "Postscript" to *Jude the Obscure*, Conrad deplores the severe misunderstandings which clouded his novel's initial reception and defends himself against those readers whose objections were made "on the ground of sordid surroundings and the moral squalor of the tale."[1] He admits that on rereading *The Secret Agent* he finds it to be a "grisly skeleton" indeed and concedes that its ending might be painful. But unlike Hardy, who gropes for conceptual terms to define the purpose and genre of *Jude*, Conrad justifies his work on purely artistic grounds. Confident of his originality and control, the novelist whose first piece of fiction had been published in the same year as *Jude* implies that his ability to reduce into "manageable proportions" the story of Winnie Verloc should be regarded as the only criterion for his successful creation of a "perfectly genuine piece of work."

Conrad's essentially aesthetic justification of his work's integrity stems from post-Victorian notions about fictive reality. More than the novelists before him, Conrad is willing to admit the deeply private nature of his art: "A novelist lives in his work. He stands there, the only reality in an invented world, among imaginary things, happenings, and people. Writing about them he is only writing about himself."[2] Despite his belief in the artist's autonomy, however, Conrad is "Victorian" enough not to dis-

1. "Author's Note," *The Secret Agent*, Canterbury Edition (New York, 1924); all future references to this edition are given in the text.
2. "A Familiar Preface," *A Personal Record*, Canterbury Edition (New York, 1924), p. xv.

miss completely the old Arnoldian notion that a work of literature ought to inspire its readers instead of causing them anxiety
and pain. Even though he stresses his craftsmanship in the "Author's Note," he also feels compelled to explain that "there was
no perverse intention, no secret scorn for the sensibilities of
mankind at the bottom of my impulses." His entire treatment of
the tale, he suggests, should prove his complete detachment and
demonstrate his intention to protect the reader from the "anar-
chistic end of utter desolation, madness and despair" to which
Winnie Verloc is led. Conrad thus emphatically rejects the
accusation that *The Secret Agent* was written solely to shock
or to cause pain: "Even the purely artistic purpose, that of applying an ironic method to a subject of that kind, was formu-
lated with deliberation and in the earnest belief that ironic
treatment alone would enable me to say all I felt I would have to
say in scorn as well as pity."

In *The Secret Agent* Conrad writes a modern novel which is
also a tale of the nineteenth century, "a simple tale" that is set
not in the exotic lands of his previous fiction but in a grimy
Dickensian London of the 1880's, in the time of gas lamps and
horse-drawn carriages. His return to an earlier setting is deliberate, for Conrad applies a new form and treatment to a
question which plagued him as much as the English novelists
before him: namely, how can man adhere to a moral code in a
world that seems anarchic and devoid of meaning. Hardy's answer to this question had been exaggerated in its despair: Jude
the idealist is drained of his lifeblood drop by drop. Conrad, on
the other hand, relies on understatement in his portrayal of a
world as indifferent "to heaven's frowns and smiles" as Hardy's
cruel "nature." His ironies, unlike Hardy's, are not pronounced,
but subtly and gradually produced. The simplicity of his tale—he
refuses to call it a "tragedy" or even a "novel"—is highly deceptive. To understand even its plot we must supply some facts
and carefully piece together those that are doled out to us; like
Inspector Heat or the Assistant Commissioner we must go by
hints, loose fragments, surmises, and keep away from misleading

pieces of evidence. We must rearrange the thirteen fragments—one hesitates to call them chapters—into which the novel is divided. Although we must experience them in the order in which they are presented, we must at the same time be aware of their true chronological sequence.

Like *Our Mutual Friend*, then, Conrad's novel relies on the accumulation of fragments which at first do not seem to cohere at all. In Dickens' bulky panoramic novel these accumulated fragments result in a fairy tale by which we can laugh away the absurd world of the Veneerings and Podsnaps; in Conrad's taut and compact tale, however, the reader is carried to the "madness and despair" perceived by Winnie Verloc. What accrues therefore is not an alternative to an absurd reality but an interpretation of that reality. Only by gradually understanding its absurdities, by looking into the contradictions slowly taking shape before our eyes, can we avoid the sudden disenchantment of a character whose "tragic suspicion that 'life doesn't stand much looking into'" fails to protect her from the nihilism that lies at the core of Conrad's universe. The delineation of that universe is not completed until the thirteenth and last fragment of the book when we hear of Winnie's fate through the fragmented clichés of an impersonal newspaper report. It is then that we comprehend, that we realize for the first time that we have been drawn into a tragedy and that Winnie—and not her husband or even her brother—has been the central figure in that tragedy. It is then that we also recognize that Conrad's ironic and elliptical method has protected author and reader alike from succumbing to the vortex of "madness and despair" which draws Winnie to her death.

Conrad's narrative method presupposes an absolute alertness from the reader. Although the narrator's ironic voice sets the tone for the story, this voice is disembodied; despite his omniscience, the narrator effaces himself and forces us to hear and see only those details he has carefully screened and selected. His suppressions offend our yearning for order, continuity, and explanation. The reader, irritated by the narrator's elusive voice, almost feels like apostrophizing him much in the way that Mr.

Vladimir apostrophizes Verloc: "Voice won't do. We have no use for your voice. We don't want a voice. We want facts—startling facts—damn you!" (ch. 2). Verloc, of course, has no facts to reveal to his employer. Conrad does. Precisely at those points at which the novelist seems most evasive, "startling facts" are actually dangling before our eyes. We remain dependent on his voice. By projecting his own voice and bellowing out into the street, Verloc engages in a meaningless and absurd action. But even though Verloc has no facts to offer to Vladimir, the facts Conrad wants to convey to the reader are there in Verloc's body, inert, corpulent, lethargic. It is the fat man's uselessness, the absurdity of his role as Vladimir's agent, that makes this spurious anarchist an apt agent for Conrad's vision of a truly anarchic existence.

## I

The "ironic method" of *The Secret Agent* is impressionistic: there are no overt guidelines to sort out the experiences we observe at first hand. The juxtapositions of scenes, symbols, phrases, words, force the reader into assessing the significance of each of the details to which he is exposed. Conrad's oft-quoted statement about his artistic intentions places the burden on the perceptiveness of his readers: "My task which I am trying to achieve is by the power of the written word, to make you hear, to make you feel—it is, before all, to make you see."[3] The rationale for this method is provided by Ford Madox Ford, Conrad's friend and collaborator: "We saw that life did not narrate, but made impressions on our brains. We in turn, if we wished to produce on you an effect of life, must not narrate, but render . . . impressions."[4]

The opening sentence of the book illustrates these contentions. Seemingly simple, a befitting introduction to a simple tale, the

3. "Preface to *The Nigger of the 'Narcissus,'* " *Conrad's Prefaces to His Works,* with an introductory essay by Edward Garnett (London, 1937).

4. "Joseph Conrad: A Personal Remembrance," quoted in *Critical Writings of Ford Madox Ford,* edited by Frank MacShane (Lincoln, 1964), p. 73.

sentence establishes a relationship between two characters: "Mr. Verloc, going out in the morning, left his shop nominally in charge of his brother-in-law." The emphasis is on the named, active man; the unnamed brother-in-law is cast in a subordinate position. The only word that might give us pause is "nominally"; its use is explained in the three sentences which complete the paragraph:

> It could be done, because there was very little business at any time, and practically none at all before the evening. Mr. Verloc cared little about his ostensible business. And, moreover, his wife was in charge of his brother-in-law. (ch. 1)

The reader is set at ease. The paragraph has moved from a relationship between two characters to a triangular relationship by its casual addition of Mr. Verloc's wife in the last sentence. Though in the act of leaving his shop, Mr. Verloc presumably remains in the forefront. We assume that he and not his wife or brother-in-law must be the likely protagonist of a book entitled *The Secret Agent*. To be sure, the four sentences do raise some further questions. Why does the shopkeeper care so little about his business and why is there hardly any business transacted before night? Moreover, why is his wife in charge of the brother-in-law "nominally" in charge of the shop? The questions seem unimportant. Perhaps Mr. Verloc trusts his wife more than his brother-in-law; perhaps the brother-in-law is only a small child. Like the untroubled Mr. Verloc who cares so little about his ostensible business, we are willing to move on, to follow him in his steps.

And yet this paragraph contains much more than a simple introduction to a simple tale. By being more interested in the shopkeeper than in his unnamed brother-in-law, the reader is led into doing exactly what Mr. Verloc will do himself, led into being far more interested in Mr. Verloc's fate than in that of Stevie. Moreover, by riveting our attention on the secret agent of the book's title, we miss the fact that the other two points in this triangle—Stevie and Winnie—will become far more important than he is. It is true that Mr. Verloc is an agent, "the famous and trusty secret agent, so secret that he was never designated otherwise but by the symbol △" (ch. 2); it is true also that the man who gives such a poor account of his activities to his new master at the Embassy also serves the interests of the anarchists and of the police. But this bumbling triple agent is an incidental figure. His wife, so casually introduced, is the book's true protagonist. And her relationship to Stevie, rather than Stevie's to Verloc, constitutes the strongest line in the triangle defined by the first paragraph.

As the chapter progresses, we realize our mistaken priority. For Conrad does not focus on the emerging Mr. Verloc, but rather forces us to linger in the shop he is leaving behind. Going back in time, the novelist describes a typical day at the shop; he provides us with the names and identities of Mr. Verloc's wife and brother-in-law; he introduces a fourth character in the person of Winnie's mother. The emphasis has altered. Mr. Verloc is no longer dominant, but neither have the relationships between him and the other characters become any clearer. The bits of information we are given seem truncated, incomplete. Each fact doled out diverts us from the unfinished implications suggested by the previous fact. Who are the evening visitors that come to the shop? Did Mrs. Verloc marry her husband to protect Stevie? Is Stevie a lunatic? Conrad compels the reader to examine more closely the details he has been provided with, to reassess their importance. Why does Stevie draw circles? Why are we asked to notice the fluffy, golden hair on his drooping jaw? The clue, we sense, somehow lies in Winnie Verloc herself, but the narrator does not allow us to share her thoughts and feelings. He deliberately relies on the limited point of view of Winnie's mother in assessing "Winnie's fondness for her delicate brother" and "Mr. Verloc's kind and generous disposition" (ch. 1). Three times the narrator resorts to the same adjective in describing Winnie: she preserves an "unfathomable indifference" towards her customers, she maintains an "unfathomable reserve" towards the lodgers in her mother's house, she meets Verloc's request that she be nice to his political friends with a "straight, unfathomable glance." The upshot is that Winnie remains "unfathomable" to the reader as well. Nonetheless, the chapter which opened with her husband's exit ends with a glimpse of her. Standing in the back of the shop she glances at Stevie "from time to time with maternal vigilance" (ch. 1).

The first chapter thus employs the cinematic techniques that are so essential to Conrad's "ironic method." Like a film-maker, this novelist achieves his effects through abrupt changes in pace, placement, and focus; he enlarges one subject, foreshortens another, and blurs a third. Time is frozen, cut up, and broken. After Verloc is stopped in mid-motion, the action dissolves into a series of flashbacks until the vivid image of Winnie's "maternal vigilance" returns us to the moment of time at which the action had begun. By coming last, just before the chapter break, her image stays more firmly impressed in the reader's mind; only after it has left its impression on our brains, can Mr. Verloc again resume his slow steps in the next reel.

Just as the order of the first chapter fails to observe a strictly chronological sequence, so Conrad deliberately disrupts the temporal sequence of the book's thirteen fragments to heighten his ironic effects and to gain an absolute control over his reader's awareness. In chapter four we learn that the expected explosion has taken place. The newspaper that Ossipon hands to the Professor, a "good-sized, rosy sheet, as if flushed by the warmth of its own convictions, which were optimistic," informs us of the event: "Half-past eleven. Foggy morning. Effects of explosion felt as far as Romney Road and Park Place. Enormous hole in the ground under a tree filled with smashed roots and broken branches. All round fragments of a man's body blown to pieces" (ch. 4). In hearing about the bomb outrage as a piece of secondhand information, we are as yet unaware that another gaping "hole" has been punched by the novelist himself. Misled by the seeming continuity of chapters three and four, we do not yet know that chapter eight—with its exposition of the triangular relationship binding Stevie, Winnie, and their mother

—should have chronologically followed the action depicted in chapter three, which placed the triangle formed by the Verlocs and Stevie against that formed by the three revolutionaries, Yundt, Michaelis, and Ossipon. Likewise, the first portion of chapter nine—which follows the events of chapter eight by dwelling on Winnie's satisfaction over Verloc's solicitude about Stevie—brings the action up to the morning of the Greenwich explosion which has already taken place in chapter four. Chapter eight and the first part of nine thus fill in all the events skipped over between chapters three and four: Winnie's mother's sacrifice and relinquishment of her maternal role to Winnie, Stevie's encounter with the cabman, the increasing rapport between Stevie and Verloc, their joint walks, Verloc's assurance to his wife that Stevie would profit by being sent to Michaelis' cottage in the country, their trip to the country, and Verloc's resumption of his walks. The second part of chapter nine resumes the sequence stopped at the end of chapter seven when the Assistant Commissioner, converging on the "open triangular space" of Brett Street, stood poised, ready to enter the shop.[5]

Conrad's disruption of the time scheme of a novel centered around Vladimir's attempts to have Verloc blow up Greenwich Observatory, the first meridian which lends order to the motions of a civilization ruled by time, serves his purposes in more ways than one. Vladimir wants to unsettle this impassive, orderly world and shake its optimism through an "act of destructive ferocity so absurd as to be incomprehensible, inexplicable, almost unthinkable" (ch. 2). The novelist, however, is less nihilistic in his aims. Although he too wants to jar the reader's complacency, he explodes time so that he can order his fictional universe by controlling and gradually widening our understanding of its nature. By forcing us to adhere to the unchronological sequence he has adopted, Conrad can delay the crucial information provided by chapter eight and the first part of chapter nine. By delaying this information, he induces us to share the limited

5. The actual chronological sequence of the thirteen chapters thus is as follows: 1, 2, 3, 8, 9a, 4, 5, 6, 7, 9b, 10, 11, 12, 13.

points of view of the characters themselves and, at the very same time, conditions us to see beyond their restricted perspectives.

Unaware at first that chapters three and four are separated by the gap of a full month, we are led to believe in their continuity. Since Vladimir's plot is presented in chapter two and Comrade Ossipon is introduced in chapter three, the reappearance of Ossipon in chapter four and our discovery, through him, that the explosion has taken place cause us to assume that there has been no serious interruption in the sequence established by the first three chapters. Moreover, using a tactic he will employ again in chapters five, six, and seven, Conrad diverts the reader as he induces us to become absorbed in an entirely new character, the Professor. We sense that the role played by this terrifying little man is important and become fascinated by the incongruities he represents. The Professor, more than Vladimir, seems to be the prime mover in Conrad's world, a man who regards all others as mere "agents" for his destructive vision. His juxtaposition to Ossipon confirms his superiority to the other revolutionaries of the Central Red Committee. Only when the Professor casually tells Ossipon that he gave his detonator to Verloc himself do we become reminded of the fat secret agent; from Ossipon's reaction we gather that Verloc must have exploded with the bomb and that consequently he no longer need interest us at all. As in chapter one, Verloc seems to have diminished in importance. When we finally are apprised of the time lag between chapters three and four through Ossipon's recollection that he has not seen Verloc for a month, we only become diverted by a new "fact," Ossipon's interest in Verloc's "widow." Like Ossipon, the reader is encouraged to "fasten" himself on those that remain behind without troubling himself about the actual events that took place at the bombing.

Chapter five continues to encourage the reader's belief that Verloc is dead. Again, we become distracted by the appearance of a new character, Chief Inspector Heat. But the juxtaposition of Heat to his antithesis, the Professor, like the earlier juxtaposition of the Professor to Ossipon, highly absorbing as it is, is jostled by a new "fact": Heat's earlier discovery that the man whose bloodstained remains have been pieced together was a "fair-haired fellow" (ch. 5). The reader now knows more than Ossipon, who will continue to assume that Verloc was killed in the explosion until he discovers the dead man in chapter twelve. Verloc is obviously still alive. But where is he? What has happened? Just as in the opening chapter, the obese secret agent has somehow slipped away from our view.

Conrad restrains our curiosity about Verloc's whereabouts and about the identity of the dead man by relying once again on the devices used in chapters four and five: he creates new characters and immediately juxtaposes them to their opposites. Chapter five introduces still another key figure, the Assistant Commissioner, and concludes with his juxtaposition to Inspector Heat. Chapter six introduces the Lady Patroness of Michaelis; chapter seven pairs off the Assistant Commissioner and Sir Ethelred, the Minister of State. For four chapters our interests have been diverted from the bomb incident at Greenwich Observatory. Although all the characters are reacting to the explosion, as eager to reconstruct the sequence of events as the reader, the events themselves have not been unearthed. Our suspicion that Stevie has been reduced to the bits of flesh we have read about in chapter five may be strong; but we lack the evidence. The narrator's characterization of the "unexpected solutions of continuity, sudden holes in space and time" that occur in the relations between conspirators and police (ch. 5) applies to our own relation to characters who, like Verloc and Stevie, may seem prominent and yet disappear from our view. Our expectations of continuity have been disappointed. Teased by the events contained in chapters four to seven, we yearn for the missing fragment that would fill the important hole in space and time that Conrad has punched out.

When that fragment is provided to us in chapter eight, we do not immediately recognize it as such. For chapter eight begins by focusing on Winnie's mother, the "heroic old woman" who like, Betty Higden in *Our Mutual Friend*, removes herself from others "as an act of devotion" (ch. 8). Gradually as the narrative shifts from her to Winnie and Stevie and moves to the young man's pity for the horse flogged by the cabman, we realize that this long-delayed flashback contains the link we have been searching for. Stevie's reaction to the cabman's maltreatment of the horse and his identification with the brute comes at the novel's midpoint. Though, chronologically speaking, the incident should have come after chapter three, its position is appropriate because emotionally the event is at the novel's very center. We witness Stevie's horror, his anger, his pain. The narrator informs us that, Comrade Ossipon's proclamations to the contrary, the young man is not mad, but perfectly reasonable. There is a logic in the questions he poses to the sister who will avoid asking these same questions until the end of the novel. Like Father Time in *Jude the Obscure*, Stevie sees a heart of darkness, an oppressive nature: "It was a bad, bad world." To him, as to Hardy, people are like animals; he believes in the cabman's equation between the two: "Poor brute, poor people." But unlike Father Time and very much like Jude himself, Stevie is a moralist who wants to counter the cosmic evil that he senses. While Father Time accepts Sue Bridehead's contention that the evil ways of the world cannot be resisted, Stevie is dissatisfied with his sister's evasion of his moral questionings. He refuses to accept her stoic philosophy ("Come along, Stevie, you can't help"). He wants to help. And help he does by innocently aiding Verloc in the attempted dynamite outrage. The irony of chapter nine, which documents Verloc's walks with Stevie and records Winnie's approval ("Might be father and son") is almost unbearable in its intensity. For by then the reader knows what Winnie yet has to learn: that her brother has been "blown to fragments in a stage of innocence and the conviction of being engaged in a humanitarian enterprise" (ch. 12).

Conrad's irony, however, is a necessary defense against the mindless circular world perceived by the demented Stevie.

Whereas the narrator in *Jude the Obscure* fails to protect himself against the pessimism of Father Time by implicitly endorsing Sue Bridehead's dispiriting view of the world, Conrad maintains his detachment as an impersonal observer. But unlike Overton in *The Way of All Flesh*, whose defensive irony blunts all feeling and precludes the reader's identification with Ernest's suffering, Conrad allows us to like Stevie and to partake of this "moral creature's" pity for human wretchedness. The ironic inflections of the narrator's voice merely deny us the sentimentalizations into which Dickens or Hardy would have lapsed. These ironies, made possible by the disrupted time scheme, are carefully controlled, directed at the reader, at Stevie himself, and, most important at Stevie's sister. The reader must recognize that our pity for Stevie is belated; we are allowed to appreciate Stevie's humanity only after we know that he has become a bloody mess of bits and pieces. Our earlier impassivity, so like that of the smug police constable, proud of restoring Stevie's body ("He's all there. Every bit of him. It was a job." [ch. 5]) comes to haunt us now that we have restored him to his true position of significance and have recognized that he is the "agent" for Winnie's disillusion and tragedy.

Stevie, we are now informed, "had liked all police constables tenderly" (ch. 8). Told by Winnie that the metropolitan police is hardly "a benevolent institution for the suppression of evil," the young man inquired, "What are they for then, Winn? What are they for? Tell me." Winnie replies that their function is to return stolen goods. In the next chapter she will face Inspector Heat who has come to return the triangular piece of cloth with the name tag she had sewn into Stevie's coat lest it should be stolen or he be lost. The police, like the detectivelike reader, can reconstruct evidences, but neither can arrest the mindless evil perceived by Stevie. Winnie, whose answer is "guiltless of irony," has yet to learn of the bitterly ironic absurdities the reader begins to perceive, yet to face the chaos suggested by "those coruscations of innumerable circles" drawn by Stevie (ch. 11).

Winnie regards Stevie as being only "a little, a very little peculiar," but he sees something that she will not see until her eyes, too, become distended and her jaw drops like that of her brother. What she comes to apprehend will be more devastating than Stevie's straightforward outrage over a "bad, bad world." For Winnie's brother dies instantaneously, happy in his unshaken belief that he is doing a good act for a man who is "obviously yet mysteriously good." Winnie is denied such comfort. Responsible for Stevie's blind faith in Verloc's goodness, she can no longer nourish any such illusions herself after Verloc returns and is exposed by Heat. She has been a fool. She must reconsider her notion that life does "not stand looking into very much." Her vision becomes more anarchic than that of the humane lunatic whose trust in goodness made him recoil from all physical harm. After a "white-hot iron" seems to be drawn across her eyes, Winnie tries to close them "desperately"; but the "night of her eyelids" only reveals the same vision of a "rainlike fall of mangled limbs" (ch. 11). She opens her eyes and becomes "clear-sighted" and "cunning." When Verloc wants some "wooing" after he has gorged himself on what proves to be his last meal, she knows what to do. The unfathomable Mrs. Verloc has become a tragic Clytemnestra who defiantly clutches her knife. With it, she expects to sever once and for all the stifling bonds represented by the "gold circlet" of her wedding ring (ch. 9). The freedom she hopes to attain is short lived. The reality she tries to puncture proves to be as circular and slippery as her obese husband.

## 2

Winnie Verloc becomes truly "clear-sighted" only after her betrayal by Ossipon shatters her last illusions and convinces her that she cannot escape from the contradictory reality she had previously refused to fathom. Before we look at her tragedy and its implications, however, we must first examine what being "clear-eyed" actually means in Conrad's fictional universe. For Conrad, as for Dickens, the world is divided between seers and nonseers; moreover, like Dickens again, the novelist who wants "before all, to make you see" relates the act of "seeing" to man's capacity for feeling. Yet whereas Dickens' suffering visionaries, figures like Betty Higden or Lizzie Hexam, can emotionally testify to the existence of a moral order invisible to those bound by the logic of the everyday world, for Conrad the task of seeing involves a confrontation with an existence painfully devoid of all such higher laws.

To wrest meaning from the meaninglessness of the world at large, Dickens invites the reader to partake of the transformation undergone by Eugene Wrayburn and John Harmon, the resurrected men whose river-baptism permits them to flee their dehumanized and fragmented surroundings. Conrad, on the other hand, encourages us to identify with that sober spectator of life's absurdities, the slightly "splashed" Assistant Commissioner who enforces laws yet knows that they are anachronistic, arbitrarily superimposed on an existence that remains erratic and disordered. The Commissioner, who walks the wet streets of London wearing a disguise, resembles that other man of many masks, John Harmon. He, too, is a just man, an idealist possessed of strong "crusading instincts" (ch. 10). Based, as Conrad explains in his "Author's Note," on the figure of "an obviously able man with a strong religious strain" who actually held the position "back in the eighties," the Commissioner is a man of feeling endowed with an absolute integrity. Yet his skeptical ability to "see"—his sad apprehension of the mindless chaos at the core of Conrad's universe—greatly hampers his role as moral crusader. In *Our Mutual Friend*, feeling alone could dispel John Harmon's pessimism and blend his aims with those of a child-man who steadfastly believed in the power of the golden heart; in *The Secret Agent*, the Assistant Commissioner's awareness of the disparity between his idealistic code and the intractable quality of a world unresponsive to questions of good and evil, separates him from Stevie, that Boffin-like believer in goodness. Still, the Assistant Commissioner also refuses to be ground by the stern reality that destroys the aspirations of

Jude Fawley; though he may tilt at windmills, he is closer to the "Quixotic" Dorothea Brooke than to Hardy's "tragic Don Quixote."[6] He is "an energetic Don Quixote," a "cool, reflective Don Quixote, with the sunken eyes of a dark enthusiast and a very deliberate manner" (chs. 6, 7). To see and feel is a burdensome task in Conrad's world. But Conrad invites the reader to share this burden by converting the self-divided Commissioner into our mutual friend. We must partake of the paradox which sustains this dark enthusiast. Only by preserving the illusion of order can men prevent their surrender to the chaos of total despair.

Like Marlow in Conrad's other novels, the Assistant Commissioner possesses the widened awareness the reader gradually must share with the implied author. He is, like Marlow, "one of us." But like the reader, the Commissioner remains an outside observer whose direct participation in the action is severely limited. In Conrad's fiction—and *The Secret Agent* is no exception—the active characters inevitably fall into three distinct groups: there are first of all those who can neither see or feel; secondly, those who do not see but who can feel; and, third, those who can survive only if their seeing rules out their capacity to feel. Those who both can see and feel must stand at the periphery of the circle described by these three types.

## The Unseeing and Unfeeling

In his "Author's Note" Conrad describes how a monstrous town, "a cruel devourer of the world's light," disturbed his "quieted-down imagination" and replaced his earlier vision "of South America, a continent of crude sunshine and brutal revolutions, of the sea, the vast expanse of salt waters." In *The Secret Agent* the unseeing and unfeeling Nature of Conrad's previous fiction gives way to London and its inhabitants, the masses of nameless and faceless people who engulf the Professor as he walks the streets, the cabs and carts and vans, the shy young

6. *Middlemarch*, ed. Gordon S. Haight (Boston, 1956), ch. 76; *Jude the Obscure*, ed. Robert B. Heilman (New York, 1966), Pt. IV, ch. 1.

men who come to buy pornographic literature at Verloc's shop, the self-satisfied constable whose shovel picks up "what might have been an accumulation of raw material for a cannibal feast" (ch. 5). The myopic Privy Consellor Wurmt, the idiotic Toodles who worries about "beastly Cheeseman" and the Fisheries Bill, the Great Personage himself—Sir Ethelred the Minister of State—are drawn as Dickensian caricatures who lead a blind existence, undisturbed by contradictions, unconscious of the emptiness they try to fill.

Conrad's hollow men are the equivalent of the Veneerings and the Podsnaps. Like Dickens' puppets, they are mechanical yet remain convinced of their indispensability as cogs within the larger machinery of society. The smugness of Toodles, the secretary with the Dickensian name,[7] stems from sheer mindlessness; the complacency of his employer, Sir Ethelred, from a desire to avoid facing the possibility of a meaningless world. As head of the social mechanism, the Minister of State wants to be screened from the same world he supposedly controls. Like Wurmt, he is terribly nearsighted; his room is fitted with green shades to protect his weak eyes from the intrusion of light. He wants the Assistant Commissioner to be lucid, brief, to avoid all disturbing complications. When the Assistant Commissioner ventures that the existence of secret agents is a sham brought out by the political absurdities of "an imperfect world," Sir Ethelred claims not to understand (ch. 7).

Sir Ethelred can function only by remaining nearsighted and uncomprehending. He is the nominal head of a circular world, a world repeatedly described as a green aquarium, a slimy sea. The unseeing and unfeeling refuse to fathom that sea, to get wet by immersing themselves in its destructive elements. The Assistant Commissioner must conduct his "crusade" in private, without the Minister's knowledge. He does not mind getting a "little wet, a little splashed," for—like Conrad's Marlow or

7. In Dickens' *Dombey and Son* (1846–1848), Robin Toodle, known as "Rob the Grinder," acts as the agent for the sinister Mr. Carker, but is finally restored to "respectability" by entering the services of Miss Tox.

Conrad himself—he is a former adventurer who has already ventured on the broader sea of life. Lacking the "saving illusions" which shelter the Great Personage, the Assistant Commissioner works within the system with a full awareness of its weaknesses: "A square peg forced into a round hole, he had felt like a daily outrage that long-established smooth roundness into which another man of less sharply angular shape would have fitted himself" (ch. 6).

Chief Inspector Heat is that other, less angular man. His "unphilosophical temperament" is only slightly unsettled by "the general idea of the absurdity of things human" (ch. 5). The Inspector much prefers to catch thieves than to hunt down anarchists. To him, thieves are worthwhile antagonists, "sane, without morbid ideals, working by routine, respectful of constituted authorities, free from all taint of hate and despair" (ch. 5). Since they play a conventional game and submit to the "sanctions of a morality" he understands, thieves can be neatly fitted into the orderly structure he is called upon to defend. Anarchists, however, are another matter: "There were no rules for dealing with anarchists. And that was distasteful to the Chief Inspector" (ch. 5). Heat fears the Professor far more than the little man's detonator. He must brand the "unwholesome-looking little moral agent of destruction" as a madman and lunatic, for only by doing so can he protect himself from the disturbing thought that his own job involves perpetuating the same irrational chaos the Professor is committed to expose. Heath cannot face this possibility. He must reject the likelihood that the explosion may have been a totally meaningless act, quite unconnected with the revolutionaries. He needs a rational system and therefore is forced to devise his own rules. Yet the rules he creates to rid himself of contradictions are themselves marked by contradiction. Since he must find a culprit, he is willing to arrest Michaelis even though he is fully aware of his innocence. Heat's "rules" demand that to enforce justice, he must be unjust. In his efforts to protect Sir Ethelred's circular world, he has been caught in a vicious circle of his own making. The man who prefers thieving because it "was not a sheer absurdity" becomes the victim of the absurd logic ruling that world.

It is not Heat, however, but rather the informer he tries to protect, Adolf Verloc, who truly epitomizes the circular world of the unseeing and unfeeling. The triple agent triangle is himself a living absurdity—an anarchist who complacently thinks of himself as a guardian of organized society. Verloc is deeply shocked when Vladimir brutally forces him to examine the inconsistencies in the existence he has led. He tries to assure Vladimir that he is useful, that he is doing the job for which he gets paid. Confronted with the fact that his reports have been useless, prodded into committing an act of true anarchy by his reactionary master, this petty bourgeois cannot bring himself to face the uncomfortable paradoxes he has denied. Verloc persists in his former blindness. Even after he reluctantly lives up to his expected public role by becoming the agent for Vladimir's and the Professor's visions of anarchy, he fails to see the personal chaos he has unleashed, unaware that he has forever disrupted the tenuous harmony that reigned in his household.

"You've been getting wet," his wife says to him, still solicitous because unknowing. "Not very," he replies (ch. 9). He has refused to get splashed. All that Verloc sees is that his indolent existence has come to an end; all that he feels is a sense of personal injury at having been unfairly displaced from his previous comfortable way of life. Stevie's death does not touch him; he is oblivious to Winnie's internal agony. Verloc cannot be shaken out of his torpor. Like a Dickensian puppet, he finds comfort in his former mechanical habits. To placate his uneasiness, to re-establish regularity in his life, the man responsible for Stevie's accidental butchering repeatedly indulges his voracious appetite. The irony is macabre: "the piece of roast beef laid out in the likeness of funereal baked meats for Stevie's obsequies, offered itself largely to his notice. And Mr. Verloc again partook. He partook ravenously, without restraint and decency, cutting thick slices with the sharp carving knife" (ch. 11). After eating, Verloc lies down on his couch and expects his wife to make love to him. He is as satisfied as any ordinary well-fed citizen after a normal day's work, unconscious of Winnie's abnormal expression, of the dilated eyes that now are fixed on his wet feet.

Only when the carving knife descends on his breast does he faintly begin to fathom the feelings of this unfathomable and "mysterious" wife. He does not see "the resemblance of her face with that of her brother." Lying on his back and staring upwards, he merely perceives "the moving shadow of an arm with a clenched hand holding a carving knife." The movement is leisurely, "leisurely enough for Mr. Verloc to recognize the limb and the weapon." As in a slow-motion film, Conrad forces us to behold details that could not have been perceived through a more rapid presentation. He devotes an entire paragraph to the thoughts flashing through Verloc's mind during the brief moment that elapses while the arm moves back and down. Verloc's body cannot carry out the elaborate "plan of defence" concocted by his brain. The inertia which has characterized him in life also characterizes him in this last moment before death. The grotesque, sensual man pays for his lifelong inability to be moved. The agent for anarchy who never really understood anarchy must die as the victim of the anarchic feelings he has so unknowingly unleashed in his wife. If the angular Assistant Commissioner is a square peg forced into a circle, the rotund Mr. Verloc is a circle who finds that he cannot be encompassed either by the triangle formed by his three conflicting masters or by the triangle formed by his relations to Winnie and Stevie. By failing to grasp that it was Stevie who kept this triangle alive, Verloc has precipitated his own death. With Stevie's extinction, the single, feeble line which connected Verloc to his wife is all that remains from the former triangle; with the linear sweep of her armed hand, this line, too, is erased. Verloc dies like a deflated balloon. After Winnie's exit from 32 Brett Street, "a round hat . . . rocked slightly on its crown in the wind of her flight" (ch. 11). The spherical motions of the bowler hat are emblematic of the coruscations of Verloc's world of unfeeling and unseeing creatures, yet they also signify the circularity about to destroy the last member of his household, the feeling but still unseeing Winnie.

## The Feeling but Unseeing

Michaelis "the ticket-of-leave apostle," the old aristocratic lady who is his patroness and disciple, the "old heroic woman" who is Stevie's and Winnie's mother, Stevie, and Winnie herself, before her second betrayal, are Conrad's innocents. All these characters are motivated by fellow-feeling; all are capable of self-sacrifice and renunciation. Still, the ideals and principles by which they guide their actions seem hopelessly out of tune with the absurd reality that the true seer must face. Michaelis' utopian faith in human perfectibility is but a personal projection on the universe, belied by actual experience; the old lady who sponsors him, though possessed of a temperament "which defies time with scornful disregard" (ch. 6), is nonetheless a victim of temporal change, an eccentric who belongs to a bygone age. Similarly, the personal sacrifices made by Winnie's mother, Stevie, and Winnie herself prove to be meaningless gestures unrewarded by the happiness that each had hoped to produce. The faithful Stevie's "humanitarian enterprise" is a grim joke, as absurd as Winnie's devotion to Verloc, "the kind, the good, the generous" (ch. 12). Their mother's resolution to move into a charity home to insure Verloc's continued protection of Stevie is equally ironic. The old woman regards her decision "as an act of devotion and as a move of deep policy" (ch. 8). She has been prompted to take this step out of "love for both her children," hoping to strengthen Stevie's "moral claim" on Mr. Verloc; yet not only does Stevie's greater dependence on Verloc have exactly the opposite effect from that which she had intended, but even her other child, who might have been expected to approve of her move, fails to understand the reasons behind it. Winnie is scandalized by her mother's willingness to throw herself on charity: "Whatever did you want to do that for?" (ch. 8). She fails to see that her mother's action is prompted by the same spirit of self-denial that led her to marry Verloc rather than the young man she loved.

Like Hardy and Butler before him, Conrad can no longer give his unequivocal support to those enthusiasts who are guided by the promptings of the heart. Nonetheless, he clearly respects the incorruptibility of Michaelis, the Lady Patroness, Winnie's mother, and Stevie; what is more, he pities Winnie's removal from the camp of the feeling and unseeing to the small group formed by those forced to come to terms with the center of indifference that lies at the core of his anarchic world. Though he does not spare these characters from the ironic treatment he accords to their blind and insensitive counterparts, he guardedly endorses their blind devotion and regards them as individualists, "hardened in the fires of adversity" (ch. 8).

Conrad's greater kindness to these blind idealists is seen in his treatment of Michaelis. Although he associates Michaelis with Karl Yundt and Alexander Ossipon, he simultaneously is careful to stress the differences which separate this gentle apostle from his two revolutionary counterparts. Like Verloc, all three men are living contradictions. Their conversation in chapter three is circuitous; they are incapable of communicating with each other, unable to relate to other human beings even though their concern is presumably for humanity itself. Yundt, the fierce anarchist whose talk of cannibalism and bloodshed terrifies Stevie, is full of empty swagger; his wrathful creed is belied by his total impotence: he survives only because he is fed and kept alive by the devotion of a woman he had once tried to shake off. Ossipon's creed, too, is a sham; his pseudoscientific stance is but an evasion of reality. "Without emotion there is no action," is his watchword, but the only actions he truly cares for are money and sex. He is emotionless, calculating. All he can see in the death of Comrade Verloc, a fellow member of the Red Committee, is that Verloc leaves behind a shop and a voluptuous widow. Though he regards himself as a foe of the bourgeoisie, Ossipon shares its love of property. When he jumps off the railway carriage he immediately passes as a member of conventional society;

he is believed in, accepted by the crowd, because he *is* one of them. He is a confidence man, a thief, who goes by the rules of the game that Heat respects. And he plays that game with consummate skill. The man Winnie regarded as Verloc's foil proves to be as dispassionate and unromantic as her husband. At the end of the novel, his resemblance to Verloc becomes apparent to the reader. He too has done a day's job, even if that job involved the death of another human being; he too rests and becomes lethargic. Like Verloc's, his eyes stare at the blank ceiling: "And suddenly they closed. Comrade Ossipon slept in the sunlight" (ch. 12). The man who looks at reality by the light of science is as blind as Verloc himself. He, too, has chosen to put out the light by dulling himself to all questions of feeling.

Michaelis, by way of contrast, bases his creed on feeling. Although he is as unaware of the inconsistencies of his beliefs as the others, and, like Verloc, is "round like a distended balloon" (ch. 3), he is not a hypocrite like his counterparts. His words about "art, philosophy, love, virtue—truth itself" (ch. 3) are but an extension of the monologue that he had conducted in prison; he is isolated from the very reality he wants to improve. Yet, ludicrous as he is, Michaelis is a saintly fool. It is no coincidence that he should be the friend of the humanitarian madman, Stevie: "his ideas were not in the nature of convictions. They were inaccessible to reasoning. They formed in all their contradictions and obscurities an invincible and humanitarian creed, which he confessed rather than preached, with an obstinate gentleness" (ch. 6). His ideals are scoffed at by Yundt and Ossipon, the activists impatient with his gentle philosophy of nonresistance. Ossipon is correct in denouncing Michaelis' quietism, his belief in the value of waiting: "Then it's no use doing anything —no use whatsoever" (ch. 3). And yet the integrity of his beliefs sets Michaelis apart from the others. It is the friendship that he has inspired in that other social outcast, the Lady Patroness, that leads a man who feels *and* sees to become his mutual friend, as well.

The Lady Patroness epitomizes the power of feeling that

moves Michaelis, Stevie, Winnie, and Winnie's mother. To the Assistant Commissioner, the nameless old lady is "kindness personified," the "specially choice incarnation of the feminine" (ch. 6). She represents a female principle and thus also typifies the other two women, as well as the celibate Michaelis and the asexual Stevie. She is at odds with the world headed by that other aristocrat, Sir Ethelred. The Commissioner intervenes in Michaelis' behalf not only because he feels compelled to rescue an innocent man (like Dorothea Brooke in *Middlemarch*) but also because of his admiration for this irrational being. He admits that he could not otherwise have faced this old women who "had escaped the blight of indifference" that marks men like Sir Ethelred or Chief Inspector Heat. Like Vladimir's kinder predecessor at the Embassy, the Baron Stott-Wartenheim who prophesied the "moral insanity" of Europe's children, she is a relic of an earlier age of innocence; like Stevie, whom the Assistant Commissioner never meets, she is a "moral creature" who persists in her steadfast belief in an order based on the heart. She, too, is incongruous, a trifle foolish, enveloped as she is by the inconsistencies of Conrad's absurd world. But she represents a "genuine humanity" which the Assistant Commissioner and Conrad himself are unwilling to give up. The Assistant Commissioner can become the reader's conscience only because the old lady is his own conscience, his moral center in a swirling and unstable world. Although this moral center may not exist, men must act as if it did. To do otherwise is to yield to the chaos of seeing without feeling, to be a cynic—like Vladimir and the Professor—or to become a tragic victim like Winnie Verloc.

### The Seeing but Unfeeling

Vladimir and the Professor see the true anarchy at the circle's center. Their personalities seem as opposed as their political beliefs: the urbane and witty diplomat who frequents ladies' salons and is a member of the Explorers Club serves the interests of the most reactionary of the European powers, Czarist Russia; the lonely misfit who denies himself all social intercourse serves the Red Committee, although he is quite willing to give his deadly explosives to any man. Both men, however, have ventured into the heart of darkness and, having seen its horror, want to terrorize the well-regulated world ruled by the Great Personage who shades his eyes. Both men are inciters, *agents provocateurs*. Though Vladimir chooses to scare ladies at the salon, while the Professor tries to intimidate Chief Inspector Heath, both are united by their joint desire to destroy the faith in legality, morality, and "usefulness" by which the orderly British guide their lives. Both enlist Verloc the pseudo-anarchist for this task of destruction.

Obsessed by the madness they see in the universe, both men rationalize their destructiveness by assuring themselves that they are working for useful causes: Vladimir, for the perpetuation of a repressive system of order; the Professor, for the advent of an apocalyptic revolution. Their rationalizations are as precarious as Verloc's and Heat's far more disingenuous beliefs in their "usefulness." They hide a pathological delight in anarchy for its own sake. Both men resentfully nurse a personal sense of injury. Vladimir the Slav, "descended from generations victimized by the instruments of an arbitrary power," is "racially, nationally, and individually afraid of the police" (ch. 10). The Professor, too, bears a grudge against the society that has betrayed his aspirations as a scientist. To shatter the normalcy of the social order regulated by Heat is for each man an obsession that springs from a private desire for revenge.

And so it is that these two antithetical figuers are motivated by identical interests. Their common master is anarchy itself. Vladimir exults in his superiority to the sentimental old Baron Stott-Wartenheim, his predecessor at the Embassy; the Professor scorns the professional revolutionaries, Yundt and Michaelis. He is the true revolutionary, he asserts, because all he wants is the perfect detonator—a first principle far more real than the moral abstractions devised both by society as well as by those reformers who would rebuild it. Like Vladimir, he has "worked alone for years" (ch. 4). Yet, ironically enough, the two men work in consort with each other when they turn over their own antagonistic ferocity to Verloc, the harmless triple agent. Vladimir provides the idea; the Professor provides the bomb. Like the bomb, the idea is clever, almost perfect—almost, but not quite.

Vladimir chooses Greenwich Observatory as his target because he knows man's enslavement to the temporal order of routine. The atemporal orders of religion or art no longer bind men; an affront to them would not be universally felt. In the absence of a belief in God, that onetime First Mover, time itself has become man's first principle. Those unwilling to be shaken out of their complacent belief in order could easily dismiss a bomb outrage against a church as the act of an atheist or some dissentient sect; the explosion of a restaurant or a theater, more modern structures, could likewise be attributed to a private motive. The act must be incomprehensible and unaccountable. Vladimir tells Verloc how to move the men and women of Sir Ethelred's unseeing and unfeeling world: "The sensibilities of the class you are attacking are soon blunted. . . . You can't count upon their emotion either of pity or fear. A bomb outrage to have any influence on public opinion now must go beyond the intention of vengeance or terrorism. It must be purely destructive" (ch. 2). His words to the pseudo-anarchist anticipate the Professor's words to the pseudo-scientist Ossipon: "Ah, that multitude, too stupid to feel either pity or fear" (ch. 13). Both Vladimir and the Professor are uninterested in evoking the emotion of pity, being pitiless themselves. But they want to spread fear, for they are themselves fearful of the capricious power of the unseeing masses. Men fear only that which they cannot understand. And since modern men claim to understand everything by science, Vladimir commands Verloc to explode the observatory whose telescopes scan the intelligible universe which has replaced the old cosmology based on faith. Though serving the forces of reaction, Vladimir has seized on an act of anarchy which the revolutionaries of the Red Committee would never have dreamed of, an act of ferocity so "absurd as to be incomprehensible, inexplicable, almost unthinkable; in fact, mad. Madness alone is truly terrifying" (ch. 2). Vladimir is correct. As we saw, Heat dismisses his deep fear of the Professor by calling him a "lunatic"; the dying Verloc can explain Winnie's action only by calling her "raving mad"; Ossipon, who takes Verloc's place, declares Winnie to be as "mad" as Stevie to account, as scientifically as possible, for actions and emotions incomprehensible to him.

Since men are no longer capable of the emotions of pity and fear through normal channels, fear must be instilled, not by tragedy, but by their terror of absurdity. Vladimir's idea is brilliant, yet Conrad goes a step beyond his creation. Like the great Victorian novelists before him, he wants to instill pity as well as fear. Vladimir wants to destroy the Observatory; we cannot pity its ruins. Conrad destroys Stevie; we can pity his mangled limbs. By forcing us to pity Winnie's tragedy as well, to share her emotions of pity and fear, Conrad steers the reader beyond Vladimir's emotionless nihilism.

Vladimir and the Professor fail. They fail not only because their agent has fumbled the dynamite outrage, but also because Verloc's lack of pity and fear after Stevie's death only proves that the "sensibility" of the class of men he represents can never be shaken. With monstruous fatuity, Verloc tells Winnie: "He's gone. His troubles are over. Ours are just going to begin, I tell you, precisely because he did blow himself up. I don't blame you. But just try to understand that it was a pure accident; as much an accident as if he had been run over by a 'bus while crossing the street" (ch. 11). The incongruity of the "accident" that has claimed Stevie does not disturb his complacent brother-in-law. His total impassivity demonstrates that his nation of shopkeepers will always remain immune to the terror of absurdity. The Professor's fear is justified: "What if nothing could move them?" (ch. 5). The world at large remains as indifferent at the end of the book as it had been before. Its rhythm persists; nothing has been moved. The order headed by the Minister with feeble eyes survives because of its blindness.

## The Seeing and Feeling: the Assistant Commissioner

The Assistant Commissioner, however, does see; to a point, he also does move. He protects the "idealistic conception of legality" that both the Professor and Vladimir so despise by saving Michaelis and by intimidating Vladimir. Yet he protects it against Heat as much as against the enemies of the system. To fulfill his role, he must remain both within and without society. Like Conrad himself, this onetime traveler to the tropics is a foreigner among the English. When he squares off against Vladimir the Slav, it is he, and not his antagonist, who seems the more exotic of the two.

The Assistant Commissioner combines the intelligence possessed by the Professor and Vladimir with the power of feeling possessed by those other outcasts, Michaelis and the Lady Patroness. Though on the side of "conventional morality," he is an unusual and unconventional man. Unlike Heat, he immediately recognizes that the bombing incident is a "ferocious joke" that cannot be blamed on the revolutionaries; long before Heat, he senses that Stevie must have been Verloc's accomplice; on getting to Verloc before Heat does, he knows that Vladimir is his man. When he wraps up the case in chapter ten, Vladimir is amazed, "almost awed by the miraculous cleverness of the English police." But the Assistant Commissioner hardly typifies the English police. While he has descended on 32 Brett Street, Inspector Heat, that creature of regularity, has calmly eaten his supper and "even gone so far as to think of getting into his slippers" before deciding to re-emerge on the wet streets in the role of Private Citizen Heat.

For all his perspicacity, however, the Assistant Commissioner never penetrates into the inner triangle of the novel. He drops out after chapter ten, before Winnie's confrontations with Verloc and Ossipon. Conrad makes it clear that this character—the most intelligent and sympathetic of the book—is not omniscient. Though seeing more than all the others, though acting as a kind of deputy-novelist who pieces fragments together again, the Assistant Commissioner cannot mend Winnie's fragmented personal life. He does not interrogate Winnie, but merely asks her to fetch her husband; she in turn, notices only his "kindly mouth and probing eyes" (ch. 9). The ties which had bound Winnie to Stevie and Stevie to her husband, though known to us, are never grasped by the Assistant Commissioner. In reporting to Sir Ethelred, he speculates that Verloc might well have been "fond of the lad—who knows?" but cannot explain why Verloc would have risked Stevie's arrest. The narrator stresses that the Commissioner's "ignorance of poor Stevie's devotion to Mr. Verloc (who was *good*), and of his truly peculiar dumbness" (ch. 10) prevents this shrewd detective from a true valuation of the three characters who lived at 32 Brett Street. By assuming Stevie to have been a rational being, he misjudges Verloc as an irrational, "impulsive man" and underestimates Winnie's importance, unaware that she is about to kill his star witness. Moreover, by failing to know of Stevie's "peculiar dumbness" this humane Don Quixote will never know his kinship to the lunatic humanitarian who also chose to tilt against the windmills of a circular world.

The Assistant Commissioner thus can carry the reader only to the threshold of the novel's inner triangle, to the rim of its domestic tragedy. There is no reason why he should carry us further. He has seen enough; he knows the ways of Conrad's world; he is capable of pity and terror. He has shown us the way by getting a bit splashed, a little wet. But we, the readers, must penetrate deeper by witnessing the story that still remains to be played out after he leaves the Verlocs. The Assistant Commissioner has done his job, though Heat soon botches it when he shows Winnie the triangular piece of cloth and thus indirectly causes her to murder Verloc. Unlike all the other "agents" in the novel, the Assistant Commissioner is an agent for construction rather than destruction; yet he cannot avert Winnie's tragedy. We must confront her pity and terror without his guidance. We must get splashed on our own. The Assistant Commissioner has defused the sequence of events which was initiated by Vladimir and which culminated in the premature explosion of the time bomb. Now, a new and shorter sequence starts. A new time bomb begins to tick, but we have no Assistant Commissioner to defuse it for us: "Dark drops fell on the floor-cloth one after another, with a sound of ticking growing fast and furious like the pulse of an insane clock" (ch. 11). The ticking sound is that of Verloc's dripping blood. Terrified, Winnie escapes the house; she regards the blood as the "first sign of a destroying flood." Like Maggie Tulliver, this tragic young woman will soon become engulfed.

## 3

Winnie's tragedy is that she is too abruptly moved from the camp of the feeling but unseeing to the camp of those who see. Like her mother, she has practiced self-denial for Stevie's sake. She has repressed her passion for Ossipon just as she had once stifled her love for the young butcher's son. The young man who wanted to become "her companion for a voyage down the sparkling stream of life" had room for "a girl-partner at the oar, but no accommodation for passengers" (ch. 11). When that passenger, Stevie, is butchered by the man she married, Winnie turns to Ossipon. His betrayal compels her to jump from the passenger ship that both were to have taken. The freedom toward which she expected to sail proves to be an illusion.

Winnie felt contented as Verloc's wife, secure in her role as Stevie's substitute mother; but after Heat shows her the strip of cloth, she sees with new eyes. And so do we, for until then we have not suspected the prominence of this silent and "unfathomable" character. In novels like *Richard Feverel*, *The Mill on the Floss*, or *Jude the Obscure*, the reader is at once apprised of the centrality of the tragic victim whose destiny will be traced, step by step. In *The Secret Agent*, Winnie's suicide comes abruptly and anticlimactically; it is an irrational, yet logical, act designed to instill us with a terror and pity far greater than that which Vladimir and the Professor had hoped to produce.

Conrad tricks the reader into believing that Winnie has become an exalted tragic figure when her monomaniacal desire for revenge leads her to plunge the carving knife into Verloc's heart. The passion she has kept under control explodes; her heart—the heart which had led her to marry Verloc for Stevie's sake—becomes "hardened and chilled into a lump of ice" (ch. 11). Her outrage leads her to identify Verloc as the murderer of the brother she regards as her child. But Winnie is not a Clytemnestra reacting against a definable crime. She needs an object for her hatred because she cannot yet bring herself to accept the full absurdity of Verloc's guiltless guilt. Her true tragedy comes only after she has recognized the absurdity that infects the world.

In a letter to R. B. Cunninghame Graham, Conrad once wrote: "What makes mankind tragic is not that they are the victims of nature, it is that they are conscious of it."[8] Winnie thinks that she has ceased to be a slave on meeting Comrade Ossipon, the libertarian whose shamelessly inviting eyes she has avoided as long as she was Verloc's decorous wife. She wants to celebrate her newly found freedom. Like Sue Bridehead, she now thinks herself capable of defying the conventional morality she has so long upheld. But she does not know that Ossipon is even more conventional and immoral than the husband she has killed in order to be "free." Verloc was indifferent to Stevie, but cared about her. The revolutionary who professes to care about the "emotional state of the masses" is concerned only with the state of his pocketbook. Verloc may have cheated her out of seven years of her life, but Ossipon soon cheats her out of life itself by robbing her of her last sustaining illusions. Her seven-year sleep has been in vain. Her freedom is illusory, for Comrade "O." belongs to the very same circular world she tries to escape.

Ossipon sees, but misinterprets, the resemblances between

---

8. January 31, 1898, in *Joseph Conrad: Life and Letters*, ed. G. Jean-Aubry (New York, 1927), I, 266.

Winnie and Stevie. Winnie does not see the resemblances between Verloc and Ossipon, between her past enslavement and
her present "freedom." She gives Ossipon the money of the man
into whose breast she had plunged a knife; he takes the wallet
and plunges it "deep somewhere into his very breast" (ch. 12).
By obtaining Verloc's money, Ossipon assumes his identity.
He has no need for Verloc's useless shop or for a woman whom
he brands as a dangerous, "murdering type." Winnie thinks
that Ossipon wants her. She sees freedom and passion where
there is none, meaning where there is absurdity. Only on recognizing her mistake, does she become truly "clear-sighted."

Unlike Stevie's death, Winnie's death is tragic, for she dies
aware of being deluded by her expectations. Her gesture of
killing Verloc has been meaningless; she might as well have
stayed among the unseeing many. Lacking the support by which
others manage to counter chaos—the altruism of those who feel
or the hatred of Vladimir and the Professor—she cannot survive.
She is defenseless against the full anarchy she sees at last. The
madness to which she succumbs is far more ruinous than the
madness which led her to strike against evil in the shape of
Verloc. Her first words as a "free" woman come to haunt her:
she melodramatically welcomed Ossipon as her "saviour . . . the
man who was the messenger of life" and told him that he rescued
her from tasting the "cup of horrors." Winnie must jump off
the cross-channel boat; she cannot cross into a better existence.
The wedding ring she leaves behind matches the round hat she
had left behind at 32 Brett Street. Of the triangle with which the
novel started, there is nothing left, only a zero, nil, a circle.

It is easy to read Winnie's death as being an act of self-
assertion, to convert her into an existentialist heroine who finds
meaning in meaninglessness only through the meaningful decision of committing suicide, but such an interpretation would
be erroneous, at odds with Conrad's avowed intentions. Winnie's act is, as we are reminded by the disembodied newspaper
phrase that haunts Ossipon, an "act of madness and despair." It
is a madness and despair that is not only possible but even logical

in Conrad's demented world; nonetheless, it is an action for which the novelist deliberately provides alternatives. Although Winnie gets sucked into the vortex of the whirlpool, Conrad's entire purpose—like that of the Victorian novelists before him —is to spare the reader from that vortex. Even though he wants us to see—to share Winnie Verloc's disenchantment—he wants us to see in order to survive. And we survive because we can still feel. Like the Assistant Commissioner, we must get splashed; like the Marlow of "Heart of Darkness," we must be infected by fever. We emerge fortified on the periphery of the circle, because we have been splashed, have had the fever, and can yet believe in the simple morality represented by the Lady Patroness.

Although technically Conrad moves beyond Hardy in his portrayal of a grim cosmos emptied of meaning, he also takes a step backwards by returning the reader to the same circular world he has so meticulously exploded. *The Secret Agent* thus describes a spiral. Whereas to Hardy all idealism must be sacrificed to an implacable reality, for Conrad the ideal is possible amidst the very absurdities he depicts. Father Time's suicide is logical; Winnie's, partakes of the same contradictions that inform all actions in Conrad's world. The contradictions of the Assistant Commissioner, who holds on to his beliefs in a world that lacks any moral order, is preferable therefore to Jude's exhausted acquiescence to despair. It is better to be an "energetic Don Quixote" than a "tragic Don Quixote" like Jude. Stevie, blown up near St. Stephen's cathedral, is as much a martyr to his idealism as is Jude, whom Sue Bridehead calls "St. Stephen" at one point in Hardy's novel. Hardy's martyr dies drained of all hope; Stevie, however, dies in blissful innocence. Although his simple distinctions between good and evil are those of a madman, his morality also becomes his saving grace.

When Vladimir is cornered by the Assistant Commissioner, he protests, "What do you want to make a scandal for?—for morality—or what?" (ch. 10). It is at this point that we realize that Conrad is still a moralist, like the great Victorian novelists before him. For the answer, which the Assistant Commissioner slyly avoids, is "yes." He has acted out of morality, inspired by the example of the old Victorian lady who is Michaelis' protectress. She is an anachronism, yet she is his tutelary angel. Like Rokesmith, Dorothea Brooke, or Mr. Harding, the Assistant Commissioner must tilt against the mindlessness that destroys Winnie. And Stevie—whose innocent love for men and horses recalls Boffin as well as Dobbin the trustful man with a horselike name—must also persist in his absurd crusade against evil. We can empathize with his futile quest in a way that we cannot identify with the prematurely wise Father Time.

## 4

*The Secret Agent* culminates the sequence traced in this book in several ways. Its ironic form allows Conrad to express the same complexities experienced by novelists affected, in varying degrees, by the hostile reality of a world seemingly impervious to all ideals. Like *Vanity Fair*, that other novel about the effects of time, *The Secret Agent* relies on hindsight, understatement, and concealment for its ironic effects; yet at the same time, this most ironic of novels also perpetuates the wishful fantasies by which earlier writers resisted their inclination toward despair. In the comedy of *Barchester Towers* Trollope defended another quixotic figure by admitting that although Mr. Harding could not be spoken of with "conventional absurdity as a perfect man," he was nonetheless to be regarded as a "good man without guile." In *The Secret Agent* the "seraphic trustfulness" of Michaelis has become even more absurd, yet despite the tissue of complexities which mock his beliefs in human perfection, Conrad still tries to vindicate "goodness without guile."

From the conniving Mr. Slope we have moved to the sinister Vladimir. Both men are intruders, both possess guile, both are defeated. In 1857 Trollope could still rely on pure comedy to laugh away the anarchy represented by London and its emissary, Slope; fifty years later, the anarchy represented by Vladimir, the Professor, and their bomb seems far less laughable. The reality of the "monstrous town," London, cannot be avoided. But Conrad still clings to the goodness without guile that unites Michaelis, the Lady Patroness, and the Assistant Commissioner into a shadowy society of mutual friends. For goodness without guile is all that separates these characters from the chaos that leads Winnie to self-destruction. In this sense, this "Simple Tale of the Nineteenth Century" still follows the precedent of those nineteenth-century novelists who relied on their art to protect themselves and their readers from "madness and despair." In this sense, too, the progression traced in this book, far from being linear, has likewise been in the shape of a spiral.

# Index

Addison, Joseph, 44, 45
Aeschylus: his Clytemnestra, 228, 252, 269; quoted by Jude Fawley, 218; reviled by Ernest Pontifex, 219
Andersen, Hans Christian: and Dickens, 164, 164n
Aquinas, St. Thomas, 190
*Arabian Nights, The*, 66, 67, 131
Aristophanes: hailed by Ernest Pontifex, 219
Aristotle, 218, 224
Arnold, Matthew, 10, 41, 111, 208, 241; on despair, 207, 230; Hardy on, 214n; compared with Thackeray, 51–52. WORKS: *Culture and Anarchy*, 51; "Dover Beach," 51–52; Preface to *Essays in Criticism*, First Series, 214; Preface to *Poems* (1853), 206–207, 230
Arnold, Thomas, 111–112, 216
Austen, Jane, 3; *Pride and Prejudice*, 39, 115, 184

*Barchester Towers, see* Trollope, Anthony
Bible, the: kicked by Ernest Pontifex, 214; references to: *Matthew*, 105–106, 161; *Revelation*, 174; *Timothy*, 32
Bichat, Marie François Xavier, 179
Blake, William, 97
Bowen, Elizabeth, *Anthony Trollope: A New Judgment*, 48n
Brontë, Anne, *Agnes Grey*, 84
Brontë, Charlotte, 49, 83, 87; on Emily's work, 84–86; *Jane Eyre*, 84, 109, 110, contrasted with *Wuthering Heights*, 85

Brontë, Emily, 49, 83, 84–108 *passim*, 135; in relation to her characters, 86, 98, 105, 107–108; and her public, 84–85
WORKS:
*Gondal's Queen*, 86, 86n
*Wuthering Heights*, viii, xii, xiv, 26, 84–108, 111, 117, 151, 177; contrasted with *Barchester Towers*, 25, 45, 86, 96; its comic closure, 96, 102–105, 114, 127; and *Jane Eyre*, 84, 85; its double narrators, 86, 90–96; nourishment and starvation in, 98–99, 101, 103, 104–105; and *The Ordeal of Richard Feverel*, 118, 119; and the reader, 87–90, 118, 139; religion in, 98, 102, 105–106; its tragic substance, 96–102, 105–106; contrasted with *Vanity Fair*, 87, 89, 90; and *The Way of All Flesh*, 211, 219
Browning, Robert, 96, 214
Bunyan, John, *The Pilgrim's Progress*: and *Jude the Obscure*, 209, 209n; and *Middlemarch*, 191; and *The Mill on the Floss*, 135; and *The Ordeal of Richard Feverel*, 124; and *Vanity Fair*, 52; and the Victorian novel, xii, xvi; and *The Way of All Flesh*, 209, 209n
Butler, Samuel, 200, 202–220 *passim*, 227, 230–239 *passim*; P.N. Furbank on, 239; and his public, 203, 204, 207–208; Yeats on, 239
WORKS:
*Erewhon*, 206n
*Erewhon Revisited*, 208, 236
*Life and Habit*, 212n

*275*